OUT OF THE
SALTBOX

Out of the Saltbox

Saltbox

The Savour of Old Vermont

by Ruth M. Rasey Simpson

Published by

CRANE HILL
P U B L I S H E R S
2923 Crescent Avenue
Birmingham, Alabama 35209

Illustrations by Kathleen Voute, except
cover illustration by Scott Fuller

Library of Congress Catalog Card Number: 93-71110

ISBN: 1-881548-06-6

For Jimmie, Cindy and Eddie
part of whose heritage is Windy Summit
and
for Eleanor
who helps to promote that heritage

Books by the author

Out of the Saltbox: The Savour of Old Vermont
Hand-Hewn in Old Vermont
Mountain Fortitude (Poetry)

ACKNOWLEDGMENTS

So many relatives and friends have contributed encouragement and anecdote to the writing of this book that it is impossible to name them all. First however, I am indebted to my forebears, who gave us our hill; to my brother Arthur (Bob in these pages), who still shares in the work on Windy Summit; to my brother Lewis (Joe), who no longer is living; and to my sister, Ruby (Mrs. James Leslie Tyler), who is herein named Sally. All their memories have supplemented mine.

To my cousin, Mrs. Anna Harwood Sheldon, I am deeply grateful fore her gift of school-district records and old photographs, as well as for her loan of *Conant's History of Vermont* and *Hibbard's History of Rupert*, from which I have drawn proof of many facts presented herein. To other cousins-Burr Harwood, an expert cheese maker; Wayne Harwood, who loved to reminisce of the past; and Dr. Edward Sheldon and his wife Dorothy, who have supplied historical records and anecdotes-I am also most grateful for their sharing of their sources of knowledge.

Others who have given abundantly of their invaluable knowledge, without which this work would have been incomplete, are: Mrs. Henry Barden, who has supplied me with papers and pictures portraying Rupert a century ago; Chriss Monroe, the mail carrier, who has added much to my "R.F.D."; Dr. and Mrs. George Russell, in whose Vermontiana library at Arlington I read from *Thomas Canfield*, and with whom I have discussed old customs; Mrs. Pauline VanVoorhees Bentley and her assistants in the North Tonawanda Library, where I have verified historical and biographical data in the *Encyclopedia Americana*, *Britannica*, and *Compton's*; our former Congressman William H. Meyer, who as Executive Director of the Vermont Forest and Farmland Foundation supplied me with many details of Champion Birch Grove; the Andrew Painters, who welcomed me back to

ACKNOWLEDGMENTS

the old schoolhouse and gave me some facts after it became their home; Bertram Shaw of Old Sturbridge Village, who clarified my knowledge of blacksmithing; Mrs. and Mrs. Edward C. Falk of Brant, who demonstrated the working of an old mill, and John Cross of Arlington for clarifying "Togglery" data.

To the Rev. J. Duke King of Rupert and the Rev. John Harrer of the Congregational Library in Boston, I am indebted for access to printed reports pertaining to the church; and to Jay Beebe, Town Clerk of Rupert, for access to the records of my home town.

Mr. Richard Westwood, editor of *Nature Magazine*, in which "Rock Spring," "The Pasture," "The Home Meadow," "The Dooryard," and "Champion Birch Grove" were first published, has been most encouraging by his urging that I write this book for the perpetuation of our knowledge of Americana.

Mr. Walter Hard, Jr., editor of *Vermont Life*, which published an excerpt from "Twenty-two Feet by Twenty-six," and Dr. Arthur Peach, deceased editor of *Vermont History*, in which "The Old Mill on Hagar Brook" first appeared, have likewise been a source of encouragement.

To the host of others who by their generous comment and interest have kept alive my enthusiasm through the past several years of research and writing, I give my deep appreciation also.

Last but not least, I owe my greatest debt of gratitude to Grandfather Seymour Harwood, whose diaries, letters, lyceum papers, books, and other possessions provided the main reservoir of early Americana and Vermontiana from which this material has been drawn; and to Mother, who transmitted to her family not only her father's possessions, but also many a legend of life in the early days on Windy Summit.

The real names for Bob, Joe and Sally in this book were Arthur, Lewis, and Ruby. Those used here are the ones by which we youngsters sometimes called one another for fun.

FOREWORD

"Nothing ever really belongs to you until you earn it. And a hard-working man needs to be well fed, body and spirit." That was Great-Grandfather's philosophy, as it had been his father's before him and has been his descendants' ever since.

As pioneers who helped to open the colonization of Vermont at Old Bennington in 1761, and later at our Rupert Mountain community, Great-Great-Grandfather and the rest of those toil-hardened, stout-hearted men drew sustenance from the nutrients of their saltbox home. It was a symbol of a homespun and rugged democracy, of folkways that spelled survival by sheer ingenuity, arduous labor, and eternal pressing toward a definite goal.

We often are reminded that from our exploration of past events comes our inspiration for future success. As we read of the old-time kindly simplicity unhampered by complicating intrigue, we can only poignantly realize that facing every issue directly, with just consideration for all concerned, resolved what must also have seemed in those olden days like insurmountable difficulties. We discover, too, that such direct and personal interest provided the energizing force and sound basis of satisfying human relations. But that indispensable contribution of the past is all too often overlooked or misunderstood unless the story is recorded.

When our old farmstead on Rupert Mountain was sold in 1938, family possessions of nine generations were removed to new homes. In the old curly maple and cherry desk, fashioned by Great-Uncle Zach in his mill from trees grown on the home place, we found a score of Grandfather's diaries, bundles of his and his ancestors' personal papers, and several of their long-used books. Those crumbling yellow pages told a thought-provoking tale of nearly two centuries of life on Windy Summit. The lives of those men and women who dwelt in our old saltbox house are symbolic of the entire race of hard-working countrymen who helped win our America from the wilderness and shape a democratic way of life. Details of a part of their struggle are recorded in the following pages.

Some of that work continues on the mountaintop today. Those upland acres are now an experimental and demonstration area—known as the Merck Forest and Farmland Center Foundation—for promoting the woodland to its utmost, long-term productivity, and providing educational opportunity in the form of field trips and project development to numerous student and youth groups.

Our old home itself, like most saltbox houses, has disappeared from the landscape. With it have gone the mill with its great water wheel and grinding stones, the district's little red school house, the blacksmith shop with its ox-sling and forge, the cheese factory. But their savour remains in our heritage, our American democracy.

May these chapters help sharpen our awareness of and appreciation for that savour. And may we twentieth-century Americans find in it some inspiration for greater achievement as we continue to possess and promote our heritage with "well-fed body and spirit".

R.M.R.S.

ADDENDUM TO FOREWORD

Since this book was first published, the author has received over 2,000 "fan letters" from readers throughout the United States. A retired woodsman in a home for the aged wrote a most touching one. Another was from Bess Truman whose Vermont forebears pioneered to Missouri about 1869. A most unusual one came from a wealthy Singapore aristocrat, who was associated with the library ans school systems of his country. Numerous school boys and girls wrote in amazement and inspiration about life in OUT OF THE SALTBOX days. All testify to a deep-rooted appreciation of the building of America by means of dedicated effort.

Table of Contents

1 THE SALTBOX HOUSE   15

2 THE DOORYARD   39

3 THE BARN   48

4 THE HOME MEADOW   63

5 ROCK SPRING   72

6 THE PASTURE   76

7 CHAMPION WHITE BIRCH GROVE   83

8 THE SAP HOUSE   89

9 UP THE MOUNTAIN NORTHEASTERLY   101

10 TWENTY-TWO FEET BY TWENTY-SIX   113

11 THE VILLAGE STORE 125

12 THE BLACKSMITH SHOP 133

13 THE OLD MILL AT HAGAR BROOK 139

14 THE DEPOT 147

15 THE CHEESE FACTORY 160

16 R.F.D.—"MAGICIAN" 168

17 THE TOGGLERY 176

18 THE TOWN HALL 188

19 THE OLD WHITE MEETINGHOUSE 197

20 TOPICS INDEX 217

OUT OF THE SALTBOX

1

THE SALTBOX HOUSE

Great-Great-Grandfather Zachariah whoaed his horse to a stop in a grassy clearing on Rupert Mountain summit one June day in 1788. Twenty-seven years before, he had come from Amherst, Massachusetts, into the section of land west of the Connecticut River known, under the New Hampshire charter from the King of England, as the New Hampshire Grants, bordering the New York colonies. Then a boy of nineteen, he had put all of his share from his deceased father's estate into the fund set up by his mother's and three other families to buy from Benning Wentworth, Governor of New Hampshire, the township at the foot of Mount Anthony.

Now desiring more space than that growing town of Bennington allowed, he had bought this pitch (or chosen claim) from his widowed daughter-in-law, whose husband John had died before he had finished clearing his mountain acres.

Alighting from his saddle, Zachariah stooped and crumbled a handful of his new ground through his fingers. It lay richly dark and moist against the green of grass and leaf. Beyond the trees, in all directions, extended mountains near and far. As he drew erect his slightly bowed, angular six feet in butternut-brown homespun jeans, his deep-set grey eyes glowed with new purpose. Here, on untouched and well-drained land, with a wide-range view, he would build a new and better home.

According to a then-prevalent belief, evil spirits possessed little power on a hilltop, where the soul could look afar and be at peace. One need not fear lurking danger in the vistas his eyes could encompass. Fear attacked one's reason only when vision was hampered. Good spirits, he had been told as a boy, liked spreading trees and green grass all around.

So, with high hope and long days of toil, Great-Great-Grandfather and his six sons dug the cellar hole for their house in the midst of the grassy clearing, bordered by tall oaks and elms and maples, near the barn site and near the road. Like many another builder of that time, they shaped their dwelling by the lines of their family saltbox.

Great pines, felled in clearing pasture and meadow and sawed at the mill in White Creek Flats to the west, provided plank and beam. With sheets of tough bark from the woodlot's giant birches and with hand-rived shingles, they roofed it well. Wide pine boards were laid for floors and erected for partitions around the nine-foot center hearth and chimney.

According to custom, the "two rods square" new house faced the south. Set back thirty feet from the narrow, packed-dirt road, its gable ends were set due east and west. Each of its six-over-six small-paned windows of handblown wrinkled grey-green glass looked out upon the mountains.

To their new home Great-Great-Grandfather brought his family before snow blocked the road in November of the following year.

The door at the center front swung wide on its strap iron hinges to welcome them across its threshold, just as for many years to come it would swing wide to welcome kindred, friend, and stranger.

Through the hall at the foot of the stairs, into the front room and downstairs chamber, came the brace-back Windsor chairs, cord bedsteads, and sundry chests. Into the smaller bedroom off the kitchen went the canopied four-poster, the trundle bed, and the cowhide trunk with Great-Great-Grandmother's initials in brass tacks. And into the great kitchen itself came table, bench, splint-seat chair and rocker, as well as the numerous iron pots and kettles, pans and basins so indispensable in pioneer cooking.

Above the wide mouth of the kitchen fireplace was hung the ancestral saltbox, fashioned in the 1660s from a black cherry tree of the forest near Boston. Colonial symbol of good cooking and provident living, there it functioned well until pantry and cookstove replaced open hearth and brick oven in the 1840s.

With crackle of blazing log and clink of bake kettle on the hearth, with ring of happy voices and eager feet, with glow of rushlight above the pewter porringers of apple-fragrant mush and milk, the saltbox house took its first family into its arms and heart.

But during those first eight years on Windy Summit, tragedy struck twice. Diphtheria claimed the youngest girls the fifth winter, and the front room was a sorry sight, indeed, with the three little handmade wooden coffins tightly closed against the dread disease and swathed in the whitest homespun linen of the previous May sun's bleaching. With heavy hearts, family and neighbors rode on horseback, two by two, down the road behind the sleigh that bore the caskets to the meeting-house burying ground.

Three years later, the stage driver brought a letter from Old Bennington to the saltbox door. When Great-Great-Grandfather broke the seal of spruce gum stamped with the handle of a pegging awl, he read an urgent plea for him to return to his former home.

The fatal smallpox was ravaging the town. Great-Great-Grandmother's beloved youngest brother had just been stricken. Ten years earlier Zachariah had had singular success in treating a similar out break, and now his services were desperately needed at the community pesthouse.

That was a raw spring, and supplies in barn and bin were running low. Great-Great-Grandfather Zachariah and his diminished family packed all their household belongings onto cart and sled, herded their animals together, and the little caravan set sadly forth down the very road up which they had come with such high hope that happier time eight years before. The fires were dead in the saltbox house, and evil spirits seemed, after all precautions, to have invaded the hill.

But young Joseph remembered the words in his copybook in the one-room log schoolhouse where he had conned his lessons aloud these past five winters. "That the hour of emergency must be the hour of triumph is one of the great underlying principles for the success of a venture or a country." "To be brave, to be skillful in whatever one sets his hand to do, to accomplish all things undertaken, and to surmount difficulty gives life a perpetual goal and meaning."

As sixteen-year-old Joseph looked back at the home he was leaving, he thought of those words and resolved that he would return.

Return he did, in late October of 1801, bringing with him his new bride. During the years of his absence, Brother Perez, who owned a neighboring farm, had worked the land on shares, filling the barn with stock and crops. Bride and groom were not expected until a day or two later, however, so only gray ashes, birch bark, and dry logs lay upon their home-to-be hearth.

From deep among her chests and "thirty-pound live goose-feather beds," her brass kettles and spinning wheels on the lumber wagon, young Vesta drew her warming pan, filled with glowing coals from her Grandfather Blackmer's hearth, one of the first ever to have been lighted in the

Benning Wentworth Grants. Flames leaped again in the wide-mouthed fireplace, and again the Concord saltbox was hung below the mantel.

Pride and happiness shut out all possibilities of homesickness as Vesta and Joseph, to whom his father had recently deeded Windy Summit, unpacked and settled their "setting-up things." Upon her cherry dropleaf table, lovingly pegged by her father's hard brown hands, the newly capped bride spread a creamy homespun linen cloth. Having woven it in a glossy "M-and-O" pattern the previous winter, she had fitted it to this table and had knitted oak-leaf lace to edge its border. Oak leaves were strong and clung to their branches in spite of winter storm. So would she cling to their home here on the mountaintop.

Like the Roman guardian of the household, for whom Great-Grandmother had been named, her home was her constant care and content throughout her sixty-odd years to follow.

On one broad leaf of the cherry table, before the first year was spent, Great-Grandfather reverently opened his sheepskin Bible and in its "Family Record" inscribed with his sharpened goose quill the date of birth of their first child, Harriet.

During the next twenty years, two more daughters and five sons each in turn kicked, and squalled his wants, and was rocked to comforted sleep in the hooded brown cradle in the busy kitchen. The flax and the wool wheels thumped and hummed. The click of knitting needles, clack of the reel at every fortieth turn, thud of loom, and hiss of hot tallow filling the candle molds mingled their melodies with "Go Tell Aunt Nabby" and other lullabies. For their accompaniment, too, was the ever-recurrent scrape of the wooden spoon against the big blue glass milk bowl, in which Great-Grandmother mixed her endless loaves of bread and hot cakes, or against the sides of the black cooking-pot that hung from the crane. The slice, that tended the fire to heat the brick oven for baking, clanked its overtones. And at the end of each day, before the family went to their rest, there was the harmony of all their voices, from Great-Grandfather's strong, deep tones to the toddler's childish treble, repeating the Psalms and the Proverbs. The daily "I will fear no evil for Thou art with me" inspired hope and faith to face the rigors of life upon this hill.

The quarter of a century during which Harriet and Abigail, Joseph and Zachariah, Ruby and Franklin, Oliver and Seymour came into being were rugged years for the Joseph and Vesta who came in 1801 to establish their home on Windy Summit. They had need enough for Psalms and Proverbs.

Each storm-riddled winter brought lung fever, croup, and crippling rheumatism; each heat-infesting summer brought dysentery, typhoid, and many another often-fatal disease to the hill community. Every family stood ready night and day to help any neighbor or stranger in need. Many a winter, Great-Grandfather and Great-Grandmother spelled each other at a 72-hour watch over a little one with the croup threatening to shut off its breath.

Almost from the very first, the red elms commonly called slippery elms, which grew in Great-Grandfather's dooryard, were his source of medical aid. The mucilaginous substance in the bark was both healing and nutritious, he had learned from the friendly Indians who sometimes came to trade their barks for Great-Grandmother's gingerbread. Each fall thereafter Great-Grandfather stripped off a supply of the inner bark and dried it by the front-room chimney. This he then pulverized as fine as powder in his iron mortar with its heavy pestle. Whenever a distressed knock sounded on his door, his first thought was of his great canister of pulverized slippery elm bark in his front-room chest.

"For putrid sore throat, dysentery, diarrhea, or daily subsistence," a notation in the yellowed pages of his "Family Remedies" prescribes, "mix a level teaspoonful of the pulverized bark with as much sugar and a little cold water. Stir well. Add enough hot water to reduce it to the desired consistency. Make it of sufficient thinness, and it is one of the best of drinks to be used constantly by the sick."

For poultices to draw out inflammation, his recipes called on some of his wife's household supplies. One was her keg of soft soap, which she kept on the cellarway beam and with which she scrubbed her floors, dishes, linens, and family's clothing in big kettlefuls of rain water heated on the crane. Another was her yeast jar, its frothy content supplied by the hops that grew at the edge of the meadow. And often it was the saltbox by the kitchen mantel.

Great-Grandfather's faded handwriting still gives the "receipts":

"Put one tablespoonful of fine ginger into half a pint of hot water, then stir in dry bread that has been pounded fine, till it is about as thick as molasses. Stir in gradually a teaspoonful of fine slippery elm, and if this does not make it thick enough, add more of the bread. If it is to be used in a high state of inflammation, add two tablespoonfuls of soft soap and one of fine salt.

"Leave out soap and salt, use milk instead of water, and it is one of the best poultices to be applied to burns, scalds, felons, freezing, and old sores.

"With the addition of a little pulverized root of yellow lily this is excellent for ulcerations and other sores. It is the best application for a swelled or caked breast, in which let the liquor be yeast.

"Fresh yeast may be mixed with maple charcoal pulverized and applied to putrid sores or may be taken inwardly, when there is danger of mortification in body or limb."

In 1816, by some peculiar development in the atmosphere, snow fell in June and July, as well as in every other month of the year. During this time of sadly diminished household stores, Great-Grandfather, his children, and the hired man peeled innumerable yards of inner bark from the red elms in pasture and woodlot. This pulverized bark, along with finely ground birch bark, added to the carefully rationed wheat, cornmeal, and hemlock tea, no doubt saved the lives of the family in that year of distress.

All eight survived, including the sixth child, baby Franklin, whose birth in January, 1817, nearly took his mother's life. Her own strength depleted by the limited food supply, anxiety for her family, and the endless cold that cruelly gripped every minute and every mouthful all that preceding year, she came to her labor nearly a month before her time.

Fourteen-year-old Harriet huddled her brothers and sisters, each bravely clinging to "The Lord is my shepherd" in their fear and bewilderment over the awful thing happening to Mother, into the front room as far as possible from the "borning room" adjoining the kitchen. The hired man saddled the fastest horse in the barn and thundered through the black night down the icy road to get Brother Perez's wife.

Frantically, Great-Grandfather struggled to stop the hemorrhage and to blanket his feebly whimpering new little son in the zero-wind-chilled bedroom. Child-voiced prayer, Great-Grandfather's vinegar sponge and pepper tea, and Great-Grandmother's own indomitable will to live for her family brought her through the crisis just before Brother Perez's horse came pounding up to the door. And slippery elm bark solution added to her own meager supply of milk finally brought her wailing, puny infant to a thriving summer.

Another "hour of emergency" in Great-Grandfather's life had proved an "hour of triumph." With satisfaction he knew, too, that all his children, as well as their parents, had been brave. Life had tested them and they had proved their mettle. Having come to grips with life and won, they need never fear the worst that future days could bring.

But Great-Grandfather knew that being brave was not enough. He must also "be skillful in whatever he set his hand to do." After much consideration, therefore, he and Great-Grandmother took from the secret cupboard beneath the chamber stairs twenty hard-earned and carefully hoarded dollars of their potash money. These were invested in "the first right of preparing and using the System of Medical Practice" set up by Dr. Samuel Thomson, a New England botanic physician of those mid-1800s.

Soon after Great-Grandfather's certification, he discarded a "cure-all" that he and his small sons had worked out beside the kitchen steps. The Spanish Fly blister treatment was highly esteemed in both Europe and America at the time. Great-Grandfather had read about it in *The Vermont Gazette* or *Freeman's Depository* which the post-boy brought from Bennington each Tuesday. But the Spanish Fly was $16 a pound and so not to be considered.

After much experimenting, the resourceful Joseph discovered that his potato bugs, drowned in cider vinegar and dried in the sun, would likewise draw the coveted blister. Although this treatment was highly rated by his townspeople, Great-Grandfather preferred botanic medication. He and Great-Grandmother therefore turned their attention to butternut bark pills for worms in children, dogbane snuff for catarrh, tincture of lobelia, and numerous other saltbox-home-concocted remedies. These they administered to ailing townspeople any time of night or day. In later years, their youngest son Seymour and his wife Mary Ann perpetuated the small hill home tradition.

The Stars and Stripes in 1944 gave high praise to one of Joseph and Vesta's descendants, who had spent many youthful hours in our old home and who was then a captain in the Medical Battalion of the First Engineer Special Brigade. As I read the glowing comment, I recalled that oldtime saltbox-house medical center. The words citing young Captain Harwood for his lifesaving skill, as well as for his bravery under fire on the Normandy Beach and in de-mining the area, thus making the "hour of emergency an hour of triumph for the success of a venture and a country," spelled out the refrain of the words young Joseph had committed to memory as his maxim a century and a half before.

Numerous other descendants of those who first opened their eyes in the saltbox borning room are today members of the medical profession. From North Dakota to South Carolina, from New England to California, as doctors and nurses, they abundantly fulfill their professional oath of service to humanity. When my sister Sally hurries forth with her first-aid kit to ease community distress at any time of day or night, I am reminded of that Joseph and Vesta who long ago so generously shared their home-grown knowledge and resources from their house on Windy Summit.

Regardless of the pressure of endless demands in the struggle for survival, family life in that homestead represented unity and the satisfaction of creative achievement. As elders and young ones gathered around the hearth or lighted table each evening, all were busily preparing for the young folks' future homes, as well as supplying necessities for the present one. Great-Grandfather often read aloud from *The Watchman* or *The Depository* as Great-Grandmother and the girls clicked off the pillowcases full of linen and of woolen stockings for each daughter's dowry. There, too, the twelve quilts for Harriet, for Abigail, and for Ruby were planned and cut and set together with tiny stitches. What a family history those blocks and hand-set stitches proved to be in years to come.

There was time, too, to hem the strips of linen Harriet wove for curtains and to knit pineapple lace denoting hospitality to edge those for the front-room windows.

On one linen square, Ruby's sensitive fingers painted a horn-of-plenty with the brown of butternut juice. This she filled with luscious fruits and vegetables done with the juices of various berries, beets, and herbs. Hung above the Queen Anne curly maple drop-leaf table between the front-room windows, the "picture" drew much admiring comment.

The boys also at an early age left off building corncob houses and helped to whittle the endless bobbins and shuttles for wheel and loom; the numerous flails for each threshing season; the butter paddles and bowls, and even pegs for the homes and barns they would some day build for themselves.

As busy fingers flew, tongues were likewise busy with the events of the day at home and abroad, with bits of gossip if cobbler, peddler, or other regular caller were making his annual rounds, and with personal views of every sort and topic. A huge bowl of apples from orchard or cellar or a panful of doughnuts there nightly regaled five generations of family and guests, and always the evenings were leavened by the joy of sharing with interested listeners.

The fall of 1824, Great-Aunt Abigail chose her mate at an Apple Paring there in her home. A dozen or more wagons rumbled up over the frozen road and into Windy Summit yard that October evening. Beams of light from tallow candle and crackling fireplace shone out from the windows of kitchen and square room in warm welcome. The heavy latch clanked, door slammed, and merry voices filled the rooms to their mellowed beams and rafters.

In the lower chambers the women stowed hoods, shawls, and cloaks on the plump beds, donned blue calico aprons over their homespun gowns and assembled in the kitchen. There the men and boys had hung their coats on the row of pegs along the western wall. In their shirtsleeves, they were setting out the heaped-up bushel baskets and hollowed-out tree-butts of ruddy apples to be cut. Other empty baskets and butts awaited the parings, which would later go to barn and sty. Pans, sharp knives, and wire needles threaded with tow string were passed, and chairs were pulled into companionable circles. Amidst the clatter of voices, shy looks from youths a-courting, and the semisecret sharing of the latest bits of gossip, twenty bushels of the pungent, juicy fruit were finished by ten o'clock.

Two great brass kettles were heaped with pared and cored quarters for the morrow's cooking on the crane. One batch, combined with maple sugar and sweet cider, would provide the season's apple butter. The other, well sweetened with honey from the pasture bee tree, would be stewed for applesauce. Some stored in jars in the cellar, some frozen in a keg at the back door, would bring healthful variety to many a meal throughout the winter. Scores of long strings of the browning slices were festooned along the chimney wall; barrels and baskets were thrust into cellarway and back yard, and the floors were cleared in the center.

The girls in the front room had found their partners for the evening by casting an apple paring over the right shoulder. Harriet's had formed a V, but no boy with that initial could be found among the crowd. Abigail's luck was better. Her D stood for Danforth, that young man opined, and black-eyed Abijah, grinning with elation, joyously stepped forward. Their partnership through "Needle's Eye" and "Come Philander," where forfeits were paid with kisses, proved pleasing to both. So, too, it was as the thirty couples, old and young, whirled and clattered merrily through Virginny Reel. By the time they had sat together on the hearth settee for a supper of doughnuts, cider, pumpkin pie, and cheese, everyone knew that Abigail and Bije were "sparking." That winter Abigail's thirteenth quilt—the bride's quilt—was finished.

One lilac-scented evening the following May, she and 'Bijah stood up together in the southeast corner of the front room for the parson to pronounce them man and wife. At the last words of the ritual, the two families thus united flocked to Great-Grandmother's long-used dowry table, again spread with her oak leaf-bordered bridal cloth. Over cups of blackberry cordial and plates of pound cake, good wishes showered bride and groom. A panful of coals from the well-banked fire in the kitchen fireplace Great-Grandfather placed last on his daughter's dowry load, and the young couple set forth to kindle their own hearth-fire a mile and a half down the road to the east.

A few years later, Sister Ruby had a neighbor boy stepping around her. The winter of 1831 he started coming in to play checkers with Brother

Zach. As kernels of corn moved briskly across the board squared off with red ochre and soot blacking, Ruby popped corn on the fire shovel or picked out the meats from the butternuts and hazelnuts that Franklin and Oliver cracked by the firelight. Before the wheezy purr of the clock striking 12 sent Seth out into the night, he must have a "bite to eat." Soon he appeared more interested in Ruby's popping corn and carding wool than in the game of checkers.

When Ruby and her mother decided to stencil the front-room walls, Seth gathered the elder twigs and chewed their ends for the brushes. He helped, too, to gather the huckleberries and prepare their rich purple juice into which the brushes were dipped to work the color through the tin stencils onto the plaster. The lovely borders of fleur-de-lis along baseboard and ceiling, around door and window casings, and above the mantel filled him, too, with pride. He and Ruby had worked together and had found the going good. The next year Ruby made her departure similar to Abigail's. By then, half wistfully, half tartly, Harriet had conceded that hers was the spinster's lot, in every meaning of the word.

When Joseph, Franklin, and Oliver reached their majority and took neighbor girls for their wives, their father gave each a farm of his own. For Zach, father and brothers all helped to build his mill. Only Harriet and Seymour were left on the homestead with Great-Grandmother when Great-Grandfather went to his final home the summer of 1843.

The following fall, Grandfather Seymour's twenty-first birthday was celebrated, as his brothers' had been; by the piecing of his "Freedom Quilt." Symbolic of his having become a free man, the quilt would later be his gift to his bride. Twenty girls, ranging in age from eighteen to twenty-one, assembled in the Summit parlor and kitchen that November afternoon. Each brought along her needle, thread, thimble, and cut pieces to stitch for the quilt-making. Great Grandmother had yards of fine white cotton ready for the "set" to combine the finished blocks, "Hearts and Gizzards," "Chips and Whetstones," "Straight Furrow," "Barn Raising." Amidst the gay clatter of girlish voices, the motley patterns grew and were all set together by 6 o'clock supper.

The tables groaned beneath Great-Grandmother's best cooking, served now on blue chinaware with silver spoons. But only visiting and singing to Seymour's fiddle provided the evening's entertainment for the girls and the boys who had joined them for the supper. Great-Grandfather had gone too recently to his grave to permit more merrymaking.

As the tall, fair-haired, hazel-eyed Seymour admired his quilt top, the four corner blocks arrested his attention. "Yankee Pride" their maker told him was the name of the red, white, and blue patchwork diamonds set in an intricate pattern. He liked that design best. All the other blocks had workaday names and dull greys and browns, but "Yankee Pride" showed vision. Perfect workmanship, too, he noted, and lively industriousness. For the unusual beauty of her part in his quilt Seymour that night chose Mary Ann from the bevy of charming young ladies to become his life mate.

It was four busy years, however, before he could claim his plump little bride. At last, on March 17, 1847, he brought to Windy Summit its third mistress. As was true of her predecessors, her home was her life interest. Unlike them, however, she pinned no cap to her brown curls, clustered above rosy cheeks and wide blue eyes.

Many another change likewise marked this home, now modernized, extended, and painted Venetian red with white trim. Grandfather's eyes had glowed the fall before, as he applied the last coat of ochre, baked red in the oven, linseed oil from his flax field, and buttermilk from his dairy, from which his paint was mixed. To his happily whistled notes of "Yankee Doodle," he graded the lawn and banked his house with leaves and straw for the winter.

The ell containing cheese room, woodshed, wagon-house, and privy had required the help of all his brothers and their hired men in building, but it spelled efficiency. In the loft were a loom-room for Harriet, a shop for himself, and plenty of drying and storage space for the endless bunches of herbs, barrels of nuts, and numerous other household supplies. At one end were set the wool wheel, flax wheel, wool cards, flax-breaker, and reel. Candle molds, brass kettles, and dye pot were likewise shelved at one side, each to await its season. No longer would they clutter the kitchen.

All his equipment and his needs were now roofed in. His father's words rang again in his mind: "To be skillful in whatever one sets his hand to do gives life a perpetual goal and meaning." Sawing and splitting sled-length fireplace logs into stove-length sticks had been no slight chore. Progress had its backaches, but the results were rewarding. A year's supply of dry wood for kitchen, parlor, chamber, and cheeseroom stoves was tiered up here in the shed. No more digging logs from the snow for burning. His shining red cutter and string of bells, his newly painted carriage and democrat were housed against the ravages of storm. The inside privy, too, was a comfort beyond words in rain, wind, and icy weather. Mary Ann would find her new home among the township's best. Yes, life had a goal and a meaning.

Harriet, too, was pleased with the loom-room. There the sunlight streamed in through the branches of the tall crabapple tree right across her weaving bars and beam. There she felt free from all interference as she sat on her weaver's bench, tramping the treadles of the loom. Her hands flew to the rhythm of the humming shuttle and the drumming batten beating up the web. Weaving strengthened one's soul in its demand for patience and concentration on the pattern as it grew from the drafted design—each one so like a person's life.

Her years of weaving had supplied her family's many households well with their linens and blankets, their coverlets and jeans, tow-cloth and frocking. Her first weaving in the loft, therefore, was a new venture, a rag carpet for the parlor. Her sisters, brothers' wives, and neighbor women sewed endless balls of carpet rags from their families' worn woolen garments. These Harriet dyed to harmonizing shades of greens and blues, reds, greys, and browns to fit the pattern she drafted. The stripes in the six strips, each five and a half yards long and a yard wide, must match and lie true.

By October of 1846 the last strip was woven. Two weeks before Mary Ann came to the hill, the sewing of the strips had been completed and the carpet tacked in place on the parlor floor, well padded with clean straw. By ingenuity and hard work, Harriet had created a thing of beauty and comfort which had cost hardly a penny. There was all that discarded red flannel from Oliver's drawers and Abigail's petticoats making a nice stripe against Seymour's and the other men's well-worn breeches of butternut brown. The achievement of her goal filled her, too, with satisfaction. Mary Ann would like this parlor.

Vine-patterned grey paper now covered the stenciled walls, and white-wash the ceiling. But pineapple-bordered curtains still hung at the windows. Mary Ann's mahogany settee and chest, her Boston rockers and Hitchcock chairs brought new elegance to the old room. Above the Queen Anne table Grandfather hung bookshelves he had fashioned. *The 1790 Book Of Psalms, The Algerine Captive*, written by Vermont's Chief Justice Royall Tyler, and left by the author after a stormbound night on Windy Summit, mixed with Grandfather's sheepskin-bound schoolbooks and his father's *Materia Medica*.

In the kitchen, a shining black stove replaced the open hearth. What a miracle for cooking was this new iron invention that closed in flying sparks and ashes! Although Great-Grandmother Vesta's eyes were misty with memories as she took down from the chimney hooks the last ham and side of bacon ever to be smoked in its wide throat, and watched the removal, brick by brick, of her old fireplace and oven, she found joy in the nine-foot pantry and the range that replaced them. Above the buttery broad shelf where she, her daughter-in-law, and two succeeding generations of women would mix and roll their baking, her son pegged her saltbox. There it reigned for another ninety years, until my mother's determined small hands wrested it from the wall to take it with her when she sold Windy Summit and moved to another home.

Even in my day, a barrel of flour and another of sugar, maple at first, white later, flanked the pantry door. A great jug of vinegar, a demijohn of molasses, and a cask of corn meal stood along one wall. On a platform were lined up the grey and brown two-gallon crocks. One held crusty brown loaves of wheat bread, another corn bread, muffins, and bannocks. One provided doughnuts for mid-morning and evening lunching, and another the plump sour-cream cookies that dropped velvet crumbs as one munched their goodness.

On the shelves above were ranged the seasons' bounty of pies. There came in turn the mince and pumpkin, the apple, and the strawberry, blueberry, and many another berry, oozing thick red or purple juice. Generous wedges from these brought never-failing comfort to soul as well as body. The pantry shelves, ever laden with good things, spelled satisfaction and security for old and young alike. "Man is a better citizen when well fed" was the creed of the saltbox.

When Mary Ann arranged her blue Staffordshire and Chelsea Harp-and-Wreath sets beside Great-Grandmother's old pewter and woodenware, her King's Rose tea-set and her Blue Willow, the top shelves of the buttery nearly overflowed. Well-stocked they needed to be for, to quote Grandfather's diary, many days brought a "prolific lot of visitors" to his homestead.

One day that first April, Great-Grandmother and Mary Ann pushed their two cherry tables together and set eighteen places thereon. A strangely assorted group of men and boys scraped their chairs up to their places to partake of the savory steaming tureens and platters. Two Iowa Congressmen, studying Grandfather's flock of Merino sheep bred from those imported from Spain some years before by a fellow-Vermonter, American Consul William Jarvis, sat at Grandfather's right and left. Next sat a Baptist preacher and a Unitarian minister, both hoping to win pledges of support for their churches from their host, who had corresponded with them to ascertain their religious views. Grandfather's two hired men, the county judge searching for data from Grandfather's surveying records, the schoolmaster, and Mary Ann's father and brother filled six more places. A tramp looking for work that he never seemed to find, a runaway Negro, two of the town's listers (men on their annual rounds to appraise personal property for the town's tax list), and three ragged little boys who had come from their nearby cabin to sell Grandfather the horseradish they had dug in his meadow completed the motley assemblage. The three womenfolks took turns waiting on the men, and ate their own meal from the broad shelf in the pantry.

Even when a surprise party to celebrate Seymour and Mary Ann's silver wedding anniversary, Great-Aunt Harriet's birthdays from her seventy-fifth to her ninety-third, and Independence Day picnics in my childhood brought sixty and seventy to the family gatherings, Grandmother and Mother prided themselves on being able to supply at least "a dish and a spoon" for everybody.

By 1866, two sons and four daughters had joined the hilltop family. The first, a nine-pound boy who lustily bawled the announcement of his arrival in the borning-room, was named Joseph Lyman for his two grandfathers. Two years later his sturdy younger brother Frank kicked and crowed in the hooded cradle between the kitchen stove and marble sink, or in front of the sunny east window. Nearby Lyman's little rocker creaked in rhythm with his grandmother's, as she taught him, too, the Twenty-third Psalm, "Hickory Dickory Dock," and "Baa, Baa, Black Sheep" while the teakettle sang on the hob.

The big brass dinner bell on the corner shelf of the pantry was used to call the men to dinner from the farthest fields. One August afternoon its clanging iron tongue urgently summoned Grandfather in from his haying. That night he wrote in his diary: "At six o'clock this eve Mary Ann was delivered of a girl. The women say she is not a fool. Praise God for His mercy."

How well he knew that God should be thanked for His mercy. His cousin on a neighboring farm had fathered an idiot son who for the twelve years since babyhood had been chained like a dog in the cellar to hide the family shame. Grandfather's heart ached for parents and child alike.

During the next few years, however, his and Mary Ann's grief seemed endless. Two baby girls and then their sixteen-year-old son sickened and died of whooping cough and of lung fever. Great-Grandmother soon followed. For months Grandfather could write nothing in his diary. At last he inscribed on an otherwise blank page, "Even so, Father, for so it seemeth good in Thy sight."

His barn and fields, his cheese-making, and his community's welfare, however, clamored for his attention. Courageously Grandfather plunged into each day's duties, finding solace in activity.

Evening after evening during the Civil War, he worked out his town's military roll on the old cherry table. As first selectman, it was his duty to secure volunteers, issue the bounty money and, hardest of all, enforce the draft. Night after night his graying head bowed over the names of his nephews and neighbors, distress in his heart for those who he knew must go into battle. Great was his joy when one by one the boys in blue knocked on his door to announce a safe return to "Aunt Mary Ann and Uncle Seymour," as they were termed throughout the neighborhood.

During those first two years of the Great Rebellion, Grandfather was sent to the state legislature to represent his town. Proud though he was to be chosen, the honor presented a hardship for him and Grandmother. Never in all their years of married life had they been separated. The preceding March 17th he had confided to his diary: "Fourteen years ago this morning I was married. Have not been sorry yet."

The evening before he was to set forth, he worked by candlelight until nearly midnight to finish the shoes he was making for Grandmother and to paint the sled he had just completed for his sons.

The next morning Grandmother smiled bravely as she tenderly combed her husband's hair and beard, handed him his tall black hat, and stood with Lyman and Frank on the marble doorstone to watch him go down the hill road and out of sight. Then she sent the boys to help with the chores and turned to her churning.

The following weeks of superintending and assisting the hired hand in the cheese room were trying ones. Seymour had always had a special knack for breaking the curd in the cheese basket and for regulating the rope of the press. But she and Tom made out. When the cows were dried off in December, the final tally showed the usual record for the season, approximately two tons of cheese, a hundred wheels, each weighing forty pounds and packed five to a cask. Grandmother got her nephew Charles to take the last load of seven casks to peddle at 7 1/2 cents a pound in Old Bennington thirty miles away. When he returned two days later with "$20 in gold, $30 in silver, some bills and an order on the town for $34, totaling $105," she knew that Seymour would be pleased. He was, indeed, pleased when he returned from Montpelier. Mainly, it was good just to be home again with his folks.

Following his term of two sessions in the legislature, Grandfather served as head of the town's listers. Around the kitchen table, for three days that April he, Cyrus Hopkins, and Abel Denio recorded the polls and personal property and made out the Grand List, consisting of "one per cent of the appraised value of the real and personal estate, added to the taxable polls."

After eight days of assessing land that June, when they worked from seven in the morning until nine and ten at night, the listers again met in the saltbox kitchen to list the assessment. At the end of the job, Grandfather noted in his diary: "Finished making out Land Assessment and sent it to Town Clerk's Office. Town of Rupert Dr. to one day's work revising Grand List $1.25."

When Grandfather was town poormaster, his home again was a community house. Two of his diary entries tell the story of typical days. "Got a curious customer here tonight—he has bunked on the floor—his wits seem to be broke by study."

"Mrs. L—came here today determined to throw her youngest boy on the town. I persuaded her to keep him and take care of him & gave her an order on Simons for a pair of shoes for herself and boy."

As justice of the peace for many years, Grandfather used the Windy Summit kitchen as his courtroom. Lively discussions and heated arguments took place in the east end of the big room, where loom, spinning wheel, quilt frames, apple barrel, and cradle had in turn occupied the floor. Complaints of wives against husbands for drunken abuse, for nonsupport, and for "fear for my life" were heard and resolved. "Breach of the peace," unpaid debts and unjust bills, declarations of bankruptcy, contested property lines, and swapping swindles were but a few of the cases brought across the aging threshold.

Within the haven of the saltbox walls, too, many a youthful couple exchanged their marriage vows. Often, Grandmother and Aunt Harriet were the only witnesses to Grandfather's performance of the legal ceremony. Always, the new husband and wife tarried long enough for a piece of cake or gingerbread and a glass of grape or blackberry cordial. As a little girl, Mother often helped with the serving and sometimes gazed in wonderment at strange couples who came with pinched pale faces or overly flushed ones, murmured their vows and thanks, and hurried on. In my girlhood, a white-haired couple from Wisconsin knocked at our kitchen door one summer afternoon. They identified themselves to Mother as a pair for whom Grandfather had performed the marriage ceremony long ago.

"We just wanted to see the place again," they explained. Then the woman added with a smile, "Si was always quick-tempered, and I didn't know how to handle him at first. When he'd get mad at me, I'd bake gingerbread as a peace offering. He's always been fond of gingerbread ever since the night we were married here in this room, and you folks treated us to some."

Her eyes grew misty with remembrance. "Your mother wrote out the directions and gave them to me that night when we were leaving. I still have her receipt, and I always say it kept Si and me together those first years. All our children and grandchildren like it, too. Every Christmas I make seventeen gingerbread men to hang on our tree."

Those thirty-five years since Grandfather had pronounced that couple man and wife in 1874 had marked many a change on Windy Summit. Frank had married and moved away from the hill. Grandfather and Grandmother, Sister Harriet and Daughter Ida had "moved on into Eternity," and Daughter Hattie had married and become the mother of Bob, Joe, Sally, and me.

When Grandmother and Mother had been left alone on the farm in the 1890s, neither wanted to leave their beloved hill. At first the neighbor men worked the place on shares and helped with the chores. Rheumatism had crippled Grandmother so that cooking, sewing, and knitting were the extent of her activities. With aching heart she watched her youngest, so like herself but unaccustomed to hard work, take on the heaviest household duties and many of the chores around the barn. Bravely, cheerfully, and with never a word of complaint, Hattie donned her black "bloomer suit," a novelty in those days, and set forth each morning and evening to fodder and milk the diminished dairy of five Jerseys. Slightly less than five feet tall and weighing just under a hundred pounds, the dauntless little figure successfully superintended the hill farm for six years. Like her forefathers, she, too, could "surmount difficulty" without wavering.

Then one August day in 1898 when crops and herd were especially problematic, a tall, dark, good-looking stranger knocked at the kitchen door. Having focused an interested eye on Windy Summit and its independent little mistress for several months, ever since his return to his nearby home town after thirty years of roaming the West, he had come to ask to work the place for a year. Grandmother was eager to accept the proposal, but her daughter demurred. At last, however, the arrangement was made, and the new manager moved his personal belongings into the upper west chamber. He, too, gazed at the mountain view, and after his long travels it was good to "look afar and be at peace."

A year later our father and mother were married. Great-Grandmother's dowry table and oak-leaf bridal cloth were set with Mary Ann's harp-and-wreath for their first night's supper. But Mother's favorite gold-and-silver cake replaced the traditional poundcake and gingerbread.

Among my earliest memories is the Christmas when I was three. Dad reported that the mercury read forty below zero, and two feet of snow blanketed our hill. Bob and Joe and I had been told stories of Christmas trees and of the mysterious filling of stockings hung for gifts on Christmas Eve. That cold, white morning we awoke in our snug featherbeds in the downstairs chamber and ran to the living room to dress beside the welcome warmth of the crackling wood fire in the big black stove. No shining tree greeted our eyes, but most wondrous of wonders—there were our stockings, not just one but a pair apiece, tied to the back of our Great-Grandfather's rocker, and bulging with tempting surprises.

What a torment of excited anticipation possessed us as Dad, Mother, and Grandmother peeled off our outing-flannel nighties and buttoned us into our plaid woolens and high leather shoes. Then came the stampede for the treasure—linen ABC books with gay-colored pictures; a boy rag-doll for Bob and for Joe, a girl-one for me; a wooden-ball-in-a-box carved by Dad for each of us; name cookies, and a big golden orange wrapped in tissue and tied between each small pair of stockings. Most of the morning Granny rocked us and our dolls, read us our ABCs, and helped us roll our balls-in-the-boxes. Memory of that morning's delight still sheds a halo around that worn old rocker.

The next Christmas was Sally's first and Granny's last. That year there was a Christmas tree—a sturdy little spruce set up on a stand that Dad had fixed to hold it and its many successors. Chocolate candy boys, more picture books, woolly wee sheep on wheels, new red mittens, and many another love-inspired gift were hung upon the woods-sweet boughs. Dad held Baby Sally up high so she, too, could see the tantalizing treasures amidst the strings of popcorn and the tinfoil flowers that bloomed on this miracle tree. Wide-eyed, we older ones crowded close to Granny's knees, as she sat in the arm-chair which she pushed from place to place to help her walk. And even more wide-eyed, we clutched each precious bit of the tree's bounty as Mother gave a share to each of us. What a merry clatter filled the old house that day.

But the clatter was silenced, our merriment subdued, not long after. Granny had gone to sleep never again to awake, our mother told us. Never again would she push us in her armchair, when we would crowd into its broad seat for a ride. Never again would she mend our toys, pare our apples, and scrape one for the baby. Never again would she hear us read our ABCs and tell us the stories of Bo-Peep, The Three Bears, and "When Your Mother Was a Little Girl."

It seemed so strange to see her big chair empty, but before we could weep for our loss, we were comforted by our mother's explanation. "Grandma was a part of God's loving plan for our life here on earth," she said. "Now she has gone to be a part of His great life hereafter. We cannot see her in that place, but we can still show our love for her by being kind to one another and by doing everything we can to help others every day, just as Grandma did."

We were awed when a bent and feeble woman who lived at the other end of the neighborhood knocked at our door. From the voluminous folds of her shabby black shawl she brought forth a beautiful calla lily, snow-white with a gold candle gleaming in its waxen cup. Her mittened hand trembled and her voice broke as she handed our father her flower.

"Mary Ann always liked lilies, so I brought her mine."

She turned and would have stumbled the long way home, through mud and slush, but Father harnessed a horse and took her.

Mother wept as she laid the lily at the head of the casket. To Bob and Joe and me, solemnly standing with hands clasped behind our backs beside her, she explained, "Your Grandma was always good to her, and the poor old body has given just about all she had to make her own days bright. Humanity is blessed by such as that. It is something no money can buy."

The fall after Grandmother left us, Bob and I took our first step out of our hilltop home into the wider world. We started school. Fortified by a knowledge of our ABCs and the stories in our mother's primer; by number facts our father had taught us in gathering eggs, bringing apples from the cellar, and putting pennies in our banks; and by our laboriously attained skill in writing our names correctly, we set forth that bright September morning for the little red schoolhouse a mile down the road. Mother put our lunch pails in our hands, kissed us good-bye on the kitchen threshold, and bade us to "Be a good boy. Be a good girl."

When we returned at the end of an eventful day, the greatest satisfaction of all was sharing its glowing details with our dad and mother, Joe and Sally around the lamplit supper table.

Through the years, a daily family journal was spelled out above the ham-and-egg breakfasts, the pie-capped dinners, and the supper stews and sauce. A community journal was likewise compiled there when road builders, hay-makers, threshers, and innumerable others thronged the kitchen. Amidst banter and news, the great platters and bowls went around, the men fell to, and from the table's abundance they filled their need and found their comfort.

Around that same table, all four of us young ones first learned to read and write and do our arithmetic. There we pored over the delights of *St. Nicholas, Pilgrim Visitor, Boy's World,* and *Girl's Companion* while our parents shared the pages of many a book, magazine, and newspaper. On its broad leaves we passed many a wintry or rainy hour at games of dominoes, muggins, authors, and Pedro.

There, too, we girls learned to knead bread and roll a pie crust, to shape a dress and braid a rug. There Sally cut and basted her nurses' training school uniforms. There Jim doubly resolved to win her for his wife after eating her warm raspberry pie.

On the kitchen table, too, Bob and Joe shaped their bows and arrows, carved their jack-o-lanterns, and planned their crops for field and garden as they thumbed the numerous seed catalogs. Great-Grandmother's dowry table found versatile fulfillment in the saltbox kitchen.

So, too, did Grandmother's in the parlor. On its weekly polished top lay the family photograph album. Beside it was the stereoscope with its crocheted basket of "views" of the Great Stone Face, Pike's Peak, West Rutland Marble Quarries, and other fascinating places. There, also, was the opalescent shell-covered box our father had brought from California. Among its treasure-contents were a silver dollar from the Columbian Exposition, a gold eagle from the Denver mint, and a silver watch that wound with a key. A map puzzle, an animal matching game, and *Frost's Pictorial Wonders of History* offered additional joys to us who went exploring in the parlor each Sunday afternoon. From the 1790 *Book of Psalms* we likewise often learned our Sunday School memory gems.

Stretched full-length on the rag carpet our mother had woven to replace Great-Aunt Harriet's 1847 one, or curled between the arms of the ancient rockers and sofa, we visited far places, dreamed our youthful dreams, and enjoyed the contentment of just being. Whether sunlight streamed in through the small-paned windows or the wind hurled sleet against the grey-green glass, the old room provided a sense of well-being for body and mind. And beyond were always the mountains.

Upstairs, the boys' west chamber and the east room that we girls shared likewise gave us young ones a sense of security. In the tall bureaus made by Great-Uncle Zach in his mill, each of us had his own space for personal treasures. There privacy was never violated. In our rare days in bed, the old patchwork quilts inspired our mother to tell absorbing stories of the long ago. Birds twittered and chipmunks scampered over our low roof in the early dawn. The tall maples budded, dressed their stark grey limbs in green, and then shed their gold and scarlet garments outside our windows. Frost etched intriguing pictures upon the wintry glass. Each season inevitably brought change, brought dormancy, brought renewal. We early sensed that it was good to be one with our universe.

When one particularly frustrating failure in the 1930s filled me with bitterness and despair, I found healing peace and inspiration in that low-ceiled chamber. It was the first morning after my return from a long absence. Rain torrents drummed on the shingles and streamed down the blurred panes. An orange-and-black caterpillar was desperately trying to crawl up the flooded glass to a sheltered ledge where it would spin its cocoon. Repeatedly it was buffeted back toward the cataract of the sill. But it groped persistently upward. At last, drenched and barely able to crawl, it clutched the edge of the dry cranny, clung, and inched its way in. The hard tight knot within me let go. Instinctively the caterpillar would move on into the existence for which it was designed. So must every living thing. So must I.

Thunder cracked, rolled heavily across the immovable mountains, and subsided. So it had crashed and rolled years before, when lightning destroyed our barn and later half our cattle. Bravely, without complaint, our parents had shaped new plans, stretched their resources and, with many a sacrifice, rebuilt both barn and herd.

Rain lashed with increasing fury against the window. So it had beaten against us young ones innumerable times when we had struggled our way home from school or to bring cattle and sheep from the pasture. So it had whipped the men again and again as they rushed a year's crop to its cover or a load of wood into the shed.

How could one who had grown up in this house forget even momentarily the doctrine of this hill—that rugged perseverance in winning the goal toward which one is guided defines the dimensions of one's life!

The tantalizing aroma of bacon frying and the coffeepot bubbling crept up the stairs along with my mother's whistling of her favorite tune, "There's Nothing Like a Jolly Good Laugh."

Thoroughly awake at last, I slid out of the old four-poster. To meet the day's challenge was joy, a gaining of strength thereby.

Cherished memories again and again called Bob and Sally and me back to our family home for vacations and holidays. Invariably, our mother's lighted lamp in one front window shed its beam along the last mile up the road. Always, her merry blue eyes and glad smile greeted us at the wide-flung door as soon as our wheels had crossed the rattling planks of the hilltop bridge. And until his last day on earth in 1932 our father's work-lined face beamed his happy welcome above our mother's. Joe, his dog Bowser, and the pet cat, too, all added warmth to our homecoming. .

Though the weathered house on Windy Summit showed physical marks of aging in its later days, its spirit remained undaunted. Its front door still swung wide to welcome friend or stranger and to minister to any need. Great-Grandfather's pine medicine chest still yielded tincture of lobelia, pulverized dried tansy, and many another herbal remedy to family, kin, and neighbor. Great-Aunt Harriet's homespun linens, blankets, and cover-lets likewise still served both bed and table.

Certain innovations, however, supplemented earlier household equip-ment. In the former cheese room, a great wooden tub on kegs with a hand-turned iron mechanism on its cover each week groaned and ground its way through the family washing. We young ones took turns at furnish-ing the power. The machine's efficacy was considerably enhanced by the corrugated metal scrubbing board, the copper boiler of rain water over the hottest griddles of the range, plenty of soft soap, and a pair of stout arms.

The heavy black sadirons used for smoothing the dried garments were well named. Heated to the hissing stage over a hot fire in the stove, they produced excellent results in the hands of a dedicated worker, but at a sad expense of sweltering in the torrid days of summer. But the dozens of garments and neatly folded linens airing on the long clothes bars behind the range were a genuine satisfaction when the long hours' task was finished.

The ice-cream freezer, with its center paddle to be licked when the custard had begun to freeze in its ice-packed bucket, offered cool comfort on those hottest days. The chore of turning its crank was lightened any time of year by happy anticipation of the great creamy scoopfuls of sheer joy to come from its frosty interior.

Daily throughout the summer, the ten-quart tin canner in which we processed the glass quart jars containing bushels of beans and peas, corn and tomatoes, beets and chard from the garden, berries from the fields, and fruits from the orchard appeared on the stove top. Those hundreds of jars stowed away in the cellar cupboards against the winter's need were a source of pride to our mother as well as deep enjoyment to her family. "Willful waste makes woeful want," she used to admonish us, as she made nourishing use of every morsel produced on Windy Summit acres.

Vibrant voices still enlivened the rooms, but with greater variety of tone and a wider circle of thought than of old. The Atwater Kent battery set here announced Lindbergh's safe arrival in Paris in 1927 and the results of the 1936 national election. The hand-cranked Victrola presented *Tales of Hoffman* and Nelson Eddy. Most frequently of all, the ear-pricking jangle of the party-line telephone bell on the east wall of the kitchen invited the uninhibited sharing of every neighborhood family's news items firsthand and "hot off the wire."

Regardless of the new interests, we still gathered around the lamplit table each evening to read the daily papers and whatever else the mail carrier left in the box at our gate. And above the broadshelf of the pantry, fragrant as ever with herb, spice, and the contents of shelf and crock, the Concord saltbox still held its own.

At the last Christmas gathering in our homestead in 1937 Sally and Jim's two-month-old son, Jimmie, was the guest of honor. From the pasture hill Joe brought a pungent green spruce, which he fitted into the holder on the stand that Father had fashioned years before for his children's Christmas tree. A mechanized furry puppy and a giant panda replaced the rag dolls of the long ago, but popcorn strings and tinfoil flowers again bloomed upon the evergreen boughs. A special gift for Jimmie came also from one laden branch. As Bob handed down the polished powder horn, dated 1761, Mother explained to Jim, "Great-Great-Grandfather Zachariah carried it when he helped break the trail over the Green Mountains into the Benning Wentworth Grants. Some day perhaps it will help Jimmie to feel his Vermont roots and value that part of his heritage, too."

As the Grandfather rocker creaked to Sally's lullaby in the big kitchen, redolent of sage stuffing, roasting goose, and warm mince pie, the small-paned windows shone with pride in this sixth-generation son. The lighted bayberry candles glowed upon him, too, when at twilight we gathered in the parlor to sing the ageless carols. From the sweet-toned melodeon, bought for Mother and her Sister Ida when they were little girls, swelled the notes of "O Tannenbaum", "O Christmas Tree," and "Silent Night." Logs crackled in the big chunk stove, and the ruddy flames cast flickering shadows along the walls and upon the happy faces of the singers.

The last time I left that home on Windy Summit, our mother again stood on the marble doorstone to wave good-bye. As I drove out through the gateway into the road, grief for the going blurred my eyes and thoughts. On the bridge I paused to gaze at the beloved mountains and to regain my vision. In never-ending beauty, the green peaks and blue ranges extended to the distant horizon. Strong, steadfast, infinite, symbols of the universe and of destiny. Fortified by their serene example of rugged endurance, I resolutely drove on down the road which led to the goal that life had established as mine.

OUT OF THE SALTBOX

All that is left now of Zachariah's house on Windy Summit is the saltbox by whose lines it was shaped. In its small drawer are two of the hand-forged spikes which Bob salvaged as mementoes of our childhood home, when the ancient timbers went down before the wreckers' bar and maul to make way for the new owner's building. But though the old house is gone, its spirit lives on in the hundreds of homes whose original fires were kindled by coals from its timeless hearth.

2

THE DOORYARD

It never was a lawn; it was always just a dooryard. Into it opened the doors of our old saltbox house, and out of it, toward the south, swung the gate to the crooked little dirt road that wound its way over our hill.

The quarter of an acre "more or less" was first fenced with uprooted stumps back in the late 1700s. Later Great-Grandfather set a fence of crotches and rails to enclose the yard. But in my day, a weathered board boundary appeared and disappeared among the willows and bayberry bushes along the barnyard to the west, the lilac hedge east of the gate to the south, and among the western shade and eastern apple trees.

An accommodating fence it was. Across its bottom boards we young ones set our teeter-totters. We clung to its tall gateposts, standing on the topmost board, to watch Father bringing home the cows, or to peer into the nests of baby robins among the maple branches which almost inter-laced above the great old iron-hinged posts.

Where the yard fence met the meadow wall at the northeast corner, there was a two-foot gap at the top of the bank that sheered down to the road. A bar across the tops of the posts that flanked the gap shut out four-footed intruders, but permitted family and neighbors to squeeze through when cutting crosslots in or out. Shawl and frock, sheepskin coat and small blue overalls had worn the inner surfaces of bar and uprights smooth with countless seasons of use.

Frost annually heaved the posts askew and here and there ripped out a hand-forged nail, but May sun and the heavy maul from the adjacent tool shed soon set the fence to rights again.

Directly in front of the house, beneath the row of maples, was the well. A water witch with his dowsing rod first located the never-failing vein of water. Dug straight ten feet deep into the earth with pick and shovel and groaning joints, back in 1810, the well was more than once the family's salvation.

So precious was it that it was mentioned first in Great-Grandmother's widow's dower in 1844: "We then set off . . . one piece of land, beginning on the north side of the highway from East to West Rupert, at the center of the well."

For more than a half century, a three-foot curb of cobbleheads framed the top of the well. Above this, a wooden windlass operated a rope-suspended, handmade hickory bucket, and a great dipper gourd or a tin cup hung ever ready on a square-headed iron spike in the roof. Crystal clear and ice cold, even on the hottest August day, was the water dispensed from the well's rocky depth.

In 1863 Grandfather was no longer content with the clumsy hickory bucket and windlass. To replace it, he sent away for a chain pump with a tight, four-foot wooden top to enclose it and provide a sturdy spout on which to hang a pail. Seven dollars was the cost of that pump, complete with its fixtures.

When it was finally installed, and glorified with several coats of red buttermilk paint, no more modern waterworks could be seen for miles around.

Tragedy one August afternoon in 1903 pumped the well dry. Lightning struck the big home barn, which stood less than fifty feet from the house, that Sunday when Joe was a week old. Father, bringing his cows home from the pasture for their milking, saw the flames leap high above the treetops as he came up the hill. Frantically penning his cows in an outlying shed, he rushed to his blazing barn. Torrid heat and suffocating smoke barred any entrance to his cow stable door. His young prize bull was in that holocaust—its terrified bawl came to his ears. In desperation, Father rolled back the harness room door, broke his way through the manger wall with an axe, and by main strength threw his half-ton yearling over the six-foot partition, out of smoke and reaching flame, into the open air.

Seeing the wild flames and billowing black clouds on Windy Summit, neighbors all up and down the mountain district poured on foot, on horseback, and in buckboards, into the turbulent dooryard. Each man or boy brought with him his biggest buckets or pails.

They formed a human chain from the well to near the blazing barn, and thanked God that it had been a rainy summer, as they desperately plied the pump handle to bring forth the only available water to hurl upon the end of the house, which was fast blistering from the barn's inferno. Not until the wind shifted abruptly from west to east did the precious flow refuse to come to the frantically pumping hands.

Staring in helpless agony above her baby's head, out past the grim, sweat-stained, smokeblackened men, our mother suddenly saw the flames no longer licking at the house. As she dropped to her knees there by the window, her numbed lips moved with their first sound since the horrifying roar of the fire had burst upon the hill: "Thank God for the miracle of the wind—for neighbors—for the well."

That fall a new barn was built on the site of the old. Soon we were again treading the "oxbow path" uniting house and barn. Soon, too, we children were again helping to bring the horses along the drive that formed a crescent around the front of the house, joining the barn at the west with the wagon shed in the east ell.

What fun it was to treat our own and visitors' horses to apples or tufts of grass, and stroke their velvet noses as they stood tied to the hitching-rings on the shed doors. So many horses had stood patiently there in the old dooryard—the doctor's horse while his master battled for life within; the mail carrier's, the peddler's, the parson's. And even impatiently pawing or cribbing nags of sundry suitors left their hoofmarks on the gravel. On what Grandfather termed "a prolific day for visitors," or when a bee or picnic, a funeral or wedding, called relatives and friends to the hill, the dooryard would overflow into the meadow with horses and surreys or sleighs, or, in later years, with purring engines that, at times, likewise pawed upon the gravel.

Loads of wood for the woodpile came along that drive, also. Every winter the sled loads of four-foot logs, damp and fresh from the pasture woods, were piled at the end of the ell to season. Sweet-smelling logs they were, of maple and ash and oak, of apple, hickory, and beech, promising heat for the kitchen range and warmth from the next winter's fires.

Sometimes there was spruce, also, and then we would vie with one another to pry off the acrid lumps of hardened pitch or gum. Never was there more satisfying gum for chewing than those pale gold and amber nuggets that we whittled away from the spruce bark on a zero morning.

How we wished there were no school the March day when the neighborhood sawyers came with their big circular saw and its gasoline or horse-powered engine. We could hear the huge blade zinging a half-mile away, and by the time we reached home at four o'clock, the logs would have become a great pyramid of stove-length chunks. Chunks that Father, the hired man, and the boys would later split into smaller sticks for the cookstove or grade out for the chunk burners. Toward the end of summer, when wind and sun would have made the wood tinder-dry, all four of us young ones often earned our "twenty-five cents of Christmas money" by lugging the entire pile by armfuls into the woodshed and tiering it up against the walls.

Early each November the house was put to bed in a two-foot banking of straw and leaves, topped off with dirt and stones. That insulating wall all around provided more than a barrier to escaping heat. It supplied a prime runway for flying feet in games of "I Spy." And from it even a three-year-old playing outside could, by pressing his nose against the cold windowpane, keep posted as to just the right moment for appearing in the kitchen to lick the cake spoon or ice-cream dasher.

When the last snowdrift had melted each spring, the banking posts and boards were taken down and piled out back to be used the next November. Leaves and straw were wheeled in a creaking barrow to the barnyard, and the blush roses, the garden and lemon lilies, and the clove pinks would start again their luxuriant summer banking.

The first warm May day our whole family would turn out after an early supper to rake the dooryard. The peeper frogs in the marsh across the road, the cedar-waxwings, searching for hair and twine to line their nests, and the bluebirds in the budding pear trees would spill their songs upon us as we worked. And when at last the great heap of dried grass and dead stalks would send up its acrid smoke to greet a young May moon, Sally and I would scurry away to our playhouse.

Every spring we relaid the low walls of stones for that playhouse along the back fence. Crude, indeed, were its furnishings—salt bags stuffed with hay for beds; broken china and bits of slate for dishes upon a plank-and-stove-wood table; a discarded wagon seat for a lounge. But it was a challenge to our ingenuity and a source of contentment. And when the giant crabapple tree shed its pink and white plush upon it, our playhouse became a palace. Later it would become our craft shop, too—a shop where hollyhock dolls would wear bonnets of canterbury bells and dwell amidst burdock blossom furniture set upon carpets of moss from the pasture rocks.

Other spring and summer evenings would call us to tend the flowers. Each year we loved to hear again how Great-Great-Grandmother Blackmer had set the lilac sprouts at diagonal corners of her daughter's house to guard it, as did the HL hinges on her doors, from spirits of evil. As we generously sifted lime, as she had plaster, around those lilacs, grown in our time into spreading trees, we fancied that each heart-shaped leaf and budding lavender plume might be warding off a goblin.

Tenderly we spaded the earth around the yellow roses, the snowdrops, and the tiger lilies that grew just where the dooryard orchard began. Tenderly, because several generations of buried pets were sleeping there.

As we spaded, we dreamed of gifts to come from bloom and fruit for summer and holiday giving. Most of all would be the bouquets for visitor and neighbor, for church and school, and for many a shut-in.

Too, there would be the potpourri and the rose beads that we girls loved to make from the falling petals. All year we saved all available jars to fill with that potpourri, after it had ripened in a brown stone crock. A mixture of haunting summer fragrance it was—petals of the red and yellow and blush roses, the starry white syringa, the cinnamon pinks, the late purple violets that grew at the edge of the "shade," the tiniest leaves from the Balm of-Gilead trees, mint, rosemary, and marjoram from the herb bed, all chopped with cloves and laid in layers of salt, with ambergris to hold the scent.

From the gnarled-branched Baldwin near the fence would come the Comfort Apple or Pomander Ball. A firm, smooth red apple it would be, stuck as full of cloves as it would hold, to perfume a lady's dresses when hung in among them by her favorite-colored ribbon.

Stringing the lattice for the Eglantine roses to climb to the east chamber window was among the lighter labors. As we balanced on the ladder, we recalled the story of the mother root's having been brought all the way from England to Plymouth colony by a home-sick young ancestor when she was a bride.

Less welcome in that housewife's chest, so ran the legend, had been the plantain seed that had drifted in in the packing straw. As we had tugged at the spreading weed there at our doorstone, we had thought it obnoxious until an accident revealed its value.

An ugly nail wound on Bob's shin had resisted the doctor's remedies for weeks, causing our mother much concern. Finally, one day she turned to her Grandfather's notebook of Family Remedies. Finding that plantain leaves were said to possess a healing property, she slightly wilted a handful and bound them on the stubborn sore. A few days later Bob's leg was completely healed.

The plantain was only one of the many sources of medication that grew in the old dooryard. There was the tansy with its golden bitter-button blossoms and fernlike leaves, leaves that when rubbed green on raw meat would protect it from flies, or when dried made a distasteful tonic tea to tone our systems.

Close by the tansy, in the shadow of the damson plum tree, grew the goldenrod. In early days, its oil had been distilled to make the family snuff more effective.

There, too, were the slippery elm and the prickly ash or toothache bush. When the seeds of the latter were simmered in fresh butter and kept warm on the back of the stove three or four days, they were said to produce an excellent poultice for an aching tooth when no dentist was at hand. In pioneer times, when no pain-deadening medication was available, this was often preferred to facing the doctor's great ugly forceps.

"Seven kinds of greens make a pottage to cure the ailing," was an age-old maxim on Windy Summit. Such a dish was frequently served from the dooryard largesse. Dandelion, dock, purslane, red-root, horseradish, scurvy grass, and cowslip all grew at the edge of the shade or among the willows. Nettles grew in rank abundance behind the shed, and they, too, made good greens.

Beneath the east window of the kitchen was the herb wheel. This had been renewed several times since Great-Grandfather and his young wife Vesta first set it there in 1802. The location had been chosen for its exposure to the full morning sunshine and for the good drainage of its gentle slope. After spading the soil to a depth of six or eight inches, Great-Grandfather had enriched it slightly with well-rotted fertilizer from his barnyard. He then set into the mellow earth a discarded wheel from his big old ox-cart, thoroughly coated with creosote from the fireplace chimney to protect it from the weather. He walled the stout rim with stones from the pasture hillside. Herbs need warmth, and the stones helped to retain the sun's heat.

Between the spokes of the wheel, Great-Grandmother set her cuttings and seedlings. She and her sisters and neighbors had exchanged their favorites to round out a good variety. Savory, basil, marjoram, and thyme mingled with chives and parsley, fennel, dill, anise, and coriander. The same procedure was followed each time the herb wheel was renewed. From late June until mid-September, three generations of women there annually cut the sprangled green leaves on sunny mornings as soon as the dew was dry. Our mother's starched blue-checked gingham sunbonnet would hover like some giant butterfly above the grey-green plants budding with sprays of misty blues and whites and pinks.

"We must gather them now before they burst into bloom and before the sun is high," she would observe. "If we wait, they'll lose their oil and juice, and they're what hold the strength and flavor."

Bordering the herb wheel was the great bed of sage, its silvery leaves in great demand for sausage, cheese, and the holiday bird. Like all the rest of the herbs that were gathered there, the cut green or pulverized dried leaves added zest to numerous dishes and flavor to the plainest fare.

Sprays of mint and clumps of catnip throve nearby. Many a time we watched our pet kittens roll in ecstasy among the fragrant stalks of catnip.

One hot summer evening in the 1930s that herb bed provided us with huge merriment. A couple of scientists who were visiting us were wishing for mint juleps, so they set about making some for all of us. Laboriously they crushed the ice, gathered the mint from the dooryard, and pulverized it with the mortar and pestle from the woodhouse chamber. At last the glasses were pronounced properly frosted. Delighted anticipation beamed above each cup as eager hands raised the drink. But suddenly expressions changed. Came a choke and a snort!

"Lord, Ed," gulped the first to recover his voice, "all you've got in this julep's CATNIP!" Grandfather always maintained that catnip was good for hysterics.

The bayberry, that grew tall at the northwest corner of the dooryard, in olden days gave root bark to cure the canker. The roots were dug in the spring before leafing time and cleansed of dust. The bark was then peeled off by pounding with a heavy mallet. This bark, thoroughly dried in the weathertight loft, was then pulverized by pestle and mortar. Administered a teaspoonful in a gill of warm water each day for several weeks in succession, it was considered a cure for many ills.

Although bayberry tea had disappeared from family use before my day, we still used bayberry candles "for luck and light." To collect the wax, the clusters of ripe greenish white berries were gathered from the aromatic bushes in late September. These berries were boiled in water, and the wax melting and floating on the surface was allowed to concrete as the liquor cooled. It was then skimmed off, melted, strained, and poured into Great-Grandmother's candle molds, in which wicks were suspended. The resultant tapers were pale greenish-white and faintly aromatic of the parent bush in the yard. Five successive generations of the first pioneer family on Windy Summit cherished the traditional burning of those wax-myrtle candles at Thanksgiving, Christmas, and Easter, as well as upon other special occasions.

Most fruitful of all was the dooryard orchard. Widely branching and gnarled Pound Sweet, Tolman Sweet, Pippin, Baldwin, and Red Astrachan apple trees formed a grove near the east fence. Damson plum and pear trees guarded the tangle of grapevines beside the nearby row of currant and gooseberry bushes. An August Sweet, crookedly grafted to a common fruit tree, shaded the great clump of wineplant rhubarb growing safe in its half-barrel stockade.

No table setting or lunch bucket was complete without its apple or currant jelly, its spiced grapes, plum butter, or gooseberry preserves. And best of all for Sunday night's supper were the great, yellow-green Pound Sweets, baked juicily brown and cut, still hot and redolent, into bowls of johnnycake and milk.

To insure a good crop in the days before spraying was prevalent, the men from Great-Grandfather's day even to our childhood used to burn sulphur in the cracks of those trees, when they were in blossom, to prevent insects from stinging the plums or gnarling the apples, or black-knot from forming.

"Better keep the house pretty well shut up this morning; the air is going to be pretty thick around the orchard," was the signal for us to watch the annual burning. We helped scrape the loose bark off the old tree bodies to rid them of insects' hiding places.

But our own hiding place there we cherished. The biggest, oldest Pound Sweet tree jutted a stout perch of twisted leafy limbs out over the road. What joy it was to nestle there in the friendly arms to read of *Little Men of Plumfield*, or *Hans Brinker* and of *The Five Little Peppers*. Or to hide there when someone must turn the spitting, wheezing grindstone that stood under a tall maple by the barnyard gate, for the never-ending chore of sharpening scythe, mowing-machine knife, or axe blade.

It was in the dooryard orchard, too, that Sally and I one day experienced the rare delight of finding a hummingbird's nest. For days we had trailed the flight of the gossamer-winged rubythroat that gathered nectar from the sweetpeas at our back door. At last our searching eyes sighted the exquisite two-inch cup of dandelion down and moss and lichen fastened with strands of spider web to a branch of the farthest apple tree.

Throughout October, more than one generation of boys and girls Halloweened or helped make apple butter in the dooryard. Among the weaving shadows wrought by hunter's moon and weird branches, pumpkin-lighted ghosts and gnomes chased one another or buried themselves in piles of rustling leaves. And there the romantic sought their fortunes from the Pippin paring tossed unbroken over the left shoulder. Or from the seeds, each named in secret, stuck to one's cheek while one chanted:

"Pippin, Pippin, Paradise!"
Tell me where my true love lies!"

And then it would be time to bank the house again, and to watch for further developments in the cycle of the years.

Gone now are the roses and lilacs, the old red pump and the Pippin and Pound Sweet trees. Gone, too, the catnip and tansy beds. In their place extends a broad, smooth tennis court over which run the feet of scientific, college-bred moderns. I still am glad I knew it as a dooryard.

3

THE BARN

A century and a half of footprints wore the path from our house to the barn. It was a path that yoked the two buildings together for sustaining life upon our hill. Extending straight from the north door of the house to the east door of the barn, with a semicircular path at either end to other doors of each building, the path resembled an ox-yoke in its contour. In times of heavy snow, the footprints were considerably augmented by the big scoop shovel in a pair of mittened hands. In mud-time, a plank bridged the dip between the two slightly elevated building sites.

Great-Great-Grandfather's heavy leather boots, both cobbled exactly alike, began the trail the summer of 1788. The last to tread it was my brother Joe, when the house was razed by Windy Summit's new owner in 1939. Although our saltbox home withstood the seasons' beating for a hundred and fifty years, the barn that companioned it was a three-times building. When Great-Great-Grandfather first took the deed to his mountain acres, he and his sons erected a crude log barn to shelter the summer's crop of hay and grain, their team of oxen, two horses, a sheep and a cow. That log barn, with four lean-to extensions for accommodating subsequently richer harvests and the annual increase in livestock, stood for five decades.

Buck and Brindle were the first two-ton ox team that powered the clearing of the hill acres of their rocks and stumps, as well as the hauling of the logs and lumber for building. They were succeeded by three more equally powerful and patient ox teams. In their wide stall at the east end of the barn, they munched their pumpkins, hay, and corn throughout the fall and winter; their fodder supplemented by turnips during the spring and great forkfuls of sweet, new-cut grass throughout the warmer months.

The brass buttons at the tips of their long curved horns gleamed; their sleek, well-brushed red coats shone; and their powerful muscles strained to their master's commands of "Gee" and "Haw." Each cleft hoof was well fitted with a pair of crescent-shaped iron shoes to aid the animal's grip upon the ground in pulling loads, often double its own weight, and to prevent sore or broken feet.

Fan and Bill, their grey coats likewise well-brushed and glossy, were the first of a long line of mares and horses to occupy the adjacent stalls. Those ever-willing bodies gave invaluable speed and strength for developing farm and township. Their morning whinny for their oats mingling with the cock's crow, the bleat of the jersey calf and Shropshire lamb, and the reassuring answer of Tess and Curly, the mother cow and sheep, early established the daily chorus in the barn on Windy Summit.

Upon the puncheon floor of that first log barn the men flailed the flax for Great-Great-Grandmother's spinning and weaving and the grain and beans for her cooking. There they gathered great armfuls of straw and filled the stout ticks to base her featherbeds. From its stables each day came the milk for table use and for the butter and cheese that not only fed the family but provided a good share of their income as well. Wool for that first family's household needs came from the backs of old Curly and her lambs. So, too, did tallow for candles, when the aging ewe came to the end of her days.

During the five years between Great-Great-Grandfather's leaving the hill and his son Joseph's return, his son Perez worked the farm on shares. Each fall, therefore, brought additional crops and stock to the log mows and stables.

As a pound-keeper for the town, he also used his father's barnyard to impound the strays he picked up on the highway. That rail-enclosed yard serving as a winter runway and summer milking enclosure was at times a place of confinement for free-ranging livestock as well. Around its open pool, and later its hollowed log trough under a tall white birch, the cattle and sheep, horses and oxen, geese and other poultry daily crowded for their watering.

Upon one doorpost of that first barn were pegged sundry notices, copies of which were filed among the town records. Two of these tell the story of Perez's official duties.

"Geese poundage fee Two cents (to be sold 24 hrs after advertising on public signpost) three fourths of 2¢ to the impounders and 1/4 to the key keeper."

"This may certify whom it may concern that we the undersigned have on the ninth day of November A.D. 1798 agreeable to an order recd. from Grove Moore Justice of the peace for the county of Bennington apprised a certain cow now in the hands of Perez Harwood—and by him the said Perez taken up as a stray—and do upon our oaths apprise said cow at ten dollars as the present true and just value thereof.

"Dated at Rupert the 24th of Nov. 1798—

"Moses Robinson Surveyor of Highway"

"Enos Harmon Selectman"

Family legend relates that the swearing, redfaced owner refused to reclaim his cow by paying the ten dollars. The frisky Jersey therefore became the property of the "said Perez" in payment for her keep. Although the "Mar. 27, 1799: Voted that horses Mules and swine shall be prohibited from running on the common" created some furor, it was said that Great-Uncle Perez never had to impound any such stray in his father's barnyard. Owners of stock were learning the wisdom of fencing their holdings.

Although Great-Grandfather Joseph enjoyed many years of abundance on his farm, the famine year of 1816 showed a skeletal barn. That year there was a ten-inch snow in early June, with July and August "colder yet due to a violent disturbance of the sun." The hardiest of the sheep and cattle survived on nettles and brouse, according to family papers. Only a starvation crop of brush and coarse ground coverage was brought on two-wheeled cart and sled to the almost empty mow. Finely ground birch bark helped to fill out the equally dwindled resources of the grain bin. The following winter was a bitter one, with scant supplies from the barn for loom and larder, but the family survived.

Though the baby boy who joined the family that lean and chill January of 1817 was a "scrawny and fretful infant in this time of little milk," he grew to rugged manhood. Perhaps brouse and bark Jersey milk was especially potent, or perhaps his early rigors fortified him for worse later. At least, he was one of the more fortunate who lived to tell of the storm-racked, body-stenched and nearly famished steerage passage around Cape Horn in the California Gold Rush.

Those intervening years, however, had brought bountiful harvests to Windy Summit. The summer of 1838 when another son, Grandfather Seymour, was nearly sixteen, a big new barn was raised. Friends and neighbors from miles around gathered at the building site, where the log barn had been torn down. Nearby had been assembled a great hulk of framed timbers, props, and beams. So lustily did those forty panting, sweating men respond with crowbar and bulging muscle to the boss carpenter's rhythmic repetition of "All Ready! Up!" that by chore time the new barn stood tall and solid, ready for its rafters.

Great-Great-Grandmother, looking out of a west window a few days later, when she was visiting the hill she had left years before, saw the last shingle laid in place. Then, startled, she peered again. Her youngest grandson's long legs were hoisted like a ship's masts in midair, as he stood on his head on the ridgepole to celebrate this long-anticipated and hard-earned event.

"Heaven preserve the dunce!" the farm's first mistress implored, as she hastily turned to her knitting.

And Heaven did preserve young Seymour. At his father's death a few years later, he inherited the homestead. The barn he had helped to build was his constant care and pride through all the long years he lived.

The gathering of his crops into loft and mow shaped his ways of thought, which often brought him solace. When a neighbor with whom he and his father had "traded works" for many decades died, Grandfather philosophized to his diary: "A good citizen, family head and neighbor—an honest man—a shock fully ripe. Why should he not be gathered home to rest from his labors and be at eternal peace?"

That gathering of crops also was achieved by arduous labor. In both Grandfather's and his father's time, the flail and fanning-mill sent out their reverberating echoes from the wide barn floor. There were threshed and cleaned innumerable shocks of oats and beans and flax and wheat from the surrounding fields. Many a long hour Grandfather and his hired man faced each other over a loosened sheaf, each with a flail staff, or handle, in his hand. One stepping forward, the other backward, with a step-and-a-blow, a step-and-a-blow, across the dusty floor they beat grain from stalk with the swingle or swiple of the flail, joined to the handle by a strip of cowhide.

Grandfather's diary reveals some of his trials in harvesting his crops. 1855:

July 31—"Got a cradle and cradled wheat and oats. Bound by my hired hands. 'Tis miserable slow business."

Aug. 13—"Hain't done any great scratch—hands feel neat tonight—neater than they would perhaps if they had mowed as much as they had ought to this A.M. 'Tis a little queer that 3 hands can't mow more than 1 1/2 to 2 acres of grass. Perhaps 'tis in my eyes but I thought they were plaguey lazy."

Aug. 14—"Hot. Good hay day. Went to Dorset & got Old Zip shod. Got 1 qt. gin &c. Worked at hay this P.M. My hands have done a good business today—5 acres mowed—so I will forget the past if they only keep on."

Nov. 3—"Got fan mill—cleaned up 5 1/2 bu. wheat."

Five years later his diary, however, noted considerable improvement in his farming equipment and results.

1860: Nov. 19— "Hill threshing here with his machine & I in the dust to help tend it. 114 bu. oats threshed @ 3¢ and 9 bu. wheat @ 13¢ in 2 days."

In spite of being "stuffed up" so he could hardly speak aloud and blackened from head to heels by the threshing dust, Grandfather was exultant. The speed and efficiency of this gigantic new horse-powered thresher was miraculous.

1863: July 16— "Swapped a mare for a mowing-machine. Got shaved at that."

However much Grandfather may have thought he "got shaved," later that summer he noted with relief that his last load of hay was pitched into the home barn mow three weeks earlier than before. Barns in the outlying meadows also had been filled earlier. With his horse-drawn machine, he could mow almost an acre an hour. Quite a contrast to "2 acres a day by 3 hands." Or even 5 acres, when they "done a good business" after the purchase of "1 qt. gin &c."

No machine for husking corn ever arrived on Windy Summit but frequently a husking-bee by neighbors would pile the corn ears high in one rollicking evening.

When Grandfather's son Frank brought his bride home in November, 1869, family and neighbors gathered on the barn floor for such a bee. Swift hands, sped on by merry banter and shouting rivalry in finding the red ears, made short work of the summer's crop. When stripped shocks and heaps of gold and ruddy ears were piled beneath the scaffold, the floor was cleared for dancing. Punctured tin lanterns and glass-paned ones like Paul Revere's shed their patterned glow of candlelight through the harvest-scented dusk. Melodeon, fiddles and players moved in.

Cal Smith, finder of the first red ear and so privileged to kiss the girl of his choice, led blushing Nancy to the head of the "Grand Right and Left." Frank and Dell fell in behind, and "Old Zip Coon" drove scores of dancing feet to follow. Shadows flew among the yellow-lighted lanterns along the hand-pegged beams until the cocks began to crow. Dishpans of doughnuts and the big barrel of new cider were emptied just as dawn was greying the east. Then the heavy doors closed on a silent barn. The merrymakers followed the path to the house or the road to their homes, and sleep at last pervaded the stables.

But grain and hay were insufficient for the animals' feeding. Therefore, tons of Swedish turnips, pumpkins, cabbage, carrots, beets, and potatoes were stored each fall in a deep pit dug "below the frost line" behind the barn. These, sliced in a hand-turned vegetable-cutter or chopped in a big barrel with a steel shovel, supplemented the hay-and-grain feed for the stock. Cows and ewes were given an extra ration of the chopped "roots" and sweet apples just before calving and lambing time.

Even with the precautionary feeding, however, Grandfather went through some trying experiences with his heifers when bringing their first calves. On one such occasion he noted in his diary: "May 25—Had to take a calf from a 2-yr-old heifer tonight—one foreleg was back—had to cut the muscle running from the point of the shoulder to the neck before I could get him."

And again: "Worked 4 A.M. till noon replacing inverted uterus after taking a calf from Cow Star."

In spite of such crises, when a man must be his own veterinary, Grandfather enjoyed his cattle. He and his father had given much study to choosing their breed. They had finally settled upon Ayrshires and Tesswaters, which had sprung from the British Islands' White Wild Cattle. "By judicious breeding," he once reported to his Farmers' Club, "the Ayrshire had become at home on scant pastures, steep hillsides, and sudden changes of temperature." Although he often praised the more productive Holsteins, he always concluded, "They would starve on our pastures." Besides, he was happy to note that his Ayrshires each averaged a pound of butter a day.

Upon the studding at one end of the stable he penciled his best cows' records. Such entries as "Wild Air—84 lbs." (of milk per day for two months in 1865); "Old Creamer—241 lbs. in 3 days;" and "Moss Rose— 400 lbs. cheese milking season of 1873" filled their master with satisfaction.

A small measure of grain in each manger every evening "messed" the cows for their milking. It induced them to give down their milk and to bring them barnward with less effort on the part of the one who drove them in, both Grandfather and Dad maintained. Certainly the cowbells in the lane always chimed more vigorously as their bearers neared the barn.

Anticipation of what awaited them in their mangers smartened the pace of the horses, too, as they approached their stable. It was an unwritten law of the farm that every man who drove a team on the road or in the fields must look to its needs before his own. A steaming hot horse must be well rubbed down as soon as its harness was removed, and if the barn were cold, the animal must also be blanketed. A pail of fresh water, and one only, must then be given, followed by a forkful of hay. Only when cooled off and rested somewhat was it allowed more water and its measure of grain. Never must it be heavily fed and watered while warm and tired.

Grandfather Seymour loved all young things, and his mares' box stall, his calving-pen, and his lambing-fold were his special care.

When his lambs came "like smoke" on cold March nights, he would sit with lighted lantern beside his yeaning ewes, sometimes until dawn. When the mountain winds chilled his stable, he would gently carry a woolly wee creature, closely wrapped under his coat, to a box of straw beside the kitchen fire. And when the quivering, new-born body had been warmed, he would return it to its mother. Or if it were left without a mother, as sometimes happened, Grandfather and Grandmother would bring the "cosset" up on a bottle.

One such weakly little ram, whose sire and dam were prize sheep in Grandfather's flock of Merinos during the 1860s, gave small promise at the beginning. Hopefully, however, Grandfather named him Gold Drop and patiently nursed him through the first year of his life. And the young buck amply repaid his master's care. After siring a goodly flock on the home place, Gold Drop brought $1,000 from Grandfather's closest friend, another breeder of Merino sheep.

From its earliest days, the sheep-shearing was an annual event on the Summit farm. The day before its start, the broad barn floor between hay mow and stables was swept clear of chaff, orts, and other litter. There the shearers knelt, clippers in one hand while the other held the sheep. Inch by inch the sharp blades removed the woolly fleece to within less than an inch from the animal's skin.

On those May days, men from miles around assembled at the wide doors to watch the shearing, select sheep for their own flocks, or contract for the wool. Grandfather's diary for May 28th, 1856, carries details of a typical day.

"Done up 43 fleeces & sheared 13 sheep yesterday. Pretty good for me. Today Harry Clay—21 lbs.—never saw or heard of such amount and so fine a quality. Josephine—11 lbs. Cut of washed wool from 1 yearling ewe 10 lbs. Sold her tonight for $20. 3 hands sheared 92 sheep in 2 days. E. Norton, wool man, here today—Sold 65 of my 140 fleeces—664 lbs.—$305.44. Lots of men here and some staying the night."

Those fleeces that were sold from the home barn helped to supply the nation's mills which by then were replacing the home crafts of spinning and weaving. Proudly Grandfather later noted that wool from his flock helped to clothe the Union Army. Part went, too, to provide Clara Barton with some of her desperately needed emergency blankets for hospital and battlefield.

From 1789 till the mid-1800s, Windy Summit flocks had provided wool for the family's coverlets, blankets, and winter sheets. Sally still points with pride to the Sunrise coverlet in daily use on her son's bed. Its blue and buff and cream-colored wool came from fleeces shorn in Great-Grandfather's barn in 1824. Through the years, too, those flocks provided the men's and boys' breeches, frocks, and full-cloth overcoats; the women's and girls' dresses, capes and petticoats; as well as underwear for old and young of both sexes. In their final stage, those well-worn garments became hooked and braided rugs or woven rag carpet. Some of these are also greatly admired on floors of today. The softest and finest wool was often set aside for the baby shawls, sacques, and binders. Then there was always the endless supply of yarn for mittens and socks, hoods, caps, and mufflers.

By the late 1850s, however, the wool for clothing was no longer spun and woven in the hilltop home. Grandfather's diary again tells of the labor of exchanging raw wool for those mill-woven goods. Some of these must subsequently be bartered for money or other goods.

Sept. 19, 1856—"Went to Claptown & carried some wool for myself and neighbors—started at sunrise and got home after dark. My two colts snapped the loaded wagon along at a smart pace. Left of my own wool 52 lbs. unwashed; 4 1/2 pulled; got 8 1/2 yds doe skin, 3 Satt, 5 tweed and 10 of red flannel. Changed some more wool for 50 yds. cloth at Cleveland & Lyons in Salem."

Sept. 22nd—"Sold some cloth in Dorset."

Sept. 23d—"Traded some wool for cloth with Long. Got enough for myself and boys each a suit."

Nov. 29th—"Went to Pawlet—Swapped wool for cloth. Wool $66.13 Cloth & yarn $38.68. Left about 40 yds. cloth with Loveland to sell in his store. Suffered severely. Snowed like shot all day."

Although his sheep were a profitable business for many decades, his heavy investment in his flocks brought financial disaster following the Civil War. In 1872, his $20 to $40 sheep were selling for $5 apiece or less.

That bitterly cold March he experienced further troubles. Extracts from his diary pages tell the story:

"The water has stopped at the barn so now our water has all failed but a little that we get from the well. It is a terrible time & I am thankful we can get water at all—we have to draw it for all of our stock with a team about a half mile—also some that we use in the house—4 horses, 23 cattle, 67 sheep.

"I have the blues about so little hay—and yet the Lord will take care."

The Lord did. Spring came early that year, and by the first of May the animals were feeding on lush green pastures.

That was the last spring that Grandfather marked his cattle and sheep in the traditional fashion, set by his father, before turning them out to graze. In 1812, the Rupert "Records of Marks on Cattle, Hogs and Sheep" had noted those for Great-Grandfather and his brother respectively as: "Joseph Harwood's—two half-penny cuts on the under side of the right ear & a slit in the end of the same."

"Perez Harwood's—a half-penny cut on under side of left ear & a swallow's fork on the end of the same."

After 1872 Grandfather Seymour's initials, applied in red ochre or in lampblack to their newly sheared coats, marked his sheep. His cattle were the only Ayrshire herd for miles around and were well fenced in so required no mark.

Every cow and calf, as well as every horse and colt, every sheep and lamb that lived in that home barn, had its own name. A white nose, a red or black ring around one eye, a pink streak on either ear, and many another individual marking, noted in babyhood, provided the identifying and name-inspiring feature.

In our childhood, the Spot and Daisy, Whiteface and Sukey, Speck and Blackie that came each to her own stanchion were the Holsteins that Grandfather had predicted "would starve on our pastures." By then, the railroad had made available more grain for supplementary feeding, thus improving herds and milk production.

Even so, two tawny-haired Jerseys, Queen and Princess, still mingled with our twenty or so black and white Holsteins, thus adding higher butter-fat to the greatly increased quantity of milk.

Twice a day the year around the cows were milked. To the experienced grip of strong brown fingers, their bulging udders yielded their humming pailfuls of frothing warm white fluid.

For many decades, much of the milk had been made into cheese. The rest had been set in earthen or tin pans on pantry shelves or cellar bottom to cool and for the cream to rise. That cream, removed with perforated tin scoops called skimmers, was then made into butter in the busy farm kitchen. Various types of dash and barrel churns were there laboriously employed two or three times each week to bring the great golden ball of butter from the gallons of frothing buttermilk.

In my early childhood, a twenty-gallon tin can with "gravity action" indicators and faucets replaced the pans. Soon after, a roaring, hand-turned separator that often balked at starting was used to separate the cream from the milk. But the ten-gallon wooden barrelchurn, with a glass peephole in its removable lid, still sloshed out the sweet golden butter.

In later days, Summit Farm milk was sold for shipping. Into the ten-gallon cans waiting on cart, sled, or wheelbarrow at the stable door, the milkpails were emptied. The cans were then drawn to the bubbling, spring-fed waterbox under the tall birch at one side of the barnyard for their cooling.

Believing that cows performed best in a sixty- to seventy-degree atmosphere free from drafts, Father worked to achieve the favorable condition. When the thermometer on the mid-beam of the stable registered 80 degrees, doors and windows were opened wide on all four sides of the barn, if there were only a light breeze. If the breeze were strong, two sides were left closed. Cut newspaper streamers were suspended at the openings to discourage the entrance of flies, wasps, and other unwelcome intruders.

On zero nights, we young ones helped plug cracks and knotholes with handfuls of hay. On such nights, too, an ancient three-legged iron kettle, called a Dutch oven, filled with red-hot coals from the kitchen range, comforted the chilly bossies. Its journey on a low sled from house to barn often considerably widened the connecting path.

The hay-sweet breath of the animals and the fragrance of warm milk filled the stables on such nights. How the young calves nestled in their straw beds, bleating softly in sleepy satisfaction after their feeding. And what sounds of repleteness and well-being issued from the depths of the old barn where we youngsters used to go with Dad to help him fodder. The whish of oats in the grain-box, of corn shocks giving up heavy-kerneled ears, of sun-cured hay in the manger chutes!

The rhythmic munch and contented snort of the feeding beasts brought a sense of assurance even on the wildest winter nights. Then freezing gales often howled along the clapboards and heaped blinding drifts against door and window. Though we knew we must again break our path to the house, we also knew that the lantern shedding its soft yellow glow on glossy hides and shining cans would light our way safely through the blackest night.

Grandfather's barn had outlasted by many years the boy who stood on his head on its ridgepole to celebrate its completion. Then, in the early 1900s, it was struck by a bolt of lightning.

Although neighbors congregated almost immediately, flames fed on seasoned timber and newly cured hay consumed beam, rafter, and shingle against all human effort.

When the slow days that followed had finally deadened the heat of the charred embers and somewhat eased the shock and sorrow of the family, a new barn was planned.

The man who erected that building had been a capable carpenter from early boyhood. By 1903 he had become a contractor and builder noted for the excellence of his workmanship. A few years later, John Lillie was recognized throughout the world for his beautiful landscapes done in oils. A self-taught artist, his paintings were sold in every state of the union. Some now hang in the Metropolitan Museum and in many another art gallery.

His letter regarding this building is a unique one.

"Dorset, Vt., 8/19, 1903

"Mr. R—

"Rupert, Vt.

"Dear Sir

"Have figured the Barn as closely as I possibly can, and to use such size lumber as you ought it will cost $815, if I should build the Barn for you. You would not pay one cent until it was completed and if it was not according to agreement you would not have to pay for something you did not have.

"Very truly yrs.

"John F. Lillie"

Since "Received in full of all demands due me on contract for building the Barn" was signed by Mr. Lillie the following November, the owners must have been fully satisfied.

Like its predecessors, the barn sheltered a long line of productive teams and flocks and herds. For their feeding, what thousands of tons of hay and grain thundered by hoof and wheel up the north ramp, through the wide doorway, and onto the broad barn floor. There each summer Dad and his hired men, red-faced and in sweat-darkened blue shirts and overalls, pitched heavy, streaming forkfuls of timothy and clover into the waiting mow. There Bob and Joe and other sweltering men and boys forked and wallowed and tramped the prickly mass into tightly packed storage for the winter.

Later in the season came the threshing machine. When our grey Percherons hauled the dusty red rig in through the gateway and along the drive to the barn, we young ones prickled with excitement. No boy or girl of helping-age ever went to school on threshing day. Bob and Joe's first job was to lug the stones from the meadow pile to block the grim black wheels in place on the barn floor and the gasoline engine in place outside.

The repeated cough of the motor and the snap of the belt flying off, mixed with sundry curses of the rig's exasperated owner, eventually would result in the monster's breaking into a steady, air-shattering bellow. The feeder-man would take his place at the front end of the separator, opening like some cavernous jaw. Into the shuddering, sucking mouth he would begin to feed a constant flow of huge armfuls of oat stalks, well agitated at the lip to prevent clogging the rumbling, temperamental paunch. Out the side spout would pour the grain into the hundred-pound sacks to be toted to the granary beyond the cow stable. And out from the tail would fly chopped straw and black, stifling dust and chaf. That dust choked the throat, reddened the eye and blackened the clothing clear to the skin as aggravatingly as in Grandfather's time. At least twice during the day the machine could be depended upon to break down. But the repair operation gave the threshing crew a chance to drink deep from the dipper-and-pail of cold water, switchel (a composition of ginger, vinegar, sugar, and water) or cider that we young ones were directed to lug to the streaked-faced men.

The kitchen, as well as the barn, swung into a whirl of activity on threshing day. A half-dozen loaves of Graham bread, dozens of raised biscuits, and pumpkin pies baked in dripping-pans were prepared in the early morning. Three 8-quart kettles containing, respectively, succotash, beets or carrots, and potatoes for mashing steamed on top of the range. These would be joined shortly before dinner by the long-handled black-iron frying pan full of bubbling brown or cream gravy. In the oven, a twelve- to fifteen-pound ham or rib roast of beef would be acquiring a crusty brownness, while oozing herb-savored juices. Great bowls of sliced tomatoes, coleslaw, applesauce, and pickled cucumbers would mingle with plates of cheese, freshly churned butter, and various breads on the long table set for sixteen.

Supper must likewise be an abundant meal and show some variety. Warmed-over succotash, cold ham or beef, and creamed potatoes were favorite dishes, but breads, pickles, and sauce had better differ from those for dinner. And the wedges of cake had best be generous and thickly frosted, else the housewife would be silently judged a pretty damn slack cook. Our mother spared no effort to avoid that unenviable title. And Sally and I labored with her as soon as we were ten. Our job was to help "set a good table" and to do the great stack of dishes after the men had eaten.

Promptly at noon and at sundown, the clatter and dark cloud of the thresher would cease, and the men would stream along the ox-yoke path from the barn to the house. Our reward was Dad's confidently prideful look as he headed the procession toward the table. Their faces ruddy from a ducking in the wash basin at the sink and a brisk rub on the roller-towel, their hair slicked down by the horn comb in the combcase above the kitchen looking glass, the hungry workers would sidle into the waiting chairs. Knotted brown hands grasped forks and knives, and a medley of satisfaction circled the harvest table.

Soon after the thresher had moved on to the next farm, the clacking whir of the ensilage cutter and the put-put of its engine would mingle with the whine of the autumn wind above the creaking rafters. Again the kitchen would be a busy place but to serve only half as many men.

Bunches of herbs for dosing sick animals were likewise an essential part of the annual harvest. We young ones learned early to help gather these— wormwood for an ailing horse, thoroughwort for calving time, tansey to poultice a sprained or swollen joint. Dried near the kitchen stove, they were stored in the pine cupboard just inside the harness-room door. On the shelf was the ointment for treating a cow's scratched udder. For this healing salve, our mother would bruise together a handful of sweet clover sprays and an equal quantity of lovage tops. These she would simmer, for three hours or so on the back of the wood-burning range, in 4 cupfuls of fresh butter or hog's lard. The last step was to press the mixture through a stout cotton bag and pour it into baking-powder cans to harden. One can was kept in the house for use on chapped hands. The other went to the barn for any dairy need.

Emergencies requiring quick thought sometimes arose in the stable in our time, just as in Grandfather's. When Molly one evening showed signs of distress from her overindulgence in the cabbage patch, Father devised a broomstick gag held firm in her mouth by a muzzle. Before midnight Molly's bloat had disappeared.

Bob was only a teen-ager when he there performed an operation on a choking cow one day when Father was away. Old Daisy, the best milker in the herd, must have had an uncut apple in her ration and had swallowed it whole. It had lodged in her esophagus and was fast cutting off her breath. Her eyes rolled whitely in her head, and she was writhing in agony.

Desperately Bob grabbed the wooden mallet used for pounding lump salt. Seizing Daisy's gullet in his left hand, he swung the mallet hard against the lodged apple. Luck was with him. With a lurch and a snort of relief, Daisy gulped down the crushed apple. Bob's face was whiter than Daisy's eyeballs had been, as he put away the mallet.

"I was scared I'd crack her gullet," he mumbled weakly. "But she was a goner anyway."

In early childhood, we learned of the magic derived from the manure that was shoveled daily onto the pile at each stable door. That snow- and sun-rotted heap of nitrogen and other essential elements we were told would revive the poorest land. It served as top-dressing for the meadow grass; enrichment for the herb bed, rhubarb, and roses in the dooryard; fertilizer for potato patch, cornfield, and oat piece. We saw rich crops produced from what was seeming waste.

From the stable, too, we acquired our firsthand knowledge of the miracle of life. There we saw the mating of our pet two-year-olds, Chub and Betsy. There, months later, in the deep straw bed of the calving-pen, we witnessed the final stage in the birth of Betsy's first baby. It was Christmas morning, and we had brought the animals their holiday carrots and sugar. Betsy's calf was our most wonderful gift that day. Innocently, we wondered if the animals also knew of Christ's birth in a stable.

In our childhood, too, we and our cousins, as well as our numerous pet cats and dogs, romped in the barn in stormy weather. Many a game of hide-and-seek we played in mow and scaffold, horse stall and manger. There we dramatized *Robin Hood, Mrs. Ruggles,* and many another classic. Below, the young cattle rolled wondering eyes upward at our improvised stage in the loft above their pen.

Unbeknown to our elders, we sometimes rode the horse-powered fork used for transferring hay from wagon to mow. Filled with gleeful daring, we took turns at riding, pulling, and dumping the great, sharp, steel-tined mechanism. Dad's sudden appearance on one especially hilarious occasion put an abrupt and uncompromising end to that spine-tingling sport, however.

The harness room was also a favorite haunt. There on the big wooden wall hooks, the well-oiled and polished carriage harnesses were hung beside the grass-stained work ones, smelling of clover, of seasoned earth, and of sweat-damp leather. From those hooks we learned to take, in order, the collar and hames, backpad, traces, belly-band, crupper, and breeching to harness a horse. The bridle, too, with its bit and blinders, check, reins, and straps for ears and nose, we learned to place gently on the animal's head when "hitching up." Those velvety noses would nuzzle our necks and shoulders for a pat or a tidbit as soon as we entered the stall. Many a contented hour we spent brushing and currying those patient big bodies, braiding mane and tail to make them wavy, and shining the hard black hoofs with linseed oil. We loved our home barn horses as part of the family.

From the hinged top of the grain box in the harness room, we first mounted the horses to ride to pasture or to their wagon hitching.

Beside that box was the barrel of coarse salt with its dented tin measure for salting the horses, sheep, and cattle. Whenever the animals licked at the wooden bars in the barnyard, we knew it was time to put salt on the grass beside the watering trough or on the big flat stone at the gate.

On the other side of the harness room was the low box that formed the outlet to the oat chute. There we youngsters often sat with our father while he whittled an axe helve, a fork handle, or sometimes a willow whistle, and listened to his stories of "When I was a little boy." There we watched each spring for the coming of the first forktailed swallow. There we observed the building of its woolly nest beneath the barn roof's sheltering eaves. And later the incessant yawning of the yellow-edged baby beaks, in spite of the constant darting in and out of the parents bringing food, filled us with wonder. From that doorway, each fall we learned to know the call of katydid and cricket as signs of the ripening earth.

From that oat-box, we once watched a baby chick peck its way out of its shell, in its nest in a tub in the corner. As its clucking mother hovered near, offering no assistance, we anxiously begged our father to help with the hatching process.

"A chicken must peck off its own shell or it will die," was his surprising answer. An unforgettable lesson of work we learned that day in the harness room.

Though house and connecting path disappeared long ago, the John Lillie barn still stands. Its coat of red and white paint marks its sturdy dimensions, square and strong against the mountain weather.

Stable and stall have yielded their space to the present owner's jeep and car. Nevertheless, perhaps the children who now romp on that same scaffold and mow will there learn of the barn's important part in their American heritage. And perhaps they, too, will there discover some essential lessons of life from barn swallow, katydid, and nesting pigeon.

4

THE HOME MEADOW

Great-Great-Grandfather's home meadow gave substance to his family for five generations. Those thirty acres, more or less, were the first land he cleared in the mountain wilderness, to which he gained title shortly after the Revolutionary War.

Quaint was the wording of those old deeds:

"Twelfth day of June anno Domini 1788....a Parcel of Land being and lieing in Rupert and Bounded as follows: Beginning at a Beech tree Marked....from thence North forty degrees East one hundred and Forty Rods to a stake and Stones....containing forty-three acres more or less....to his heirs and assigns forever, for and in consideration of thirty pounds, two shillings lawful money.....and also namely a certain Sixty acre Pitch in the Second Division No. twenty-three of the original Right of Wm. Kanaday, running E. 144 to a Spruce tree then No. 20 W. 45 then to a Beach Staddle the S. E. corner of Joel Harmon's 60 Acre Lot then on the South Line of Sd. Lot to the first boundy begun and Suryd by me. Eben Cobb Survr."

Throughout the long, hot summer days—the oxen standing by—Great-Great-Grandfather Zachariah and his six sons felled the forest pine, oak, and maple to clear the plot of land for the home meadow. The great logs, many of them two or two and a half feet in diameter, they hauled by ox-team down the Vermont mountainside to the saw-mill. These they brought back as planks and beams to season for building their saltbox house.

With handmade shovel and crowbar and mattock, they loosened the gigantic stumps, which the faithful oxen then dragged to the meadowside, there to be upturned to serve as boundary fence and windbreaker.

But more than stumps must be cleared from the Windy Summit field. Great patches of flint rock here and there reared a grim barrier to plow and scythe. Dynamite was not yet available, so the stalwart John, Silas, Perez, and Abel, ranging from thirteen to twenty years of age, set to work with their father at burning and digging out the huge rocks.

Arduously wielding their heavy, clumsy tools, they dug a six-inch-deep trench around each block of stone. Into this trench, with the help of Oliver and Joseph, aged eleven and seven, they packed the dry and broken tree branches. The boys piled a thick layer of the same over the top of the rock, and Great-Great-Grandfather fired the twigs at intervals with live coals brought on a shovel from the hearth of their nearby log shack. For more than an hour the branches burned, frequently replenished by busy brown and calloused hands, until the rock itself shimmered in the heat. On it then were flung in quick succession countless wooden bucketfuls of water from the clear, cold brook that sang at one end of the meadow. Great cracks broke the up-jutting masses of stone wide open, until, by repeated firing and drenching, the rocks were vulnerable to pick and shovel.

From earliest dawn until after sunset, man and ox toiled at dragging those rough stones to points along the pioneer cart track for its future roadbed or to the edge of the meadow, later to be painstakingly worked into a permanent wall.

All that summer and autumn the hill and valley echoed to the lusty blows of axe and mattock, to the crash of log and stone, and to the whistle and shout of man and boy, as these wilderness acres were broken for tillage.

Deep early November snow drove father and sons back to Bennington, where Great-Great-Grandmother and the three little girls had remained in their log cabin to tend the family's first holding in the Benning Wentworth Grants.

The following May, Zachariah and his sons returned to crop their meadow. Rich soil yielded to spade and homemade mould board, a full twelve-inch depth of friable black humus, built up from the ancient forest floor, its decaying leaf mould the priceless gift of ages.

What dreams of next winter's fare for his pet brown calf must have glowed in little Joseph's wide blue eyes, as he helped to pull thistles from the thriving patch of corn. And how he must have gloated over the prospect of family flapjacks, when bees flying over that first, sweet-smelling field of buckwheat led him to the hollow tree, where meadow and forest met, that held the dripping wild brown honey.

When the early snow came that fall, the season's harvest was gathered into the family's new clapboard home and log barn that the men had toiled early and late to complete. That was the first in a long panorama of a hundred and fifty harvests that Great-Great-Grandfather and his descendants reaped from their hill acres before the farm was sold for reforestation and a summer home.

There, each spring, the fields of wheat and oats, barley, buckwheat, or rye were sowed by hand. There each autumn the heavy-kerneled stalks whispered and fell to the scythe, cradle, and corn-knife, and later to the horse-drawn mowing machine that made its first clattering appearance in 1863.

Often the three farm owners on the hill "changed works." By that method, all the men and teams worked together in a kind of "bee," finishing one field for each owner in turn until all had been completed. Grandfather's diary one August bore the notation: "Changed works in haying this year and finished the earliest yet. So the system of 'you tickle me and I'll tickle you' is sometimes advantageous."

There, too, each October, the bleaching green blades of the corn shocks rustled their secret of golden ears to the round orange colored pumpkins that sunned at their feet.

Those ears were hard-earned treasure. When I was a five-year-old, I used to ride on the handles of the weathered wooden marker as Father drove our grey team, Dan and Prince, back and forth across the plowed and harrowed field to mark the corn rows. In later Mays, I helped to drop the five kernels of corn to a hill, two feet apart in those marker tracks, as Bob followed with a hoe, covering the seed with sun-warmed earth. And then what startling images we erected to scare away the robber crows from the tender young green shoots. Just so had four generations seeded their field before us.

There we once draped a six-foot wooden cross with a rusty black suit and fullcloth overcoat from the attic. A raveled red stocking mat of hair and whiskers we topped with a battered straw hat, firmly tied on with more of the yarn. With what confidence we left our wooden man to stand guard over the corn.

When Sally and I went through the early June dusk soon after to gather the pink wild roses that grew along the meadow wall, we fancied that we saw our scarecrow move with more than the motion of the wind. Surely that head was nodding at us. A scarecrow could not come alive. Was some real hobo trying to make off with that ancient overcoat? Hardly daring to breathe, we groped along the wall until we were nearly opposite Mr. Scarecrow. Suddenly a loud, hoarse "Ha-a ha-a!" nearly toppled us off our precarious perch, and away flapped a big black bird bearing in its bill some of our sentinel's tangled red wig. Our faith in our own cunning was somewhat shaken.

Potatoes were this meadow's banner crop, however, even the common varieties of the earliest years. Then, in June, 1863 Grandfather swapped a buckboard for a barrel of the newly developed Early Rose potatoes, getting $27.50 to boot. Thereafter they and such other choice varieties as Great Divides, Mortgage Lifters, and the Green Mountain all richly rewarded the tedious labor of dropping each eye-scored segment by hand, hoeing the long rows of the four-acre lot beneath the scorching July sun, and digging the great nuggets from their dried-vine-thatched hills with a hand hook. A ready market always awaited those satin-skinned, snow-fleshed potatoes.

When Bob and Joe and Sally and I, in our childhood, picked up innumerable basketfuls of culls to be boiled in the great black caldron kettle for the pigs and chickens, we used to marvel at this miracle of Nature. From bits of shriveling old potatoes thrust into spring earth enriched by barn creatures' waste could come what in time of necessity was man's sufficiency.

Grandfather, too, had recognized the miracle of his meadow, while knowing the joy of accomplishment, as he followed his springtime furrow. In a paper for his Farmers' Club in the 1870s, he wrote: "Seeding, growth, and harvest compose the plan of the Power that governs the earth. The plow is the instrument of promise, the preparation for the seeding as the first step in the plan. Urgency is upon the plowman as he turns his long straight furrows, opening the heart of the earth to the husbanding sun."

And again, when snow pressed dead stalks and weeds and stubble back into the earth to enrich the soil for another season's growth, he wrote upon his diary page, "To die is gain."

A narrow strip of meadow near the wall was not disturbed by the plow for many decades through the 1800s That was the place where the perennial root of the hop vines grew and spread and disappeared and grew again. The long sprays and tendrils clung to the wall and yielded an abundance of green blossoms and catkin fruit. Those prized plants were hoed and weeded as carefully as the corn and potatoes, for from them would be made the yeast for the family bread.

Each September the catkins were picked and dried on a screen over a pit of coals. Beside the screen, also over the coals, an iron kettle containing sulphur would send out its fumes to bleach the cones and kill any insect life clinging to them. The hops were then sewed into canvas bags to store for household use, and any surplus would be sold. Sometimes, too, a small linen sack was stuffed with hops to be used for a pillow that would induce sleep.

The yeast, however, was the prime consideration. Grandmother's recipe for making it read:

"On Monday put a heaping handful of hops into 3 qts. water & boil gently 1/2 hour. Strain off the liquor & when milk warm, add 1/2 pint brown sugar & 2 tablespoons salt. With a little of this hop water wet 1 lb. flour then gradually add the rest of the water. Let it stand in a warm place to brew: stir it often. On Wednesday boil and mash 6 common sized good mealy potatoes & stir them into the yeast. Let it stand 1 more day. Then strain and bottle. Will keep for months if cool. For 3 loaves of bread use 1 cup (1 gill) of yeast."

Swedish turnips were also an annual crop produced in the meadow for man and beast. Grandfather's diary of September, 1858 noted: "Harvested 41 bushels Swedish turnips from about 10 rods of land." Year after year, he exhibited samples of these at the county fair. And year after year he won first premium for them. But better yet, those turnips, stored in a pit dug into the hillside, provided healthful winter fare in both house and barn.

When Great-Great-Grandfather moved his family to his hill farm, he also brought with him a bundle of apple whips from the Bennington orchards. One of those whips was a sprout from the first apple tree ever planted in Old Bennington. It had had an interesting beginning.

On their way to establish that first Vermont settlement in 1761, the pioneers had paused near the outskirts of the Grants to eat the mid-day lunch they carried in their saddlebags. Great-Great-Grandfather's mother Bridget's eagerness to see her new home site outweighed her hunger. Pressing on, she arrived at the Grant a half hour ahead of the others, thus "gaining the distinction of being the first settler." As she dismounted in the clearing, she firmly planted in the virgin sod the apple switch that had been her riding crop all the long miles of the four-family migration. A sprout from the resultant flourishing tree was in Great-Great-Grandfather's bundle when he moved to Windy Summit.

In order that each might have plenty of sunshine, he set these whips at random over his cleared acres. Even to my day, we picked Northwest

Greenings from the gnarled old tree at one side of the meadow, Russets from another, Blue Pearmains from a fence corner, Northern Spies and Snow Apples from the slopes where the hay grew thickest. True, plow and cultivator, rake and mowing machine had to be skillfully steered around those grey-barked monarchs, but the original theory was sound.

Every fall saw the great piles of fragrant red and golden fruit heaped beneath the staunch old trees to await basket and barrel and wagon to transport them to cellar or cider mill. Gale and ice and bee and sun had so capably attended trunk and bough that an abundant crop was produced there with little or no assistance from man. A hundred bushels was the usual yield that supplied Great-Grandmother and three successive generations of housewives with their dried apple cake, boiled cider, apple butter, pies, and all the other tempting dishes concocted from the cellar's barrel and bin.

Besides the cultivated crops, numerous wild ones in the meadow brought good eating in their seasons. We young ones looked forward to picking the milkweed greens and the lush red strawberries glowing in the grass as part of each June's delight. Tender young greens, cooked with home-cured ham and followed by a plump, brown-crusted shortcake, filled with deep layers of sweet, crimson wild berries, could fortify a man to face his heaviest task with a song in his heart.

Crops were rotated annually in two-, three-, and four-acre sections throughout the meadow, to give the land a chance to restore itself. Timothy grass and clover frequently were seeded into a large portion of the meadow, however, as they provided an abundant crop of hay for the barn animals. Besides, the roots of the yellow clover, alsike, white, and red clover were known to be host to potent restorers of the essential nitrogen in the soil. How we young ones loved to play hide-and-seek among its freshly cut, fragrant tumbles or haycocks. And how we loved to stuff sugar bags with the sweet-smelling blossoms for pillows for our playhouse. The honeybees, too, gave us their choicest combs when they had fed upon its nectar.

It was Great-Grandfather, however, the little Joseph of the long before, who had found the red clover of his rowen crop useful as a medication. In his doctor book, dated 1836, are still to be found these notes:

"Fill 18-20 gal. brass kettle with heads of red clover pressed together, stone on top to hold. Pour on clean rain water. Boil 1 hour and strain through flannel, pressing out clover juice. Fill kettle again with clover and boil in first clover tea. Strain. Simmer over slow fire until the consistence of tar. Do not burn. Spread this adhesive salve on a piece of split bladder or the membranous covering of suet, lard or tallow. Good for old sores, cancers, sore lips, etc."

The weeds or herbs that had a way of creeping into the haylots also supplied valuable aids for the ailing. Among these was the squaw weed or wild aster with its purplish white blossom about the size of a sixpence. Notes for its use read:

"Bruise green roots and leaves, pour on hot water and infuse 15 to 20 minutes. Pour off and add sugar and milk. A little spirits added acts as a preservative. This is a good remedy for rheumatic and nervous affections."

The lacy white bloom of the thoroughwort, the pink-blossomed Joe Pye Weed, and the lovely Queen Anne's Lace all contributed likewise to the family medicine chest.

Great-Aunt Harriet's favorite cough syrup, tightly corked in an ancient black bottle, stood always beside her Bible on her candle-stand at the head of her bed. Her recipe stated "1 oz. each of flaxseed, stick licorice, slippery elm and thoroughwort. Simmer all together in 1 qt. soft water till strength is extracted, then strain and add 1 pt. best molasses and 1/2 lb. loaf sugar. Simmer again 20 min. Enough cannot be said in its favor."

Enough could not be said in favor of the annual field of flax in the home meadow, either, thought Great-Aunt Harriet. From it she spun the flaxen thread and wove the linens for her father's household for a half century, and for her numerous brothers' and sisters' households as well. Thousands of yards of towcloth and brown homespun for clothing, and flawless linen for sheets, pillowslips, towels, and tablecloths had their beginning in the field at the top of the hill.

Each May the flaxseed was sown, and its delicate blue blossoms were fanned by the earliest June breeze. The busy hoe tended it throughout the summer, and in mid-September horny hands pulled its seed-laden stalks from the earth. Tied in bundles, the plants stood upright to dry for a week or so. Then the seed was separated from the stalk by threshing it with a flail on a clean, stout linen sheet. The precious seed was saved for the next year's planting, for a tonic meal to be mixed with the cattle grain, for future poultices, and for many another remedy.

The stripped stalks were then packed into the clear, cold brook at the end of the meadow, there to ret or rot. That was to soften the stalk, so the valuable fiber could be separated by the flaxbreaker from the woody core, before being hetcheled or combed for spinning.

Medicine, clothing, shelter, food, and joy in living, all were supplied by that mountain meadow. But to insure abundant provision, those acres must be fenced from invasion by wandering animals, by teamsters cutting crosslots, and even from thieving winds that lift the topsoil. The upturned stumps and broken rocks of Great-Great-Grandfather's original clearing were inadequate for both space and time. Therefore, stones for many rods of wall were dug laboriously from the meadow loam each spring, as the plowshare annually turned up an incredible crop to be loaded on the stoneboat and dragged to the fence line.

Some of the space between wall and stumps had been filled in with thickly set rows of brush for many years. Then, in 1855, Grandfather's diary tells of the end of his bush fence. April 24: "Drawed stone and pulled brush." April 26: "Put up brush fence like sack all day. All the time on the bob." April 28: "Burnt over some of my meadow to rid it of weed stubble— had a fine time—worked hard to keep it out of the fences but burnt brush ones at that. Whewing about from one thing to another, busy all day and but little to show for it."

A rail or snake fence then supplemented the several rods of wall. Even to this day, those nearly a century-old hickory crutches and rails may be seen here and there fagotting the boundaries of woodlot and meadow. Here and there, too, may still be seen sections of the weathered grey board fence, supported by its tall, hand-split oak posts, which later replaced some of the wall, torn down to renew a road bed.

The raspberry and elderberry bushes and chokecherry trees early established themselves beside wall and rail and post and board. The earliest owners toiled endlessly at pulling and cutting that brush, knowing that the roots sapped a good twenty-foot margin of soil of its moisture and vitality. But Grandfather, analyzing the labor of rebuilding wall, toppled by frost and animal intruders, and of grappling with wild growth, decided to let the hedges grow. Besides, he liked to look out across his new-ploughed fields checkered by flowering fence-rows. He valued, too, the bird-life sheltered there. The brown thrasher, the catbird, and the screech owl were his allies in ridding his fields of insects, mice, and other pests.

One of his feathered allies rated a notation in Grandfather's memoranda for February 4-5, 1860. "A neighbor screech owl dove through our kitchen window at 9 o'c & puppy caught him."

"The owl that came in unceremoniously last night I did not let the puppy kill but put him in an outbuilding, for which to reward me he broke out another window light and gained his liberty. Good luck to him and a cropful of mice."

Today's "living fence," so widely recommended by scientific farmers, is but Grandfather's hedgerow refined and come of age. How it has reduced the yearly ritual of neighbors walking the line to keep their fences as guardians of justice and amicable relations. No longer do horse-drawn stoneboats or wagons loaded with seasoned rails, boards, posts, or rolls of wire and the wire-stretcher make their halting way along the line each spring. But the matted tangle of brier and vine still provide sanctuary for rabbit and bird, as well as a breaker for the sweeping wind.

When wind and untimely storm, hail, or frost out of season, drought, or other calamity swept the meadow, the family learned early to accept it as a part of life: a part to be met, to be dealt with as best one could, and to be faced with fortitude. Where one crop failed, another, by its very nature, must produce a goodly yield.

Production by prodigious effort was the end and aim and law of life upon the meadow. Great-Great-Grandfather and his succeeding generations found warmth, contentment, and repleteness, joy, and security there upon the land.

5

ROCK SPRING

Rock Spring has never failed. Its cold clear water gushes the year around from its rocky cavern high on our Vermont hillside.

Giant sugar maples, pungent spruces, and wild apple trees drop leaf and cone and fruit upon its brink. Nearby, the hermit thrushes and chewinks spill their melodies through the summer days and early evenings. And when the cold drives them away, other songsters, the chickadees and buntings, join their voices with the singing of the water. Mountain pink and brier rose, hawthorn bush and lady's-slipper, purple violet and clematis, each in its season sheds its fragrant petals on the mossy green cliff above it. And where the silvery overflow gurgles down over the black earth, clumps of peppermint and cowslip drink deep and spread their luxuriant leaves.

Great-Grandfather found the spring in 1801. Having just returned to the home his father had deeded him, he set out that October morning to look for water. The wild wood inhabitants helped him. Not ten feet from his house, Great-Grandfather spied a narrow trail of animal tracks leading up the hill. Following it, he came upon a velvet-eyed doe and her fawn, drinking from the sun-flecked pool. Startled by this strange creature, they raised their furry white flags and were gone. But they had led young Joseph to the richest treasure of the hills.

With his hand-forged spade and hoe, he dug down and cleaned out the fallen leaves and twigs, making a three-foot basin with a spillway at one side of the top.

How many thousands of years the fox and hare and deer have drunk there, or the black-faced raccoons have washed their food there no one can tell. But for more than a hundred and fifty years now, the spring at the foot of the rocks has given its priceless gift to man unfailingly and unstintingly.

When Great-Grandfather first brought his bride to their new home, they carried the water down the trail in wooden buckets dipped into the spring. Then, when sons grew big enough to help with the chore, they used a wooden yoke, made to set upon their shoulders. From each end of this yoke hung a hand-forged iron hook, from which a bucket was suspended. Although this somewhat eased the burden, water carrying for family need became more and more a backaching job.

When Grandfather Seymour grew up and settled on the gradually improved home place, he established a better water system. Enlarging the spring, he walled it up inside with small cobbleheads picked from his neighboring meadow, and laid a cover of poles over it. Then, with arduous toil, he dug a ditch a foot deep, connecting the spring with his dooryard sixty rods away.

All that winter he chopped down spruce trees four or five inches in diameter and trimmed away their branches. When he had a few more than enough of these small, four-foot logs to reach the length of his ditch, when laid end to end, he set to work with a special auger. After boring in two feet from one end of each log, he repeated the process from the other end. When each of a seemingly endless pile of these had been bored with an inch-and-a-half channel down its center, the ends were shaped to fit together with socket joints.

After he had finished boring a quarter or so of the logs, Grandfather's back and stomach cramped him sorely. Finally Grandmother persuaded him to hire someone to help. A few days later he noted with considerable relief in his diary: "Engaged a man to bore and lay some logs at 32¢ a rod."

As soon as warm weather had thawed the ground, these "pump logs," as they were called, were carefully fitted together, section by section, in the ditch. With a great sigh of satisfaction, Grandfather and his helper "@32¢ a rod" threw in the last shovelful of dirt to refill that sixty-rod ditch. Only once, the winter of 1872, when a long spell of twenty- and thirty-below-zero cold caused the frost line to burrow deep, did the water in the pump logs from the hill spring ever freeze.

What a thrill the whole family felt when they first saw the clear water gush from the end of the pump log into the great barrel right at their door. How Grandmother delighted in having all the water she wanted for washing her homespun blankets without having to depend on her rain barrel.

Grandfather set a great hollowed-out tree trunk outside the dooryard gate. Rock Spring and the pump logs fed that, too. How the sheep and cattle and horses and oxen reveled in burying their noses, eye-deep, in the fresh, clean water of this new trough.

More than Grandfather's animals slaked their thirsty throats in that and its successor troughs. Tired teams, hauling their heavy loads over the hill road, stopped there to drink and rest. Herds of cattle and flocks of sheep on their way to and from the county fair, or in the fall drives, halted there to drink their fill or to nibble the lush grass that grew at its overflow.

Most of the year the overflow spilled down freely over the home meadow, enriching its heavy growth of clover and timothy and wild strawberries; or of potatoes, corn, and oats the years that the plow turned the fertile sod into rolling black furrows.

But for a few days each May for many years, the overflow was held back at the sheep dam below the barn. There in a ten-foot pool the sheep were washed for their shearing. And there, a few days later, the water would be steeped into a strong tobacco solution. Into this Grandfather and his hired men, and later our father, would dip the lambs and shorn sheep, to rid them of ticks before turning them out to summer pasture.

Soon after water came to her door, Grandmother persuaded Grandfather to dig another branch ditch and tap the main pump log line to carry a stream of the clear, cold water back of the house. There, in the thick shade of Early Harvest and Spice Apple trees, the boys set another hollowed hickory trunk and built a rough shelter over it. Here, in the summer, Grandmother set her buckets of milk to cool before pouring it into pans for the cream to rise. Here she set her dash churn, and here she "rensed" and worked her great wooden bowlfuls of firm yellow butter. Here, too, she kept her crocks of cream and salted butter, and here she scrubbed her dairy utensils.

Here also in later years the ten-gallon cans of milk for the cheese factory or creamery were cooled each morning and evening in a big water-box which succeeded the earlier log trough.

Pump logs, replaced later by lead pipes, carried Rock Spring water to the nearby sugar bush, as well as to house and barn. In earlier years more than one big brass kettleful of boiling syrup had been rescued from scorching by water from the wooden bucket and gourd standing close by the boiling place. More than once in later years, when the blazing logs in the great stone arch outstripped the boiler's watch, the sap-panful of precious sweet was saved by the fast dipping of water from the bubbling tubful at the door of the shanty.

Even now, when up-to-date equipment fills the saphouse, the tankful of spring water is the first to be readied when tapping season opens. Spiles have changed from poker-bored sumach to galvanized steel, small wooden tubs to covered metal buckets, brass kettles to shining evaporators, and gathering-tubs on ox-drawn sleds to pulsing pipelines. But Rock Spring water has washed and readied them all for a hundred and forty-seven sugar seasons.

Five generations of planters, haymakers, and harvesters, too, have quenched their thirst at the spring. In the days of scythe and cradle, the jug of gin or rum to replenish the small bottles that the mowers swung on their snaths was suspended in the spring. Later the buckets of root beer and switchel that replaced the stronger drink were hung in the spring's cooling depths, between the rounds of the mowers. And my brothers and sister and I lugged countless pailfuls of that cold clear water itself to the farthest corners of our hill acres, to refresh the sweating men.

Rock Spring, however, has fulfilled more than the physical needs of man and beast and vegetation. When grief for the death of his hunting dog came to my younger brother, he climbed the path to the spring. There, at the edge of the woods, where they had picked up so many game-trails at the spring's outlet, Joe shed his tears where no one could see. And there, beneath the stars and beside the soothing murmur of the water, he came to know that some part of his dog would be with him as endlessly as the water would be with the earth.

When the pattern of my life demanded that I leave the old homestead, I, too, climbed to our childhood sanctuary at the rock above the spring. As memories of our beloved hill surged through my mind, the thought of leaving it seemed almost unendurable. So much that I treasured most had come to an end. Then the song of the spillway came to my ears, and peace came to my being. Nothing loved would ever be lost. Memory would keep it always, pouring it out like water from the rock.

6

THE PASTURE

The pasture has long been the Summit Farm source book. Its hundred odd acres of berryfields, woodlot, and grassy slopes spread their wisdom-packed pages upon our southern Vermont hillside, where the winding silver of the mountain brook illuminates the text.

As Great-Grandfather and his neighbors laboriously dug and rolled cobbleheads and boulders out of the earth to fence their newly cleared adjoining acres, they learned beyond all doubt that good fences make good neighbors. They found, too, as they toiled and yarned and munched their salt pork and johnnycake beneath a tall pine at midday, that men become united when they work together to produce what is good for them all.

In the hundred and seventy-odd years that have followed, they and their descendants have kept that belief alive. Each spring they have gone, with ox and stone-boat at first, with extra rails and sharpened posts on horse-drawn wagons for several decades, and with tractor and wire-stretcher in more recent years, to repair the line fence. It is as much a part of the spring ritual as turning the cows to pasture. Each man, walking his side of the line, sovereign of his own stock and domain, is a part owner in the boundaries that promote their mutual good—boundaries whose maintenance causes their owners to know and understand one another better; boundaries that separate what is best separated, but which permit the free passage of all with a right to pass. There the wild gifts are free, for no man's sweat has gone to their growing.

In 1951, the late George W. Merck, Chairman of the Board of Merck and Company, Incorporated, of Rahway, New Jersey, in conjunction with state, county and township, established the Vermont Forest and Farmland Foundation here on Rupert Mountain, bordering our old pasture. As president and principal financial support, he generously permitted public access to these hill acres to continue.

Under the present program, "studies, experiments, and demonstrations designed to improve and make more productive the forests and farm land of Vermont" are being conducted upon the 2,600 acres of the mountaintop, which include part of Great-Grandfather's early holding.

If soil, plant, and tree here contribute to future discovery as liberally as to previous lore, the findings should be rich and vast.

One of the pasture's gifts, which Great-Grandfather and all his kin have most generously shared with friend and stranger alike, is found in its medical resources.

When the deadly smallpox struck the sparsely settled hill community one fall in the early 1800s, the young Joseph recalled how his father had successfully combated the dread disease in the pesthouse at his home town of Bennington several years before.

Searching his pasture, he found a patch of lobelia with ripened seeds. These he gathered, to pulverize with mortar and pestle for the needed emetic tea. From beneath the great red oak tree at the farthest corner of his lot he filled his leather bucket with glossy brown acorns. The kernels of these he would pound fine and steep with the gold-thread root he had gathered the previous May, to relieve the horrible canker. From his meadow wall he drew a flint stone the size of a flat loaf of bread. Heated in the fireplace and drenched with strong vinegar, this would produce a curative steam.

Armed with the pasture's wealth, he returned to his sick neighbor's home. In the harrowing weeks that followed, only one of the stricken settlers was carried to his grave.

The men and women of that remote settlement helped one another through many another illness, and Great-Grandmother's services also were often in demand. Before her own first child was born, she had been gathering red raspberries that grew in the neck of the pasture nearest the house. To relieve her thirst, she chewed some of the dewy green leaves and found that the burning soreness of her tongue and mouth was relieved, as if it had been pleasantly cleansed and sweetened with a magic brush.

When her wooden piggin was full of the crimson fruit, she pinned her brown homespun skirt around her with spurs from a nearby thorn-apple tree and picked a quantity of the raspberry leaves into its folds. These she carried home to her kitchen.

For many years, her own and numerous other babies in the community had their first feeding from this berry-leaf tea, mixed with boiled wild honey from the pasture bee tree and some fresh warm milk. It proved a preventive for sore mouths, which so often developed in the new babies of olden days.

One of the most potent concoctions from the pasture resources for many years was the Balsam Honey. Considered a cure for "cough, pain in the side, shortness of breath, spitting blood, decaying digestive powers," and just about every conceivable ailment, a quart brown bottle of the magic mixture was a medical requisite of practically every family in the neighborhood for more than a century. Its end came only when the essenial Jamaica rum was no longer obtainable.

If my brothers Bob and Joe filched and munched green apples, Balsam Honey scorched away their bellyache.

When Aunt Matilda once came to "spend a time" with her brother's family, one day after a hearty dinner she took to her bed, complaining sadly of her chronic ailment, the asthma. Mother immediately administered a generous dose of the fiery family cure-all to her wheezing sister-in-law. The resultant anatomical and emotional shock brought both the complaint and the visit to an abrupt conclusion.

The treasured recipe follows:

"Gather a quantity of Balm-of-Gilead buds before they begin to burst into leaf and pulverize these. Put six ounces of the buds made fine into one pint of honey, one pint of syrup of ginger, and one pint raspberry or blackberry preserves. Simmer over a slow fire from fifteen to thirty minutes. When cold, add three gills of 4th proof Jamaica rum, and stop it in tight bottles, with grains, for use.

"In many cases the balsam will be too strong a tonic for weak patients. In such cases, it must be reduced by taking a few drops in soft water warm. In ordinary cases, it may be taken from half to a teaspoonful."

By the time Great-Uncle Zachariah had grown to manhood, three tall Balm-of-Gileads were shading the pasture bars, where he called the cows to their milking. Accidentally crushing some of the fallen buds between the top rail and his lumber-blistered hand one April evening, he was inspired by their soothing, sticky juice. The next few days, he and his father and brothers spent all the time they could spare from picking stone, plowing, and the mill in experimenting in the big brass sap kettle slung over a fire in the stone arch at the edge of the sugar bush.

They finally evolved a healing ointment. The process consisted of boiling a bushel of the Balm-of-Gilead buds in the great kettleful of water from the freshly cleaned and settled pasture spring. When only a gallon remained, the decoction was strained through a woolen sheet. To it was added a bucketful of hot, newly rendered mutton tallow, also strained.

But the pasture has given more than medicine to its several generations of owners and neighbors. Bushels of strawberries, huckleberries (long ago known as whortleberries), elderberries, raspberries, and blackberries have been gathered annually from the sunny slopes by berry pickers from miles around. As preserves and cordials, in pies and shortcakes, or even dried, pickled, salted, and frozen, they have brought welcome variety to tables ever since pioneer days.

From the pasture fence rows, Great-Uncle Oliver made a novel discovery in 1838. He was gathering wild cherries to pulverize and mix with warm water, maple syrup, scorched Indian meal, and yeast to make a cooling drink for the men who cradled his father's wheat. Suddenly he realized that the sweet elder bushes growing nearby had the only fruit-bearing branches he had seen that summer free from caterpillars or other insects. "They ought to be good for something to pay for drying up the cows in blossom time," he meditated.

For many a season thereafter, he successfully whipped green elder leaves against the limbs of the choicest Pearmain and Pound Sweet apple trees to prevent insect pests. And an infusion of the elder leaves sprinkled on the yellow and pink rosebuds and clove pinks saved the dooryard flowers from destructive caterpillars for years to come.

In the old family doctor book may still be read a faded notation: "The elder bark and young shoots given to sheep will cure the rot."

The pioneer women and girls used to beautify their homes whenever time and resources permitted. Great-Aunt Ruby especially loved color, and from the time she was twelve she experimented with the dye-pot. This black iron kettle stood at the far end of the kitchen hearth, when not bubbling and steaming from the crane in the great brick fireplace. Into this pot, in separate batches from the pasture, went all sorts of barks and twigs and roots, wild grapes and berries, nutgalls and even blossoms to steep into dyes for the flax and wool that fed the humming wheels and loom.

The elm, the sumach, and the spruce rendered lovely shades of red; the ash and tender young walnut twigs soft greens; and butternut, alder, and oak were best of all for brown. The blues from toadflax, grape, and huckleberry, and the yellows from cowslip, goldenrod, and adder's tongue blossoms, were especially tedious to prepare, for collecting sufficient fruit or bloom was a backaching job.

The well-worn garments, too, were often dyed to be cut and hooked or braided into brightly colored rugs.

When young Ruby was returning from taking the wood choppers their mid-forenoon lunch of doughnuts and new cider one fall day, she paused to gaze with delight at the gorgeous foliage of the pasture hills. If only she could keep it with her always. And why not? She gathered great handfuls of the maple, oak, and sumach, the birch and elm and woodbine leaves of the brightest hues, and then a clump of the blue fringed gentian that cupped the azure of the autumn sky in its heart, and ran excitedly homeward.

Spreading a piece of a heavy, handwoven sheet on one corner of the kitchen floor, she sorted and arranged her leaves and gentians to form an all-over pattern and border on the four-foot-square linen. With a piece of charcoal from the fireplace, she traced around them.

In the long evenings that fall and winter, by the light of the blazing logs from the pasture woodlot, she bent happily over the rug she was hooking. Having selected the desired colors from the chest where rug rags were kept, she patiently cut countless strips, each from a quarter to a half inch in width, and painstakingly filled in her design and background by drawing loops of these through the meshes of the linen with a hook that her father had made for her. Bordering the whole with the dark brown of her mother's wedding dress, to represent the tree trunks, by spring she had achieved the most beautiful rug ever seen among the Vermont hills.

When she became a bride the following year, this was her bestroom rug, and the pasture dyes and design brightened her floor until her children's children romped there. So much admired was it that the pattern was widely copied. Somewhat modified, it is still a popular pattern for rug-hooking.

When Aunt Ida was piecing quilts for her dowry, she was inspired to make one of sprigged green calico triangles, set together with white muslin, as a likeness of the tracks of the fox and the wild geese which she had seen fagoting the early autumn snow, when she had helped drive the sheep in from the pasture to their winter pen. One of her nieces still cherishes her Fox-and-Geese quilt.

In one of the oldest family quilts, preserved in an attic chest, may be seen a piece from Great-Grandmother's first experiment with dyes. As chubby little Harriet trudged along the woods road with her mother in that long ago, she tripped and crushed her tiny apronful of whortleberries against her homespun sacque. Great-Grandmother's rebuke never found utterance; the stain was an inspiration. Into a steaming kettleful of rich, dark berry juice the young mother dipped her little girl's dress. And Aunt Harriet had a royal purple gown. That gown still gives its beauty to a quaint old quilt block.

In more recent years, the great amethyst- and jade-winged luna moths and the jeweled cecropias have supplied designs for the local silversmith, ceramist and linens maker.

The family genealogy notes that Great-Great-Aunt Pamela, who passed to her reward at the age of ninety-seven, was "a devout Christian, greatly beloved by all who knew her." When she was nineteen, she came to visit her brother and sister-in-law, Joseph and Vesta, at their new homestead. One afternoon she spent with Brother Perez's family, and on the way home at twilight she missed the short cut through the pasture woods.

Somewhat after dark, she reached Great-Grandfather's, with an exciting experience to relate. Halfway through the woods, she had suddenly felt a cold nose close to her arm and a great hairy body padding along beside her. According to the prevalent belief of those days, she thought that this was Satan, come in the form of a wild animal, to tempt her to forsake her faith in God and His constant care for His followers.

Now Pamela loved her family, her neighbors, and most of all her Maker. Her conscience assured her that she had committed no evil in thought or deed, and so, secure in her belief that "Love casteth out all fear," she kept calmly on her way. Sure enough, at the pasture bars, where Great-Grandmother's candle could be seen shining across the clearing, Satan disappeared.

When Pamela finished her tale, Great-Grandfather reached for his flintlock and strode into the night. A half hour later he returned.

"Judging from the track at the barway, your Satan was the big black painter (old form for panther) that's been killing sheep around here all summer. The only reason he didn't make an end of ye was because ye didn't run nor act afraid," he concluded grimly.

Aunt Pamela gently replied, "Fear is Satan." Her brother merely grunted as he put his gun back on its hooks on the kitchen beam.

More than a hundred years later, one of our cousins was blue-berrying in the same pasture when a young bull approached her, bellowing and pawing the dirt as he slowly advanced. Ann told the incident herself. "As that red-eyed critter was coming at me, I felt numb. Then I remembered Aunt Pamela and the panther. I never let go of my berry pail but just sat there and looked that bull right square in the eye. He stopped a little ways off and finally went to hooking into a tree. As soon as his tail was toward me, I worked my way over to the fence. And was I ever thankful to be on the other side!"

"Fear is Satan" comes down the pasture wind.

Stretched on the grass at the edge of the brook one Sunday afternoon in 1862, his fishing pole beside him, Grandfather drew his notebook from his pocket and wrote for his lyceum paper—a paper to bring fortitude to his neighbors, whose faith was being undermined by the War of the Rebellion and by Darwin's *Origin of Species*. His own fortitude had been born of his long pondering as he had tramped cowpath, line fence, and woods road throughout his boyhood and youth.

"Considering the facts as Nature presents them to our minds, we at once conceive that before any of the animal kingdom were created from the dark mass of inertia to active life, the herb, the grasses, the shrubs and fruit must have been a production of the earth. Hence the herbivorous animal must have been the first created according to Nature's Book. After so much of creation had been perfected, the carnivorous animal could have an appropriate sphere of action, and Nature would point to the fact of its creation. So that creation must have progressed step by step through a long period of time, whether we denominate that period to be six days of common time or six periods of time of indefinite length. So that the creation of one thing was made to follow another, all in perfect order and in their appropriate time and place, never conflicting with the purpose for which they were created.

"So far as the *Bible* speaks about the order of creation, it does not conflict, but harmonizes, with the Book of Nature in every respect except that the *Bible* says God created all these things, while that of Nature declares that it was done and leaves the pupil to draw his own inference in respect of the creating power. Yet who can turn one leaf after another in Nature's Book without discovering the infinite power and wisdom of an Infinite God?"

Each dawn still turns the pasture pages for any who will pause to read.

7

CHAMPION WHITE BIRCH GROVE

"Our great white benefactors." That was what Great-Grandfather Joseph in the early 1800s called the big canoe birches on his mountain woodlot more than once.

During Forest Festival Week in 1957 it was announced that the national champion White Birch among American Big Trees had been found in that same area, now known as the Vermont Forest and Farmland Foundation.

As I read the announcement of its acceptance as champion by the American Forestry Association, I could but wonder whether this canoe birch is the last survivor of those "great white benefactors" of long ago.

Estimated to be possibly two hundred years old, it bears the scars of time and weather. At breast height, its fungus-invaded trunk measures nine feet, two inches in circumference. Though winter gale or summer lightning storm, ripping through the grove with hurricane fury, has torn away its top, the old giant still rears its scraggly head sixty-five feet above the dark leaf mold of its forest floor. Though its thick, horizontal branches, reaching out among its crowding neighbors, attain a maximum spread of forty-three feet, many of its limbs, in conflict with the ravaging winds and snows of innumerable seasons, are likewise jagged at their tips. This grove has been truly versatile in supplying many a decade of hillman's need.

Great-Uncle Perez used to tell tales of the wandering Indians who used the birches of this fertile mountain slope when they pitched their tepees here before the White Man came. They, too, learned early to look upon the gleaming birches as the givers of good gifts.

From gigantic trunks, the squaws ripped broad, pliant sheets of bark, tough as rawhide. Sometimes they soaked these for greater pliability in the woodland brook, then bent and poled them for shelter. When they moved on, they often took with them their roll of bark to use again for a tepee.

Along the banks of this rushing stream, the braves once or twice carefully felled the previously reserved biggest tree, from which they stripped the strong white bark in one piece. This they "toasted" to flatten it, then placed it in a form of stakes. Inside it they set their framework of cedar strips, already steamed and bent to the proper shape. Over this skeleton of their cedar-ribbed canoe they sewed the bark with long fibers from the split roots of spruce and cedar. When this was finished, they calked the seams with gummy pitch from the boughs of the nearby Balm-of-Gilead trees to make them waterproof, also. Sometimes bearing a dozen Red Men at once along the valley waterway still known as Indian River, the craft was yet so light in weight that two young boys could carry it at portage.

The squaws and children likewise fashioned dipper and bucket, basket and dish from smaller pieces of the bark, sometimes combining two layers and turning the golden brown side outward to prevent its peeling with repeated use.

In every season's weather, bark and timber from this white friend also provided the nomad's fire, his indispensable defense against hungry wolf and panther, chilling wind and zero cold. A spark from his briskly rubbed stones' friction never failed to find ready tinder in the delicate white shreds he could peel from trunk and bough. To this the greenest twig and branch gave quick fuel for his cooking fire.

From these fortifying trees, the Indian took not only bark and timber for canoe and lodge and wigwam need. From the shining trunks he also drew sustenance.

Legend has it that one cold March morning in the 1630s an Iroquois chief hacked with his tomahawk into one of these white birches to get a block of bark for his squaw to patch an arrow hole in their wigwam roof. When she returned to the tree for more bark later that sunny day, she found the "boxing" from her husband's cut filled with a most refreshing crystal-clear and delicious wonder-water. How much better, she thought, this would be than the usual snow water for boiling the venison for her husband's supper.

Scooping the sparkling liquid out into a birch-bark cup laced with strawberry vine, she accumulated enough during the day to half-fill the wooden trough in which she did her cooking. Into the birch sap then went the chunk of deer meat and the shimmering hot stones from her wigwam fire. Replenishing the hot rocks at intervals, she produced the most flavorful venison stew that her chief had ever eaten. With appreciative grunts, he demanded more. So it was that sugar, rather than salt, became the Red Man's favorite seasoning for his meat.

The succeeding days and years, the story goes, found many an Indian striking a sharp-edged implement into various trees of the forest, but only the canoe birch and one kind of maple yielded the sought-for wonder-water, and then only during the Moon of Melting Snow.

At first, those Red Men knew its use only for boiling their meat and corn. Then, by the prolonged cooking of a haunch of particularly tough bear meat one day, they discovered a miracle syrup which hardened as it cooled and could be kept indefinitely.

When the Indians shared their discovery with their new White Brothers to the South and East, those newcomers tried another method of securing the sap. Instead of boxing the tree, the White Man gashed the trunk with his hatchet, inserted a thin chip or sliver of wood, and caught the drip in a birchbark cup.

So it was, according to legend, that today's maple sugar industry is derived from the gift of the early white birch grove.

Another of Great-Uncle Perez's stories told of the Red Man's use of this tree for medicine....The patient squaw would gather wide strips of inner bark from trunk after trunk each spring or early summer. Boiling this tender by means of hot stones and rain water in the wooden trough at her wigwam's opening, she then ground the mass to a soft paste between flat rocks. The juice she carefully scooped up, again in her birch-bark cup. When need arose, her toilworn brown fingers applied the healing lotion to cuts and burns and other sores on her papoose, chief, or brave.

Great-Grandfather also had faith in the health-giving properties of his birches. A strong tea, brewed from tender twigs boiled in spring water until the liquid was a dark amber tone, was one of his favorite tonics. He often drank a generous cupful before eating his fried potato, corned beef, and dried apple pie breakfast, to keep him "in condition," he said. The inner bark, too, he and his family frequently chewed, the delicate mint flavor serving to freshen the mouth and soothe the canker.

Both Great-Grandfather and the Red Man before him found that in lean times the inner bark of this bountiful provider could be dried and used for food. When the corn supply ran low, they ground the starchy substance and mixed it with their morning mush. During the frost-every-month-of-the-year in 1816, generally known as "Eighteen Hundred and Froze to Death," vast quantities of the bark were milled to supplement Great-Grandfather's meagre grain resources for his starving sheep and cattle.

When Great-Great-Grandfather Zachariah built his saltbox home on Windy Summit, he, too, had found the canoe birches an asset. He spread thick sheets of their weatherproof bark along his roof before laying his hand-rived shingles.

When Daniel Shays was fleeing from Massachusetts, following his famous rebellion against government taxation, to seek refuge with fellow-officers of the recent Revolution in the nearby town of Sandgate the spring of 1787, it was reported that he outfoxed his pursuers by hiding in the underbrush of this Big Birch Grove. Here the tall trees were, indeed, his benefactors. From their bounty, he erected a bark roof against the elements, kindled a fire to warm and dry his fugitive body, and over quickly-glowing coals roasted what game he could snare.

Many of the giant trees in the first stand of this grove were felled for charcoal for the first blacksmith shop in the village. Here, in the early 1800s Preserved Wright, the smith, spent long hours each winter, chopping both the big trees and the smaller, to thin the grove for better growth, as well as to secure the making of the hottest fuel then available to feed the fire of his forge.

When spring came, the black-browed smith dug his coal pit, a shallow space twelve or fourteen feet square. Setting his two- and three-foot logs in a tepee position in the center, he proceeded to build the longer ones up all around this conical core. When his huge pile filled the pit area, he covered the whole birch stack with sod and dirt to keep out the air. He left a tiny opening at the front, and through this, by means of his Long Tom musket and some bits of finely shredded bark, he fired the center logs. Preserved had brought food and his blanket with him for his four-day-and-four-night vigil while his logs smoldered to charcoal. His spade stood ever ready to supply an extra scoop of dirt if the need should arise. Air penetrating the pile could send his entire winter's work up in a stack of flame. But all went well, and the slow heat finally charred his logs to a rich harvest of fuel.

Great-Great-Uncle Eleazer also drew from this grove the wood for his "dish turnery" business. Smooth, pale-yellow trenchers and plates, sassers and noggins (gill-sized mugs), piggin (a small pail or tub with one elongated stave for carrying), losset and skeel, the last two being shallow containers for milk set for the cream to rise, all came by the score from his lathe. These supplied the pioneer table for many years before silver, pewter, and china made their appearance thereon.

Great-Grandmother's dyepot was sometimes replenished with dry leaves or bark from these birches. A yellowish tan for her husband's and sons' homespun breeches came at times from the leaves; rose tan for her daughters' woolen petticoats from the bark.

Soft soap, made from waste fats and lye from the fireplace ashes, often contributed by the birches also, she used to "set" those dyes.

Her ash-container in her backyard was, itself, a birch stump barrel two and a half feet in diameter. It had been hollowed by slow fire and her husband's axe and adze. Punctured at the bottom, it was set upon a strong cask, which received the lye drained from the barrel when accumulated ashes were drenched with water from the dooryard well. This lye must be strong enough to support an egg or a potato so a part the size of a ninepence would show. Six bushels of ashes were required to be thus leached in the outdoor tub to supply a barrel of the clean, jelly-like soap for the early American household. Twenty-four pounds of grease were also required, to be boiled with the barrel of lye in the big black caldron slung by trammels over the backyard fire on soap-making day.

My earliest memory of that grove stems from a family expedition to the nearby berry lot one July day. That hot afternoon Dad lined our canvas shoes with birch-bark insoles. To our surprise, our small toes found relief from the heat that crept out of the burning rocks jutting up in the field. And when we slyly tried the shallow pools at the edge of the brook, our soles were strangely waterproof.

Dad showed us how to make drinking cups by cutting circles of bark, six inches or so in diameter, from a fallen birch. Each of these we creased into quarters and clipped "the wings" into the shape of a cone with the split end of a stiff two-inch stub of a willow twig.

A basket, too, to hold the duskiest, sweetest fruit we had ever found, he fashioned from a sheet of bark shed by one of the older trees. After lacing the nine- by eighteen-inch golden brown and white strip into a cylinder with strands of wild grapevine, he similarly laced in a six-inch round of bark for the bottom.

Each year, from the bark she peeled off the birch chunks for our winter fires, our mother made a dozen or more cornucopias to fill with candy and nuts and hang upon our Christmas tree. Stitching these into sturdy containers with bits of red and green yarn left from her knitting of numerous pairs of mittens, she made a strong loop of the same to hang each satiny white horn-of-plenty on the fragrant green boughs. To each she often attached tiny sprays of pine, wee cones, and scarlet berries. How we loved those birch cornucopias.

On one of our earliest family pilgrimages through this mountain woodlot, we came upon what has now been named the Champion Birch. Our Midas Tree, we called it that October day. Its hoard of golden leaves, through which the sunlight sifted, gave a burnished crown to the monarch's buffeted head and wealth to his silvery pockets. Gathering a handful of the "coins" that had fallen, we laughingly called them our lucky pieces.

In later childhood, my brothers and sister and I looked upon our first hike each spring along these slopes of Windy Summit as marking winter's end. Eagerly we would set forth the first Saturday after the last snowdrift had disappeared.

One of the most beautiful scenes painted upon my memory is of that grove one glorious spring day. The graceful white trunks and limbs in their feathery green stood regally silhouetted against the blue of sky and mountain. High in the top of one, a bright-crested cardinal poured forth his song, while the peeper frogs piped from the rain-pool among the great roots below. The white of bark, of drifting cloud and foaming brook were all reflected in the sky-blue pool.

Reflected in it, too, was the furrowed black knee of our great King Birch. As gigantic and majestic as ever, it stood deep in the grove, though broken boughs at its foot again bore witness to the winter's rugged challenge.

By some strangely unaccountable, though fortunate, combination of circumstances, through the changing decades man and Nature have permitted the Big Tree to outlive its fellow birches. Indian tomahawk and pioneer axe, gashing and girdling others in the grove, bypassed this gleaming trunk in its youth. Wigwam, canoe, hearth log, and timber for pulp wood or charcoal claimed its giant brothers and their seed, one by one. Gale, sleet crust, and lightning have likewise taken their toll from successive generations upon this mountainside. Scarred but stalwartly erect, the Champion Birch keeps its secret of age and survival.

Neighbored close by many a younger canoe birch, mingling with beech, ash and maple, elm, oak and hornbeam, the venerable monarch today looks down upon a woodland block, especially designated for managed cutting operations for research and demonstration. Profits from this area are used by the trustees of the Vermont Forest and Farmland Foundation for a scholarship for local youth, to point out the values of forestry.

If Great-Grandfather were to revisit the George W. Merck Birch Grove today, he might well still call the tall trees growing here, "Our great white benefactors."

8

THE SAP HOUSE

June 12 1855—"Went on the hill and put up a kind of sap shanty to set my kettle in."

June 15—"Finished my shanty 10 x 12 ft., cost not over $3."

That tiny log hut noted in Grandfather's diary a little more than a century ago was the first sap-house in our hill community. Three sides and a sloping roof were made as tight against the weather as mud-chinked logs from his woodlot would permit. The fourth side, facing the south, from which direction the wind blew least often, was left half open for ventilation and for the escape of steam at boiling time.

As Grandfather surveyed his great black caldron kettle set in an arch of stone picked from his meadow, made tight with mortar, and with a neat square opening for feeding in the wood, he felt a surge of pride. Nearby stood the wooden rack with the two big brass kettles for storage.

True, he could only partly boil his syrup in his caldron. It must still be laboriously dipped into pails and carried to the house for its final boiling down, but this was the best that he had managed yet. No longer would flying ashes, wind-blown leaves and twigs, nor insects blundering near, darken and taint his syrup. No longer would sun and wind and rain and snow beat upon the contents of his kettle.

In spare hours from doing chores and tending the sick the following winter, Grandfather Seymour with the help of his hired hand laid in a supply of "boiling wood," tiering it up for convenience beside the shanty opening.

On stormy days he whittled and with a red-hot poker bored his spiles or spills, until he could count nearly three hundred of those four-inch-long sumach cylinders, a half inch or so in diameter, upon his workshop shelf. Those would take care of the two hundred trees in his sugarbush and allow for some breakage as well.

Eagerly Grandfather awaited the following spring's tapping time. But his diary entries for April and May, 1856, tell of bitter disappointment. From December until April of that year, the mercury had frequently registered 27 or 28 degrees below zero and commonly 20 below. The roads had been almost impassable, and the first thaw came on April 17. Three days later, six more inches of snow fell. Was this to be a repetition of "1800 and froze to death"?

On April 23, 1856, he wrote hopefully: 'The winter has mostly all past with his gloom and frost & smiling spring seems to be slowly approaching to infuse new life into things which winter with its rigors has so nearly destroyed. May I hope that I may be a recipient of its blessings, for if the seeds of Consumption are not sown, my System seems almost willing to cave in, so much is its vitality injured by the severe cold. The longest, steadiest, most lasting cold and snow I ever saw."

April 27—"Pleasant and warm: May my heart be ever grateful to God for His manifold Blessings and tender Mercies."

April 30—"The last of April & a good many snowdrifts to be seen, yet grass is coming on rapidly, sheep can get their living upon a pinch—have made no sugar, put up but little fence, & have not plowed a furrow. Farewell, April."

The next spring again brought Grandfather new hope for sugar-making. He and Grandmother and their two small sons, Lyman and Frank, had survived the winter without even a touch of lung fever. The two little boys had helped him clear the snow out of the sap shanty and watched him patch the cracks in his frost-heaved arch with a heavy paste of ashes, water, and salt.

His goose quill scratched briskly across his diary page:

March 25—"Heard and saw a bluebird sing his lovely 'Cheer-up.'"

March 28—"Warm and fair for a cloudy day. On the dodge seeing to things. 'A cheerful spirit dissolves difficulties as the sun does the snow.'"

March 29—"First rate sap day—seems good—staid at home from church—worked about my sap—lost a darn good lot of syrup tonight."

His caldron had boiled so fast over the hotter fire of his arch than it ever had outdoors that Grandfather had not had enough sap to keep up with it. Nor had he brought enough water from the spring to supply his need.

April 25—"Sap run well."

April 26—"Froze like a rock last night & cold as Greenland today. Staid home from church & read nearly all day in Bunyan's *Pilgrim's Progress.*" No doubt Grandfather well knew that day how to sympathize with poor Christian bearing his burden.

The next several years, he struggled annually to produce the family's sugar. His sap shanty proved too small for his boiling, so he returned to an outdoor "camp" until he could build a larger, better constructed, and more adequately equipped sap-house. So many obstacles of War and other obligations stood in his way that it was not until 1871 that he realized that dream.

In the meantime, excerpts from his diary entries tell an interesting tale:

Mar. 29, 1861—"Mild & a good sap day. Tapped some trees, some (pail) buckets full in four hours. (These held about ten quarts each.) Worked some on arch for kets."

Mar. 30—"At work about sap and sap fixings. My hired hands have acted cross-grained for a day or two now. Some talk of trouble to the South. Hired I.H.D. for 6 mos. @ $11 per mo."

Apr. 11—"Frogs have got loose from their winter prison & today have added their joyful chorus with Nature's songsters to make the earth rejoice & cheer the hearts of men."

Apr. 17—"The boys gathered the sap buckets. N. wind and snow all day. The snow is now 10 o'clock, about 1 foot deep. Terrible times quite the whole South are in Rebellion."

Mar. 12, 1863—"To East Rupert, corn to mill. Got 50 sap tubs (pine) & a pan from T. Tobin, traded sleighs, am to have $14 to boot. Engaged an old codger, poor and lame, to chop me some wood."

Apr. 2—"S.W. wind—A regular hurricane almost. Lyman and Frank hunted after buckets, found most of them—5 lacking."

Apr. 7—"Boiled some sap—had a good deal to do in this time of young things—had to take a lamb from a ewe & a very hard job at that—had a sow pig, and she went to killing them like smoke—4 of them here in the kitchen. Fed them here after we finished the sugar at 3 A.M."

Apr. 12—"Warm. Boiled some sap & got it all in. I got to bed at 4 this morning. These late (or early) hours wear upon me some."

Apr. 21—"Syruped down some sour stuff. Fixed my boiling place over &c. Gathered in my sap tubs. Poor sugar season, not much help. Went down street to put the military roll on its way to the Adjutant General &c."

Apr. 17, 1869—"Boiled in last of sap—had 98 1/2 lbs. thick syrup. To date

1036 lbs. sugar. Probably more than 25 lbs. skim sugar that was not right. Sold 332 lbs sugar @ 13¢ a lb."

His sugar business was truly beginning to show a profit, so he thereafter annually increased the number of trees he tapped from 200 to about 1,000. Always he looked forward to the day when he could have an efficiently operating sap-house.

The fall of 1871 Grandfather knew the joy of that dream fulfilled. For years he had been drawing plans and "laying aside" what he could for the building. No mere 10 X 12 ft. shanty was this, but a strong 18 X 30 ft. frame structure of hand-hewed timbers with pegged and morticed beams, a shingled roof with a cupola above his boiling-pan, and tightly closing wide swing doors with strong iron latches and strap iron hinges. Weeks of hard work had gone to its building. He and his son Frank, then married and living on the next farm, had toiled with the help of their hired hands through the days between haying and harvest to finish it before the fall rains began.

On what was thereafter known as Sap House Knoll, Grandfather's new sugar camp stood for many decades in a grove of white birch and rock maple, at the foot of his sugar lot. Nearby, the rushing mountain brook, fed by Rock Spring, babbled reassuringly among the willows and down the glen. No more scorched syrup for lack of water would be the boiler's lot.

A new sap-house must have new equipment. First came the shining new evaporator set upon its arch of fieldstone and mortar, an apparatus that he proudly showed to his townsmen, who came to investigate the innovation.

Also entered in Grandfather's expense ledger the following March were: "500 wooden sap buckets—$150; 300 tin buckets—$105; 2 storage tubs—$23; 1 20-bbl. storage & 1 gathering tub—$25.50; 50 syrup cans $12.50; 1 tin conductor—$6.25; 48 caking dishes—$3."

Those caking dishes represented a new phase of the sugar-making industry. City people summering at Dorset and Manchester would pay outlandish prices that netted a neat profit for fancy-shaped little cakes of the maple sweet, averaging six or eight to a pound. A dozen each of plain rounds, scalloped rounds, scalloped ovals, and fluted hearts Grandfather selected and carried home to his Mary Ann.

Syrup in gallon cans was also increasingly in demand, so those containers would likewise be a good investment.

Grandfather and the "boys" had cut forty-five cords of wood from the second-rate growth of the woodlot and stacked it for the new boiling season. The prospect was bright, and Grandfather whistled "Old Zip Coon" and "Pop Goes the Weasel" more merrily than usual, as he whittled extra spiles and watched for signs of spring. But March 15 brought a west snowstorm with cold that froze brooks and wells so hard that his diary again tells a tale of struggle and at times despair. He had now lived through fifty cycled seasons, however, and his ripened philosophy and matured faith helped him accept things with greater fortitude.

March 31, 1872—"A blustering East storm of snow. Thus ends March without any thaw at all more than in the middle of some three or four days by sunshine. That so light that in two of the warmest days it took 500 maple trees fresh tapped to run 6 bbls. of sap (should have got near 69."

Apr. 3—"Nice little snowstorm again last night, warm this morning & foggy. Fixed my sap House doors where Apr. 2 West Wind racked them some. Not warm enough for sap to run."

Apr. 5—"Moderate. Started a fire for a little while and boiled some sap. The boys got completely set in a drift and had to take the horses off and leave the load."

Apr. 9—"Warm, showery, foggy & a thunder shower in the evening. Finished tapping my sugarbush—the snow in the woods is deep, 4 ft. on an average I should judge. Broke out the road—left off a pair of drawers."

Apr. 10—"Some rain in the morning—turning cold at night. Emptied the water out of our buckets. Whittled some sap spouts."

Apr. 12—"Gathered 33 bbls. today—brought up about 25 gals. of syrup, not quite No. 1 but good fair quality. Put 21 cans full & left the rest for Mary Ann and the girls to sugar off."

(Mother then aged six and Aunt Ida, fourteen, were a great help to Grandmother in stirring the soft sugar to the desired creamy whiteness just before pouring it into the caking dishes. If enough of these little cakes were sold, the reward was to be a new sprigged muslin for each of the girls for school.)

Apr. 15—"Boiled in what sap I had. Orders for Syrup keep coming but no sap—sent some Syrup & sugar to Depot today. Cleaned up my sugar things.

"Our little dog Tuck, a model of dog friendship & steady companion for abt. 14 yrs, died last night. Followed us to the sugar lot & fell in his tracks near the upper wall. Died of old age. Covered him with my old coat & left him there."

Tears blurred the page as Grandfather wrote. Never again would the warm, shaggy little black and white body curl itself comfortingly close to his chilled feet as he drove his woodshed sled home from "tapping out." Never again would velvet nose, pink tongue, and joyous yelp beg for Tuck's ball of wax from the pan of snow at "sugaring off" time. But perhaps there would be wax-on-snow in a little dog's heaven. And "Tomorrow I must start the plow."

Little Hattie and Ida had to make their old red and blue calicoes do for school one more year, but 1873 proved a better sugar season, renewing hope and assets.

March 19, 1874, saw 800 sap buckets gleaming in the spring sunshine that dappled the Summit Farm sugarbush. Bluebirds and robins bugled and flitted among the branches, and 35 gallons of syrup poured their golden stream from the newly burnished evaporator into the shining strainer cans. Buyers came to the steam-clouded door and carried away the precious product at $1.45 a gallon before the heat had fairly gone out of it.

Sugar-making became a progressively thriving part of the annual harvests on the hilltop farm in the ensuing years. Grandfather's study of the industry became so well recognized that in 1881 the Farmers' club of the mountain township asked him to give a paper on "Maple Sugar."

Grandfather credited the Indians with having discovered the art of sugar-making. He then went on to say that when the Red Men shared their secret with the colonists, they in turn tried a new method of securing the sap. Instead of boxing the tree as the Indians had, the white man gashed the trunk with his hatchet, inserted a thin chip or sliver of wood, and caught the sparkling drip in a bark cup. Almost from the first, however, the cup had proved inadequate, so a chunk of butternut or other hard wood, about a foot in diameter and two feet long, was cut in half lengthwise, hollowed out by axe or adze, and set at the foot of the tree beneath the chip spill to catch the sap.

When the buds began to burst upon the trees, the crude troughs were simply turned bottom side up, on the north side of the trunks, where they would be least exposed to sun and storm that might crack them, to await another spring.

Grandfather recalled that his first chore in the sugarbush, as an eight-year-old in 1830, had been to help dig the sap-troughs out of the snow and tip them, cleansed only by Nature, right side up. His father and oldest brother, meanwhile, bored the trees with an auger and inserted spouts or spiles, which by then had replaced the earlier splinters.

By the mid-1800s, most sugar-makers were using tubs instead of troughs. These were also wooden, both staves and hoops. One stave was left longer than the rest by about three inches, and into this a hole was bored for hanging on a handmade nail just below the spile.

Around 1860 a pine bucket became popular. This was smaller at the top and so permitted fewer leaves, twigs, and insects to enter the sap.

In his new equipment in 1872 Grandfather pointed out that troughs had been superseded by the tin bucket with one ear, by which to hang it from a nail or hook. In some places he had heard that men often hitched a broken piece of roofing slate over the top to protect the sap from dirt, snow, and rain.

Grandfather went on to say that the boiling was usually done in earlier days in the woods or bush, the snow being shoveled away from an 18-foot square. When the place was selected, a large log was laid in position for the backlog. Then a strong pole was erected either between two crotched tree trunks or in one, and from this the kettle was hung by heavy chains called trammels. Some had caldron kettles, but the old-time five-pail iron kettle was most often used.

"Usually three to five of those kettles, cast of iron an inch thick, comprised the boiling apparatus," Grandfather explained. "Each was sometimes hung on the end of a ten- or twelve-foot heavy pole with stone weights chained to the other end. The whole was then balanced on an upright tree-post, so the kettle could be swung away from the fire to fill or empty it. Otherwise the great iron receptacles were slung singly, or even five in a row, several feet apart, from a heavy pole set into crotched tree trunks or posts.

"When the buckets or troughs were set & the kettles hung, the sugar-maker, armed with a piece of fat pork, an axe, & gathering pails on a neck-yoke, was ready for business. He had considerable chopping to do, for it needed an enormous amount of wood proportionately to evaporate the sap in that open style. A piece of the fat pork was put in each kettle to prevent its boiling over.

"The sap was brought to 'camp,' as the boiling place was styled, by hand. When the sap was boiled down to the consistency of syrup, it was carried to the house by hand, after which the women taxed their ingenuity to cleanse out some of the impurities but were seldom troubled with the sugar being too light-colored; yet the power of the maple was prominent in a great measure.

"Pans for evaporation superseded the kettle, then came the evaporator. The old wooden buckets so tenaciously clung to are passing away, giving place to those made of tin.

"Our sap is now almost invariably gathered by drawing it to the boiling place with teams, in large tubs or casks, & stored in large wooden tubs. It seems to be the best that we can do—So the troughs, the kettles, the backlogs & pork was tho't by our ancestors as the best that they could do.—It seems strange to us that people should make sugar as they did fifty years ago. Fifty years hence people will think strange of our present style of management.

"Most of the sugar-makers today have their sap-houses to shelter their boiling apparatus, their evaporator set upon a tight arch of stone or brick, with an iron front and fire grates. Almost if not every sugar-maker gathers and stores his sap in wooden tubs. These are almost an abomination, for it is quite impossible to wash one with any degree of cleanness. When the tub is new and clean, the sap may carry a flavor of the wood to the sugar, but when the tub has been used, the pores soaked full of sap, what remains in the wood becomes stale & all the washing and scrubbing that anyone may bestow upon it will not make it clean.

"Sap should never touch wood at all after it leaves the tree, as the contact hastens its decomposition & good sugar cannot be made with stale sap. Some still cling to the system of putting some albuminous substance into their syrup to 'cleanse' it, but this is more apt to add to the impurity of the sugar. It will not have the delicious flavor of maple that naturally belongs to it, and all that makes it a luxury.

"It is now agreed that there should be roadways in the sugarbush, so that a team may be driven quite near to all the trees, that a large amount of lugging may be avoided.

"A sap-house is indispensable. After having weighed the arguments for housing the wood inside, I am of the opinion that the sap-house should be large enough for that purpose.

"I should advise the building of the sap-house close to some knoll or side hill where a road can be made some eight or ten feet higher than the level of the building & near by so that the sap may be readily run from the gathering tub to the storage in the sap-house. Also close by should be a good supply of water which will be found a great convenience in the necessary washing of the utensils inside.

"Sixteen to eighteen feet wide, 8 or 9 feet posts for height, and at least twice the entire length of the arch for the length of the building seems sufficient for all practical purposes. Stand the storage on a platform 3 or 4 inches higher than the top of the evaporator that the sap may run freely & quickly from the storage.

"With a good large door on each side and a large cupola for the escape of steam, so arranged that it can be shut up tight to keep out the storm, the building is ample.

"The foundation for the arch should go below the frost line, lest by heaving, the arch is damaged & the level of the boiling apparatus is disturbed. The arch should be of brick well and firmly laid in mortar. An iron front with one or two doors & fire grates for the wood to rest on while burning is indispensable. Under the grate must be an ash pit 14 or 16 inches deep for ashes and small coals to fall down and to furnish air for the fire. Grates must reach in the length of the wood; if not, coals will pile up and retard the fire.

"An evaporator should be large for a man's business; it takes but little more fire to run one 14 feet long than would be needed for one of 10 feet in length. There would be a little advantage in the extra four feet of heat.

'The chimney should reach well above the ridge of the building & have a slide damper in it in easy reach of the operator—this should not be omitted under any circumstances.

(Was Grandfather then remembering that Sunday night nearly a quarter of a century before, when he had "lost a darn good lot of syrup," because his caldron had boiled too fast above the driving, uncurbed flames?)

"It needs a very hot fire to drive the boiling of sap & it must be flame. A bed of coals will not answer.

'Tin buckets and no other, galvanized iron or tin for gathering and storing the sap by all means—metallic spouts if they can be got that are good for anything. If wood must be used, cleanse them by burning before they are put into the tree.

"When we can manage a bush of 500 or 1000 trees & bring the sugar in as nice and clean as a woman will take the sap from one tree & boil it down on the stove in a tin pan, then it will be time for us to begin to boast of our skill as sugar-makers.

"Don't forget—the watchword is Clean and Quick."

For nearly forty tapping seasons, Grandfather's sap-house served his sugarbush. In spite of his prediction of 1881 the method of production changed but little during those four decades.

When freezing nights and thawing days, the wild geese flying north, and the joyous "Hear it, feel it" of the bugle-throated robins assured us that spring had come again, Bob and Joe and Sally and I would watch impatiently as Father and Uncle Morrison, the hired neighbor, would ready the sap fixings. What sheer delight it was to pile onto the woodshod sled behind our grey team, Dan and Dick, and be whisked away to the woods each glad mid-March morning, when the drip from a break in the bark of the tall maple by the dooryard well told us that sap was starting.

What joy it was, too, to drink the first crystal clear, sweet magic flow from the shining buckets, that we scrambled to bring from the sled to the newly tapped maples, as Father and Uncle Morrison bored one after another of the rough-barked trunks with bit and brace.

How clean and new we felt as we raced along the brook by the sap-house to gather an armful of the fat and furry grey pussy willows that had burst from their shining brown cases overnight. And what fragrant promise came from the pungent leaf mold of the making earth on the sunny slope south of the brook, where the trailing arbutus, hepaticas, and adder's tongues soon would be showing.

But hard work, as well as fun, marked the sugar season in those days, just as it had in Grandfather's time, though snow seldom fell so late or piled so deep as his diary entries had recorded. Yet many a time Father and Uncle Morrison spelled each other at boiling all day and all night, while a neighbor boy helped Bob and Joe with the gathering in hip-deep snow.

Sally and I were given the job of carrying supper to the men, who "boiled," and often we lingered long after they had eaten, to watch the sap flow into the front of the evaporator, circulate back and forth in its crosswise sections, and be drawn off at the rear in a fragrant thick amber stream into the strainer can, while more sap poured into the front section again.

Steam rolled in such dense clouds up through the cupola that we could hardly see across the five-foot width of the pan, and even our eyelashes were netted with sweet stickiness as we lingered there. How the sparks flew out the chimney and how the flames roared when fresh logs were thrust through the iron arch door.

"Time to go now," Father would say, as he would pull from the receiving-can a double thickness of a corner of one of Grandmother's hand-woven woolen sheets, damp with the warm syrup it had strained, and replace it with another fresh from its scrubbing. Already Uncle Morrison would be "shaking up" the plump tick of straw at the far corner of the sap-house, getting ready for his four-hour sleep beneath the shaggy buffalo robe, before taking up his vigil at the boiling.

As we young ones would peer from the lantern-lighted mist into the spring darkness, we would often see a pair of eyes gleam and vanish. Momentarily a deer or some other woodland creature had investigated this mysterious low-hung moon, where strange clouds rolled above the trees.

Once, Uncle Morrison told us, a trio of young raccoons had come padding across the midnight snow to sniff at the sap-house door while he was having his snack of fried cakes, dill pickles, syrup, and eggs cooked in the boiling sap. Perhaps little coons were hungry, too. He had set a panful of partly boiled and cooled sap just outside the door, and soon three sharp noses and three pairs of black-ringed eyes were delving in the pan.

Sparks from a wind-damaged chimney ignited the dry shingle roof of that old sap-house the last night of the sugar season in the early 1900s.

Fanned by the wind, the flames made short work of what Grandfather had toiled so long to build. For several years no sap-house stood on Summit Farm.

In the 1940s however, a modern sugar plant was erected there. In spite of Grandfather's prediction of change, this latest structure is very similar in design to the 1874 sap-house. A tin smoke stack and asphalt shingles, stone floor instead of dirt, an iron arch and a more convenient evaporator, as well as galvanized tubs, equip a tighter, larger building, with more space for storing wood.

Electric bulbs send their arc of light where our old oil lantern shed its glow; a padded sleeping bag replaces straw tick and buffalo robe; a fire extinguisher and a radio fill the corner where a big brass bell for calling needed help once hung.

A caterpillar tractor rolls today where straining horses used to break the road. Metal spiles, with covered metal buckets or plastic bags attached, are now hung upon the trees to catch the precious drip. Tapping, too, is simpler now. Bob goes about that task these later years with a gasoline-powered drill strapped upon his chest. His three-eighths-inch bit is slightly smaller than those in Grandfather's time, and he bores a half inch deeper, that the spile may easily support its container of sap. That is deep enough, also, to reach the cambian layer where the sap rises, but not deep enough to split the bark and cause sap to trickle wastefully down the trunk. Carefully he bores each maple, the drill penetrating with an upward slant, so sap will have a downhill path as it oozes from the tree.

He estimates that an average season will have from two to five good runs of sap with drizzles between, covering a period of four or five weeks during March and early April. A snowstorm is as welcome as a freeze, but the required sunny day following either is barren of yield, if it brings a cold east gale roaring through Summit Farm Grove.

Damaging insect pests were routed from that grove one recent May by a co-operative state-spraying program. A scientist-operated spray-plane swooped above the land and sent its clouds of DDT, solvicide and kerosene upon the budding trees. This prevention of defoliation by tent caterpillars insured a better syrup harvest, by permitting well-developed leaves to manufacture sugar throughout the sunny summer days for storage against the winter's need. This method later proved impractical.

The traders in Great-Grandfather's day took his four- or five-pound cakes of hard maple sugar to exchange for alewops and shad from the Connecticut River at an average of 6 cents a pound. Maple butter from the descendants of those old trees is sold today in fancy jars at twenty-five times that price.

There has been some change, but the brook still sings beneath the willows where the boys used to cut their whistles, and small log wood from the second growth still drives the boiling of the sap in its evaporator. The basic primitive procedure of production still dominates, for the "power of the maple" is an independent power, as indomitable as its Yankee producers.

9

UP THE MOUNTAIN NORTHEASTERLY

Like some ancient scroll unrolled upon the mountain is the steep little country road that leads over the top of our old hill. Nearly two hundred years have now spelled out upon the lined brown document of earth and stone a tale of human struggle for survival and for the attainment of democratic ideals. Yankee ingenuity and good neighborliness, independence and courage, spiritual fortitude and a oneness of man with his universe are likewise written there. And wide in its margin are lithographed the sundry delights of a winding rustic road.

The earliest record of that highway states that at a meeting of the township's first settlers the second Thursday in October, in "the ninth year of his Majesty's reign, anoque Domini, 1769," it was voted, "That the road through White Creek meadow & up the Mountain Northeasterly be four rods wide."

It was further voted, "That Mr. Barnabas Barnum shall have one acre of land in the undivided - for his extraordinary labors in having the Highway through his land."

The purpose of that road was to unite the town's two earliest settled extremities, Mettowee Valley and White Creek Meadows, "lately reputed to be in the province of New Hampshire," but at that date "situate in the county of Charlotte and province of New York."

At the first proprietors' meeting the year before, those enterprising pioneers had voted "three shillings on each Right for making roads and other charges."

The first evidence of that road "up the Mountain Northeasterly" was a trail of gashes in the forest trees. A trail that was gradually deepened and widened by axe and boot and moccasin, by ox cart and pioneer sled, as the settlers increased in number and sought to communicate with one another.

Indeed, there was early necessity for communication. In 1771, soon after the New Hampshire grantees had registered their claims to White Creek Meadow, settlements were begun on the same acres by New Yorkers, who also defiantly maintained ownership there. A buckskin-clad runner carried news of the invasion to Indian River, the middle section of the present Vermont township.

Immediately along the woodland trail strode an ardent band of coon-skin-capped defenders of the New Hampshire titles, armed with stout beech clubs and muskets. And so lustily did they apply the "Beech seal" to the backs of the intruders that they gladly fled to safer holdings.

The next year, when the Albany County Sheriff came with his posse along that same trail to arrest those "Rupert rioters," he, too, was glad to flee from those "Twigs of the Wilderness." For some time thereafter, border warfare was frequently waged along that frontier highway, the same highway that today is traversed by a centralized school bus for the two townships' joint program of education maintained on the New York side of the line.

Shortly after the first land feud in White Creek Meadows, the boldest leader, Robert Cochran, joined the Green Mountain Boys and became one of their captains. Along the road "up the mountain Northeasterly," he and a band of his staunch adherents marched with knapsacks and guns, in the spring of 1775, to join Ethan Allen and other Green Mountain Boys, as they advanced along Mettowee Valley, thence to take part in the famous attack on Ticonderoga.

When Bob and Joe and Sally and I in our childhood climbed the home stretch of that road from district school, we used to wonder if those White Creek Green Mountain Boys might have paused that warm May day to slake their thirst at the wayside spring, where we loved to fling ourselves full-length and drink deep of its clear cold water. Perhaps the hermit thrushes and the chickadees, the peeper frogs and the mountain brook had sung for them as they sang for us. Or perhaps those military ears were so alert for a Tory whistle that they missed the peaceful music of the earth.

There was reason enough for the colony's Whigs to dread the few Tories in their midst. Along the two or three miles of cart track that had been widened and packed to a semblance of a road, the British sympathizers in 1778 burned the only grist mill and two of the log huts in the struggling little settlement. Following the act, they fled, pursued by their neighbors, along the mountain trail toward refuge in Canada. And all that dark night of terror, the women and children hid in the neighboring woods.

In spite of Royalist terrorizing, however, the town established itself, and 1780 saw an influx of new settlers. Over the mountain they came, lumber wagons cutting deep ruts along the tree-blazed trail. With them came the spinning wheels, iron kettles, and other necessary equipment for establishing homes in the land which had been designated since March, 1778, as part of Bennington County in the independent State of Vermont.

In 1790, the land feud between the Green Mountain State and her neighbor to the west came to a peaceable end. Although the opening of the Revolutionary War had suspended the controversy, New York successfully opposed Vermont's petition to the Provincial Congress for admission into the Confederacy in 1776 and 1777, because of these counterclaims. In 1790 however, New York re-linquished all "Grant" rights to the territory when Vermont paid $30,000 to clear the land titles. Rupert citizens at last held undisputed title to their holdings in White Creek Meadows.

About that time, too, the state enacted a ruling that the Selectmen of each town should require four days of labor on the road annually, from every able-bodied male citizen or resident from sixteen to sixty years of age, ministers only excepted.

Although highways remained comparatively primitive for many years, they nevertheless were markedly improved under the new requirement.

In the next three decades, the town reached its peak population of more than 1,600 inhabitants. Another grist mill replaced the earlier one. Saw mill and cider mill, blacksmith shop and tannery sprang up along the wagon way. A church and a store, a law office and a doctor's office centered a cluster of houses near the western extremity and again near Indian River, and the Street became a hard-packed road.

Section by section, the eight-mile strip that runs the length of the township was won from the wilderness. Ichabod Baker, John Weed, Asa Kinne, Phineas Spencer, and Cyprian Eastman, as selectmen and surveyors, underwent more "extraordinary labors" in laying out those first sections of that road and many another in the town's network than had the earlier Barnabas Barnum in "having the highway through his land."

Quaint phrases appeared in those old surveys of the main route. An April, 1791, record stated, "Then surveyed and laid out a Road in the West Society in Rupert Beginning at a stake and stones standing on the Road that leads from Noble's Mill to Continental Sam Hopkins......to the road leading from Aaron Rising's to the Meeting House."

Earlier surveys had included such details as "near the dugway," "crossing the Mill Dam Brook," and "The winding and twisting line is the center of said road."

"Said road" was the section of the main highway near the top of the mountain. There, on June 12, 1788, Great-Great-Grandfather Zachariah had purchased a "Parcel of land" and begun the frame house that his son Joseph later completed as our old saltbox home.

As the road was extended, stagecoaches made their appearance on its winding course. To accommodate these, several owners of large farm-houses along the way were granted the right to use their dwellings as inns. Two of those that kept their privilege longest were James Moore and Jonathan Eastman at the foot of the west and the east side of our hill, respectively.

James Moore's Inn, which is still the farmhouse of one of our old neighbors, was often used for town meeting. There, on March 10, 1795, it was voted: "That the road by James Moore's Inn shall remain in the same place where it is now put, (south of the said Moore's barn), provide the old road be not shut until the new one is made as good and convenient for the publick as the old one." The new one represented an attempt to straighten somewhat a highly dangerous curve at the foot of the mountain. In fact, hazardous crooks and steep pitches constituted one of the town's major problems for the next century and more.

As late as 1887, that same curve and pitch were still so much of a hazard that forty-eight of the "freeholders, taxpayers and residents" of the town "respectfully petitioned" the selectmen to alter thirty rods of it. Although a similar petition for another part of town had recently been denied, this one was granted, "with the understanding that they (the petitioners) are to build the road and the Town build the bridge and fence the road. Petition-ers notified by letter; occupant of land notified verbally." The selectmen also "appraised the damages $10.00."

Grandfather being the senior petitioner, it fell to his lot to "boss" his neighbors, mostly his nephews' hired men, on that reconstruction job. Returning from warning out his district to work on this high-way, as he had done so many times before, his diary comment was, "O, there is some dreadful pujeky folks in this world."

The bridge, which the town then supplied, was a great blue-grey flat stone, nearly a foot thick, wide enough to span the mountain brook even in time of melting snow, and so long that a lumber wagon could cross it with wheel room to spare. Topping one of the numerous "breakers" or "water bars" on that steep half-mile incline, it provided a place for teams and pedestrians to rest beneath a pair of twin white birches—a wishbone birch in effect, whereon more than one generation of lovers have carved hearts and initials.

To appease a neighboring district, whose petition for grading a pitch nearer the village was denied, the farmers of the more favored neighborhood, after haying was finished that summer, joined other men along the line in a bee to do the grading job as well.

From its earliest beginning, road building in that mountain township involved long and arduous toil, with a large ingredient of trial and error.

Surveyors having laid out the route, most often conveniently following a creekway between the hills, ox teams hitched to homemade plows were used to excavate the road bed. Tree stumps, roots, and great rocks had to be dug out by hand with heavy shovels and mattocks. A foundation of stone, laboriously picked and hauled from the adjacent meadows, was then piled into this bed, and over this the excavated dirt was heavily packed, rolling higher in the middle to aid drainage.

Considering the backbreaking effort required to wrest even a one-way strip of road from the wilderness and maintain it through freshet, New England snow, frost-rack and mud, it is small wonder that this road "up the Mountain Northeasterly" failed of its original specification of being four rods wide. Indeed, most of the way it was actually barely wide enough for two vehicles to meet without clicking hubs. In frequent stretches, until just recently, a driver had to watch several rods ahead for another vehicle so he could wait for its passing at one of the wider intervals between the deep, bordering ditches, or away from a narrow bridge. The "four rods," therefore, still is nearly twice the distance between the stone walls, or the fences of crutches and rails, that separate the thoroughfare from the pasturelands and meadows through which it still winds its way.

One July day in 1937, I was unforgettably impressed by the narrowness of that road. Mother, Sally, and I were driving up our home hill when we met Chriss, the mail carrier. In exchanging greetings, I failed to follow the example of one of our elderly neighbors, who once sagely remarked, "I don't watch much to see what's comin' my way; I keep my eye on where I'm a-goin'."

Not having kept my eye on where I was going, I suddenly found that the right front wheel of the car had slipped off the log that temporarily supported the edge of the road. Tug as I would, I could not get it back. An inch farther to the right would put us in the ditch; and a few feet behind us yawned the gully of the brook where it flowed under the bridge. What were we to do?

While Sally went to the nearest neighbor's a half mile down the hill, Mother silently wedged a stone under each rear wheel, and I ruefully remembered that our men were not at home and the nearest garage was ten miles away.

Finally Sally came with the neighbor's hired man, Bill, the rest of the men being away at an auction. Bill pried and tugged and pushed, but to no avail. Two woodchuck hunters from Rutland happened by. They also pushed and tugged and perspired. An hour passed; the sky grew dark, and thunder grumbled in the distance. Just as we had decided to go and phone for a tow-truck, Bill's eight-year-old son came wandering up the road. After watching for a few minutes, he innocently inquired, "Why dontcha jack up the bumper?" Why, indeed?

Six red-faced adults hauled out the bumper jack, and ten minutes later we were all rolling our various ways.

Building the road was not the only "extraordinary labor" connected with it, however. Its maintenance was endless in its demands. The east gales and the west, sweeping down from the neighboring mountains, blocked the highway again and again each winter, sometimes with four- and five-foot drifts and even deeper.

If the storms brought only a wading snow a foot or so deep, the men would need only to "kettle out the road." The big black iron caldron, capable of boiling a barrel of sap in sugaring time, would be rolled to the woodshod sled. Heavy chains would bind it firmly to the rear of the wooden runners so that its rounded, three-foot bottom could plow the snow. Into the kettle then would tumble as many boys as its ten-gallon maw would hold, and away would go the horse-drawn snow machine.

It was a merry ride for the teen-agers who could jackknife their knees to their chins, but it was something else for a beginning-to-be-rheumatic hired man, who sometimes drew the lot to ride the "kittle." A neighbor often used his sacks of grain and ground meal for kettle ballast, for the grist mill stood at the foot of the hill where his stretch of kettling ended.

Within my remembrance, though, there were days when Chriss had to bring the mail on snowshoes. Those were the days when all the men along the route would turn out with shovels, teams, and plow-equipped bobsleds to break the road. Father and the other men at the top of the mountain would break downward east and west to meet the road gang coming up. Often a dozen or more at a time would get warm around our kitchen stove. Wet mittens and moccasins steamed dry on hearth and oven door, as their frostbitten, blue-frocked owners gulped strong hot coffee and spun strong hot yarns.

When the road was broken and we went sailing down the hill in the red cutter, its sleighbells jingling behind bay Prince, whose flying hoofs sent up a spray of snow, the drifts would be piled above our heads like some misplaced Sierra.

But when spring thaws struck the road, Grandfather once expressed the situation well: "Mud! Mud! Mud! 'Tis monstrous muddy. The road near the cheese factory has caved in! Oh, sorrow!"

If not always sorrow, it certainly has been a tedious job to travel that road in spring and fall mud-time, when truck and wagon wheels have mired to the hub beneath their loads of milk or logs or grain, or even with a driver only.

By May, however, the frost would be out of the ground, and then the road has always been worked. Farmers along the way, anxious to work out their taxes, used to take turns hitching their teams, three at a time, to the big scraper that brought fresh dirt from the side embankments into the highway. Others, armed with shovels, cleared the sluices and opened the ditches, while one raked the scraper ridges smooth, leaving the end-lessly appearing loose stones in mounds along the side, to be picked up later on a dray.

Uncle Jase was one who raked the stones when I was in district school. We who sat near the window loved to watch him work. A shock of white hair, curbed by a faded maroon cap, shaded his bushy brows and crooked, turned-up nose. Down his nose the sweat trickled as he spat his way between his neat little piles of stones. Timing the movement of his rake to the motion of his jaws, one quid always took him up the road as far as we could see in half the time any other man required to rake the quarter mile.

The bridges, too, were forever needing to be fixed. There were eleven in the eight-mile turnpike before the meadows, claimed from woodlands, drained some hill brooks dry.

Here and there, hand-constructed stone abutments and hewed timbers are in use yet, though concrete has replaced the rattling planks of former years. They were planks from the nearby pastures' straight black oaks, sawed in the mill at the east end of town and hauled over the hill by oxen.

Although no covered bridge has ever spanned these streams, one was long considered for a fork of Indian River, where gales sucked down the valley as if it were a funnel. During one of those October gales, Bob and I, both in our teens, were going home from the village. Old Prince disliked facing the storm, so Bob got out of our high-topped, leather-curtained carriage to lead his horse. We had barely crossed the creaking timbers when a hurricane gust struck and capsized the wagon. Prince braced his forefeet, lowered his head, and waited while I crawled out. As the blast eased somewhat, we righted the carriage, climbed in, and proceeded homeward, not even aware that we had narrowly escaped a pair of broken necks. Now that section of road follows a more protected route close to the parallel hill, but the cold white froth still churns over the rocks beneath the wind-swept bridge.

In spite of occasional hardships of travel, a varied caravan has passed along that road since the blazing of its trail in 1769.

For all of nearly two hundred years, it has been the remote mountain community's marketway over which have lurched ox-, mule-and horse-drawn cart and sled or motor truck, loaded with farmers' produce. Great bales of wool to exchange for red flannel and full cloth; crocks of butter; boxes of cheese; barrels of syrup from the sugar bush; and sacks of corn, wheat, buckwheat, and rye to the grist mill, returning to the family larder for samp, hot cakes, and plump brown loaves. Loads of potatoes, too, and of red and yellow apples for bin and cider mill.

Cows passing to and from their pasture, the leader rhythmically swinging her sweet-toned bell, still frequent this highway. But the annual drives of two or three hundred cattle or of as many as six hundred sheep no longer leave their hoofmarks in the October road-side frost.

The bootmaker on his annual round, the peddler with his pack or cart, and Teacher walking home to supper with a proud and happy pupil have also disappeared from the traffic line.

No longer does the buckboard returning from the cheese factory, blacksmith shop, or an auction halt in the middle of the road to let the driver, one leg over the side, exchange political and other views with his neighbor, leaning on fork or shovel or hoe at the edge of his field beyond the fence.

Soldier boys in homespun and khaki and sailor boys in blue have gone down that byway in answer to their country's call. But beneath the bridges, other barefoot boys still fish for minnows or skip pebbles along the shining ripple.

Every first of April, too, three listers set forth, as they have ever since the town was organized, to take the list of every taxpayer's property. A social as well as a business tour, it is often marked by a match of wits.

The first piano in the town about 1865 was subject to high tax, but it was owned by one shrewd farmer whose house had been built on the

Rupert-Dorset line. When the Rupert listers drove into Mr. D—'s yard that spring, they found the piano in the Dorset spare room, but when the Dorset takers of the list called, the piano's ivory keys grinned impishly in the Rupert parlor. "Piano" was not mentioned, but the next April, by some strange coincidence, Dorset and Rupert listers drove up to Mr. D's hitching post together in a mud-spattered buggy.

For many years Grandfather was one of the listers. His memoranda for early April, 1858, tell an interesting tale. Fri.—"Throat sore and feel unwell but worked at the list. Am at Wm. Sherman's tonight after a hard day's work.

Sat.—"Have got the mumps but still at work at the list & have got around Dists. 4 & 8, tired as a horse & some sick.

Sun.—"Fair I guess. The fact is I am rather mumpy & have not observed the weather much. My hired hand has also got the mumps & both my boys. We have to do some chores which is rather hard work."

Although people in those days unwittingly carried their diseases to one another, they also generously shared their services. Any time of night or day, in fair weather or foul, men and women left their baking, haying or many another urgent task to hurry along the road to a neighbor's need.

Before the telephone had climbed our hill, our nearest neighbor's son one morning was kicked in the head by a colt, causing him severe hemorrhage. Their hired man frantically knocked at our door to ask if Father would get the doctor.

In spite of rough wheeling, ten minutes later our spirited grey gelding, Dan, arrived in the village doctor's yard three miles away. Fortunately, Dr. Austin was just climbing into his new Reo, and fortunately, too, it neither sputtered nor balked on the hill that morning.

That trip marked the beginning of the change from the staunch old doctor, making his round of mercy with a plodding horse, to the speeding medic in his Chrysler today.

Refrigerated milk truck, tractor-drawn hay baler, jeep, station wagon, bookmobile, and motorized R.F.D. now roll where ox-cart and stagecoach broke the trail.

Until about 1930, hoboes with bundle and stick had a way of frequenting our mountain township. One who had been given thick roast-beef sandwiches and blueberry cake had been discovered to have placed a mark on the post of the mailbox at the hospitable gate, so other Knights of the Highway would know where they might fare equally well. The owner vowed vengeance.

Not long afterward, one black-bearded Timothy Jenks from the other end of the county, on his annual search for ginseng, stopped at the same door one early morning and asked for "a bite to eat."

Irate Aunt Ph'lindy was in the midst of spreading bacon fat on johnny cake to give him, when his hoarse bass bellowed behind her, "Ain't ye got no pie?"

Startled though she was, she answered tartly, "Young man, if you're very hungry, you can eat what I'm a-fixing."

When her swarthy "tramp" meekly proffered a shining silver quarter, she hastily exchanged her first offering for a thick slice of ham on freshly baked bread with butter, and, yes, a huge wedge of the coveted apple pie. To this day Timothy Jenks is identified as "Ain'tyegotnopie."

That road "up the Mountain Northeasterly" has recorded a script of more than livelihood, however. Education and entertainment are written there as well.

Quilting-party, husking-bee, barn-raising, family reunion, and almost daily "going visiting" deepened the ruts and kept grass from growing between them throughout the first century.

Spelling school, lyceum and singing-school through the middle 1800s added their score to the weekly traffic.

From November through March during the 1880s the District No. 8 Farmers' Club brought forty or fifty men and women and teen-age boys and girls onto the road each Friday evening. Refreshments at the meetings in the members' homes had been limited to pans of buttered popcorn, cider and doughnuts, or crackers and cheese, so that no one need miss the carefully prepared "papers" and the lively discussions on such topics as "The Best Potatoes to Raise," "Care of Stock in Winter Quarters," and "Money for the Farmer's Wife."

Perhaps "Money for the Farmer's Wife" had brought an unexpectedly favorable response. Anyhow, at the final meeting for 1883, the women surprised the menfolk with a real treat for those days, an oyster supper. The host's hired man was taken into the secret, that he might drive to the village for the necessary gallons of oysters while the meeting was going on.

From up and down the road the Farmers' Club had assembled on foot at seven o'clock that March night, at the former James Moore's Inn. Not until they were summoned to the feast did the men suspect that their women-folk had gleefully concealed "riz biscuit," Dolly Madison cake, pickled pears, and many another delicacy beneath their Paisley shawls and volumi-nous capes, as they had picked their way over frozen hubs and puddles earlier that evening.

Some outsiders, too, whose names have won distinction have traveled that upland road. In late December of 1863, Congressman Grinell of Iowa there braved a sharp northeaster with a mutual friend, to see Grandfather's prized flock of Merino sheep.

Again the following spring he and sixty other men, including breeders from Ohio and Connecticut, as well as the Bennington County Agricultural Society, jolted up over the "thank you ma'ams" to Grandfather's sheep shearing.

Over the same road, through the early 1900s, Uncle Charlie in his three-seated surrey used to bring many a famous guest from the Dorset summer resort to our hilltop to look off. Any clear day, from June blossoming through gorgeous autumn foliage, his "summer people" might be heard calling the echo where the road winds up the east side of the glen.

One golden August afternoon, Uncle Charlie White had brought Aunt Kate Stanton and her boarders, the noted author Edwin Lefevre and his family, on one of those scenic jaunts. On the way home, Uncle Charlie's rheumatic foot slipped off the wheel-brake. If ever his pair of sleek and spirited bays had felt that loaded surrey crowd their haunches on the steep descent, Jehu himself could not have held them. Nor even Uncle Charlie.

For only a second was the brake released. Buxom Aunt Kate, sharing the driver's seat, saw what was up, and risking Uncle Charlie's ire, she firmly planted her number nine on the brake-head and stared grimly down the winding road. Nor did she relax her two-hundred-pound pressure on the vital point, regardless of the driver's high dudgeon and vexed gestures, until the safety of the valley flats was reached.

Another noted one, who often came each summer in my girlhood, was Robert Todd Lincoln. How impressed we young ones were at first, when his big black limousine with its chauffeur would glide up into the meadow above our house, where Mr. Lincoln would quietly enjoy the hour of sunset. A glorious hour it often was, as the western sky flamed with rose and gold, against which far peaks of the Adirondacks and Helderbergs serenely stood in purple majesty. Then as the afterglow gilded the fleecy clouds over the Green Mountains to the east, and moon and evening star came to the vast blue arch above the twilit land, the motor would purr back down the road to Mr. Lincoln's country home at Manchester.

Those who established the Vermont Forest and Farmland Foundation now own those hilltop acres and have begun to add their story to that mountainway, up which a hard surfaced road is slowly climbing.

Two hundred or so boys and girls from the southern counties of the State recently attended a series of three 4-H overnight Conservation

Camps on the Foundation. Along the road, from their station wagons, their exploring voices also called the echo in the glen as they and their leaders assembled for firsthand study of plant and wild life; soil, water, and forest conservation, and astronomy.

An artist's easel often stands today where my father's corn shocks leaned before the wind. But no canvas can contain the seasons' panorama of spruce shadows on the snow where fox and deer and rabbits run; of greening meadow and orchard apple bloom; of plowman whistling as he turns black- furrows for their seeding; and busy hay-fields sweet beneath the sun. Nor can the artist's palette capture here the cricket croon upon the harvest land, the lamplit window that guides the traveler home, the dawn salute of neighbors' chimney smoke, or the phantom cavalcade that won this township from the wilderness.

But that which the brush cannot portray is indelibly engraved on the innermost being of those who have traveled this Vermont byway through dappled light and shadow.

10

TWENTY-TWO FEET BY TWENTY-SIX

"Resolved to build a new schoolhouse 22 ft. by 26 the spring and summer of 1851."

By that record, inscribed with a grey goose quill in the clerk's book, our little red schoolhouse came into being.

All thirteen of the district's qualified voters, having previously read the notice of the meeting posted on the old schoolhouse door, had met in the ramshackle one-room building that winter evening in 1850. Stamping the snow from their cowhide boots and setting a big square tin lantern on the schoolmaster's desk to light the clerk's task, Grandfather and his dozen brothers, nephews, and other neighbors had been settled on the benches, ready for business, at six o'clock.

When it had been resolved, after much debate and deliberating, to build "said schoolhouse," that handful of earnest farmers returned to their various homes among the hills of the little Vermont neighborhood, content in the thought that they, too, had acted "to promote the general welfare and secure the blessings of liberty" for themselves and their posterity.

The Superintending Committee must have given generously of their time and labor between sheep-shearing and harvest that following spring and summer, for "said schoolhouse" stood ready for occupancy for the next year's winter term.

A coat of red ochre, baked in the oven and mixed with linseed oil to penetrate the wood and with skim milk to spread, gave the new building a soft red exterior. Like a hovering mother hen, it settled down there beside the road running between pasture and meadow, at the exact center of the three-mile-long district, to become the beloved Alma Mater of many a neighborhood chick.

The white wooden plaque on its gable end facing the road announced, "School District No. 8, Rupert, Oct. 1st, 1851." Though wind and rain and snow and sun beat down upon it, the lettered board gave its information to the passer-by for nearly ninety years.

When the centralized school movement caused the little red schoolhouse to be sold for a summer home in 1939, the plaque was removed. The great-grandson of one of the voters in that December, 1850, meeting one day said gravely to the new owner, "I hope you kept that sign. This was the only school my father ever attended."

"The sign" is now carefully stored in the loft, just inside that same gable end that still faces the road.

Three hundred thirty-nine dollars and forty-five cents was voted at the last district meeting held in the Old Schoolhouse on October 27, 1851, "to defray the expenses of building the New Schoolhouse, said tax to be paid by the first day of Dec. next 1851 next." But that tax burden was somewhat lightened later by the sale of what was left of the abandoned building for seven dollars, to be used as a hay shack.

At the first meeting of the voters in the new building, it was "resolved to raise a tax of thirty-four dollars and twenty-three cents on said Dist., it being to defray the Teacher's wages the first winter and other expenses." The teacher boarded around, so most of the other expenses were for wood.

Grandfather was assigned to collect "said tax" and to serve on the Prudential Committee to deliver at the schoolyard eight cords of "good body wood" for the big box stove.

It further became his duty to take his turn at dropping in at "said school" now and then on his way home from the depot or cheese factory to question the scholars. In this way it was ascertained whether they were truly fortifying themselves by learning their books.

Four months was the length of that first winter's term, beginning on the second Monday in November. On that memorable morning, a dozen or so eager-eyed boys and girls, ranging in age from six to eighteen, congregated with book and slate and lunch bucket at the broad fieldstone steps.

Little Rhoda and Cornelia and Sarah lined up on the girls' side, while Heman and Morrison, Elon and John followed Aaron through the boys' entrance. Hanging cap and hood and shawl and roundabout on the nails in the square entries partitioned out of the front corners of the building, they all filed into the newly plastered schoolroom.

There the pleasant-faced but well-muscled young schoolmaster, hired for his Herculean stature as well as his learning, directed the placing of lunch buckets in the chimney cupboard at the rear of the room. The bigger fellows vied for the back seats, the smaller fry settled down front, and school "took up."

For more than eighty consecutive years thereafter, the first day of each fall term was again an event in the lives of the boys and girls of the neighborhood. A social as well as an educational event, it was marked by new shoes and hair ribbons, new overalls and gingham dresses, and a new anticipation for what life might hold.

The memory of my own first day there at the age of five is still vivid. Seated down front, my big brother Bob, who was all of six, and I joined the school body in chanting after the teacher, "Look out not in; look up not down; look forward not back; and lend a hand."

After we had all lustily sung "My country, 'tis of thee, Sweet land of libertee," Teacher, a cousin of whom we were very fond, heard her two small new charges read the alphabet from a tall chart beside her desk. There were pictures on the pages of kittens and ponies and zebras, of little girls in red capes and blue dresses, and of boys with fishing-poles, too, so the lesson was fun.

We cut gay flowers and vegetables from a seed catalog after we did our copy and then made a pilgrimage to the spring by the stone pile out back, having discovered the magic of waving two fingers. On the way back we even paid a visit to the traditional "three-holer," after making sure there were no windows in the rear wall of School.

And then it was noon recess. We all trooped out to the flat rock beneath the maples in the front yard to eat our lunches. Small hands, sweating with eagerness, tugged at the tin pail cover. And there were the plum jelly sandwiches, the chicken leg from Sunday's dinner, a big Red Astrachan apple, and a butternut cupcake, wrapped in a crisp white napkin by a loving mother.

Shyly but happily, the two new scholars ate every crumb of their own good things, while the others traded delicacies—a practice in which we soon were sharing.

Many a recipe for graham bread and black currant buns, shaved sugar cake and pumpkin preserves found its way into neighborhood cookbooks via the schoolyard rock.

"I'm on Dixie's land, Dixie don't know it; he's got a sore toe and he can't go it," shouted the first one to finish his lunch. We played the game hilariously till the bell rang for us to line up, red and puffing.

More copy, more cutting pictures and listening to the others recite brought us to dismissal. Desks cleared, we listened while the others said the daily closing verses, verses which can still bring a measure of tranquility to those who used to say them in that long ago.

> "Now the day is over,
> All our tasks are by;
> Soon the stars will twinkle
> In the evening sky.
> "Little hands are folded
> That have worked all day;
> Little lips are silent;
> Books are put away.
> "Now we say our good-night,
> Each one has done his best,
> Homeward we are going
> For a quiet rest.
> "Keep us, Heavenly Father,
> Through the silent night,
> Soon we'll wake up safely
> In the morning light."

The fifteen-year-olds repeated the words as wholeheartedly as did the younger ones.

Teacher smiled as we finished, and we all got our things from the chimney cupboard and entry. There was only one entry by then, the other having been taken for a woodshed several years before, when co-education had progressed to the point of permitting both boys and girls to pass through the same doorway.

Bob and I were the only ones to take the road up the hill to the east, as the others lived down the road to the west or up crosslots to the south. Our father had brought us that morning in the buggy behind our pet grey gelding Dan, but Dad would be busy in the fields at closing time, and we had assured him we could follow the mile of road home. Bob took my hand protectively in his, and the road ahead looked bright in the fall sunshine.

But that was nearly a half-dozen decades after the first opening day. By then that first four-month term had been lengthened to an annual three terms of ten or twelve weeks each.

Several times the ruddy outside and the grey interior had been renewed and other repairs made "to render the building secure against travelers and comfortable for scholars." The clerk's record further stated in 1870 that a bolt and lock were added to each door, for hoboes had been surprised in their disheveled sleep beside the warm chunk stove a time or two.

About then, also, boards painted black had been placed between the two windows on either side of the building. A third one was suspended by pieces of harness strap from one wall beside the teacher's desk, which stood on a platform in the recess between the entry and woodshed. These blackboards replaced the earlier individual slates, and the last board especially was an aid in drilling the beginners who always went to the bench beneath the front window behind Teacher's desk to recite. To recite and to steal glimpses of the squirrels and chipmunks that scampered in tantalizing freedom among the trees in the yard. Or of the robins that nested on the cornices. Or of the occasional farm vehicle or peddler, or the daily mail carrier that passed along the nearby road.

In 1883 the advent of a water pail was noted in the clerk's book. The spring by the stone pile had a way of becoming "riley" or freezing up at certain seasons. Such emergencies were provided for by the pupils' drawing lots for the privilege of going in pairs to fetch a pailful of water from the supply that flowed into the big marble sink in Aunt Delia's kitchen several rods up the road. It was a kitchen that sometimes offered spicy molasses cookies fresh from the oven.

To accommodate the shining new tin pail, a broad shelf with a stout bracket was nailed beneath one west window. An equally shining new tin dipper was hung on one window casing, and it and its successors daily provided the means of slaking dozens of thirsty throats.

In my day, it was an unwritten law that those with colds should rinse the dipper after drinking and pour the rinsing into the not-so-shining wash basin beside the pail. Such a one was also expected to use the upper end of the community towel of coarse brown linen that hung on the other casing and was taken to someone's home each Friday night for its weekly laundering.

Perhaps disease germs are impotent in an atmosphere of such brotherhood and good will. Or perhaps "Kitty Corner," "Squat Tag," and "Pom-Pom-Pull-Away" at recess three times a day in the clean mountain air put germs to rout. Whatever the reason, there was seldom even a single case of the so-called "children's diseases" in the little red schoolhouse. And I never heard of an epidemic in all its close to a century of service.

Such pride was there in regular attendance that never to my knowledge was a truant officer called. True, a boy stayed home if sugaring or planting or potato-digging demanded. Or a girl might be kept out to help with dinner for threshers, but those were considered occasions of genuine need and treated as such. Besides, keeping all five points on the gold star in one's attendance chart or hearing what happened next in *Black Beauty* or the Horatio Alger classic Teacher was reading at roll call was also a genuine need that sometimes took precedence over all others and overcame such minor barriers as hipdeep snowdrifts, or forty-below-zero cold with its frost-bite and chilblains, or even the arrival of a baby brother and the *Sears Roebuck Catalog* the same day.

Understanding was a large ingredient of all that went on in the little red schoolhouse. It was understanding the need for getting the most of his education by his own efforts, while the others got their fair share of Teacher's attention, that kept a fellow studying his book till he had mastered it. It was what kept him figuring his problems on the board till all were done and right, even though more than one winter the wind and snow came in on his toes through the wide cracks along the baseboard, where his chalk rolled out if he dropped a piece. He would reclaim the chalk from the drift outside, warm his toes by the crackling chunk stove, and return to his Rule of Three with renewed vigor.

Miss Grey had understanding, too. She was the pretty little seventeen-year-old teacher, who was hired for the spring term in 1897. One blue and gold May morning, she had reluctantly noticed for some time that Bill, the big boy of the school, was more intent upon what went on outside the open window by his seat than upon his book.

"Bill," she commanded sharply at last, uncomfortably aware that this was her first case of discipline, "you may put that tenth cube foot problem on the b—."

With a sudden leap, Bill took his denim coattails, leather boots, and all across the weathered sill and away into the green world where the bobolinks were calling. When he returned to his seat with a sheepish grin next morning, no questions were asked, no explanations given. Yes, Miss Grey had understanding, as did her long line of predecessors and successors.

The little red schoolhouse ministered first of all to individual need. Beneath its wings, each pupil was a person, not a case; and a grin from a friendly heart was the only psychoanalysis needed.

Visual aids to education were there in abundance. Hills and valleys we learned at an early age from the upstanding knots in the worn floorboards.

The ditch at the edge of the yard gave us river and delta, cataract and levee each spring of the year.

By damming the nearby pasture brook with log and mud and ardent sweat, we learned the ways of the beaver. When Bob slid on a flat stone down the steep crusty slope beyond the dam, and landed in the icy water one January day, we unforgettably learned the meaning of acceleration, gravity, water displacement, and saturation in one object lesson. From the seesaw in the yard fence we laid the foundation for high school physics in accumulating facts about the fulcrum and the lever.

Each Arbor Day, too, as we cleaned the yard, we re-explored the habits of grass and tree and ground mole and earthworm. If the six or seven older ones had each brought a rake and employed it diligently, while the half-dozen smaller ones returned the playhouse boards and stones to fence and pile, the annual chore was completed by noon.

As soon as lunch was eaten, it was time to plant the young tree, which one of the biggest boys had dug up in his father's pasture and lugged to school on his back that morning.

While the strongest arms took turns at the shovel, the rest wrote their names on a sheet of paper, rolled it up, and placed it in a patent-medicine bottle. When the hole was deep enough to accommodate the tree roots, we would all solemnly form a ring around it. The donor of the tree would carefully bury the bottle of names at the center of the hole, the sapling would be set into its new ground, and the soil would be shoveled and stamped into place. Each pupil must leave his stamp upon the earth, his name within the bottle.

Otis was the last big boy to bring a young maple to the annual planting, in 1935. As he stood admiring its growth a dozen years later, he recalled that when he was in training for the Armed Forces in 1943 he was comforted by the thought of that tree. If he should fall on foreign soil, his maple with his name embedded at its root would be his memorial in the old schoolyard—the yard where he had shared friendships, played ball, and learned the meaning of true democracy.

The last day of school before Christmas was another event never to be forgotten. When somebody's father or hired man would stop out front with a loud "Whoa" the day before the exercises were to take place, we all went wild with delight. And when he dragged in the pungent green spruce, fresh from the woods, and set it up near the woodshed door, our hearts almost burst with joy.

The branches that had to be lopped off so the top would barely touch the ceiling we nailed above blackboards and windows. Out from the box under Teacher's desk came the strings of dried rose haws strung at recess and the ropes of snowy popcorn brought from home. Then came the paper chains the littlest ones had colored or cut from the brightest pages of the mail order catalogs and pasted when copy work was done.

All these we looped and festooned among the evergreen boughs until the plain old room became a fairyland. Butternuts wrapped in the gold and silver tinfoil from tobacco, carefully hoarded all year; spruce cones dipped in starch; and quilt batting snowflakes blossomed on the tree. Last of all, at the tips of the branches we clipped the little tin candleholders with their rainbow of wax tapers, not one of which could be lighted till just before the exercises. How we hated to say good-night and leave our beautiful room.

Next morning came our presents, to be hung by each who brought them at the most tantalizing angle among the fragrant boughs. How our fingers wished for the ones that bore our names as we "spelled down," spoke our pieces in one last rehearsal, and gave the room a thorough cleaning as soon as lunch was eaten.

At one o'clock the people came from up and down the road. Fathers and mothers, cousins and aunts, uncles, older brothers and sisters, even the two-year-olds. Every seat was crowded, and sometimes we scholars had to sit on chunks along the outside walls. Someone drew the green paper shades, Teacher lighted the candles, and radiance enveloped folk and tree.

"He comes in the night," "It was Christmas Eve and a beggar stood in the falling snow," "But jest 'fore Christmas I'm ez good ez I kin be," and "Oh Little Town of Bethlehem" came from weeks of rehearsing.

Then, amidst jingling bells and squeals of delight, in bounded Santa Claus to pass out the presents. Dolls' quilts pieced from the year's dresses, birchbark-covered blotters tied with bright ribbons, bows and arrows whittled after chores, the biggest, reddest Twenty Ounce Pippins from the fall picking, and dozens of other homely offerings gladdened our childish hearts.

Teacher's gifts brought the biggest thrill of all, for they were wrapped in white ribbed tissue and tied with red ribbons to prolong the agony of joy in opening them. Bought gifts they were, bought in towns where we had never been. A pink and white workbasket, a flashlight that really worked, a china cup and saucer delicate as an eggshell, a storybook with pictures. All were treasures to be shown and enjoyed with care and cherished as keepsakes.

Little folks still enjoy reading from the yellowed and tenderly mended pages of *The Progressive Primer* my mother received there "from Santa Claus" in 1870, when she was going on five. The quaint old black and white cuts of horsecar, oxcart, and boys and girls at play nearly a century ago vie for first place with the gayly colored Dick and Jane Readers of today. And "A boy is a man when he can put off self to please someone else," found on its page 19, comes as easily from their childish lips as does "Go, Dick, go. Run! Run! Run!"

Though time has greatly changed the content of the texts that the first scholars provided for themselves, frequently a different set of books for every pupil, the element of learning remained much the same even in the properly graded ones the town later supplied.

The 1936 grammar there admonished, "State your thought in simplest form, using vivid words that present your exact meaning." The grammar of 1856 stated a similar idea under Perspicuity in Writing. "Circumlocution seldom conduces to plainness; and you may take it as a maxim that when once an idea is clearly expressed, every additional stroke will only confuse the mind and dim the effect." All that was intelligible, it seems, to those who did their spelling lessons from Noah Webster's current edition.

Greenleaf's New Intellectual Arithmetic on the Inductive Plan, published in 1867, probably did not confuse the minds of those who learned its multiplication tables even unto the 24's, but it certainly has "a dim effect" on us today. "A hare starts 25 leaps in advance of a hound and takes 4 leaps to the hound's 3; but 2 of the hound's leaps equal 3 of the hare's; how many leaps must the hound make to overtake the hare?" That is a poser for even our atomic age.

Through the years, our little schoolhouse has ever been a community center for extracurricular activities, as well as for book learning.

There in the 1850s and early '60s, the neighborhood Lyceum was held. Each Friday evening of the winter months, twenty-five or thirty adults and youths of that remote mountain community would assemble by the light of candles and later of kerosene lamps in the one-room building.

Organized as "The Improver" in 1855, it soon became "The Young American Society," stating its purpose as "Devoted to general intelligence and cultivation of the mind."

The Rising Star was its publication, which defined itself as "A planet whose revolutions present the Wit, Wisdom, Sense and Nonsense of Young Americans."

As soon as "Diligent, Desirable Delight," "Land-Loving, Lady-Loving Leroy," "Jovial, Jabbering James," and the rest of the humorously recorded satellites convened, the meeting opened with "Oh say, can you see by the dawn's early light," "Mine eyes have seen the glory," or "Yankee Doodle." Grandfather as editor then read the wit, wisdom, sense, and nonsense submitted for the week. Upon those now-yellowed pages appeared a wide variety of "subjects of utility for improving the mind." "The Use of Chewing Tobacco As an Enslaving Habit," "Freedom of Thought," advertisements for a mate, conundrums, verse, and many another piece worthy of a "Rising Star" were recorded there.

One who signed herself Peace offered an essay on hope concluding with: "Hope is a telescope to man's eye, a staff to his weariness, a lever to his soul. She is the mainspring of action, the mother of enterprise.

"Hope on then, hope forever,
For hope will clear our way,
Be to our souls the lever
That rolls the rocks away."

One pert miss, who chose to write about old bachelors who continued their calls without stating any intentions, closed her remarks with: "If the old boys know bran from a leg of mutton, they will not wait for the kick; but leave tracks early, with the heels toward the door—Winnie."

Following the reading of *The Rising Star* came the debate. Those current problems covered a wide range—"Tight Lacing," "How to Split a Log," "Why a Young Farmer Should Marry."

One such, entitled "Shaving Off the Beard," deserves republication of its conclusion. "The Book says, 'Let not man put asunder that which God has joined.' It is said that there is a nerve running from each hair to the eye. For this reason the mustache had never ought to be cut off because it affects the eyes. It is said that there is a nerve running from the teeth to the beard on the chin. So by shaving it would tend to rot the teeth—Codger."

The editor noted beneath the record of this debate, "The purpose of debate is to hear how remarks from their own lips will sound when delivered to the public."

One eligible young bachelor advertised for a good, prudent, and industrious wife to help him make his cheese and butter, adding that only the pretty good-looking need apply.

Whether he found a spouse to meet his requirements is not recorded. Certain it is, however, that three grandsons of the builders of our little red schoolhouse won their mates from the young ladies who, in my time, came as schoolmistresses and remained as wives.

Those courtships added zest to our scholastic careers. DeWitt was the first such beau in my recollection. His freshly washed carriage drawn by his glossy chestnut Ned frequently stopped at the schoolhouse door on sundry errands. One June afternoon, just as we were picking up to go home from our last-day-of-school picnic, the smiling suitor appeared again. This time he carried a big bouquet of the wild red roses that grew deep in Owl's Head Woods. Teacher glowed and grew as crimson as the roses.

"Let's give Ned the rest of the cupcakes," she suggested, "and you boys and girls may pick out the pictures and other things you want from that pile on my desk."

Grinning, we took the hint and scrambled for the bounty. We always believed Teacher said "Yes" while we were so occupied, for the wedding occurred not long after.

Another courtship proceeded to the tune of "Old Zip Coon" and "Pop Goes the Weasel," played by one of the older boys on his jew's-harp. John used to drop in from foddering sheep at the barn across the road from school to beau Teacher at recess. As we do-si-doed around the big box stove, we gleefully watched the telltale giggles and blushes we had learned to recognize as symptoms. Later there was another wedding.

Harry conducted his courtship outside school hours, but when Miss Dean began to look dreamy and started the flag salute one morning during opening exercises, with "I believe in the United States of America," we guessed what was up. Nor were we mistaken.

Two of us who hold treasured memories of the days spent in the little old schoolhouse stopped in last summer to chat with the present owners, the Andrew Painters. It was my first visit there since it had been made into a summer cottage.

As I entered the beloved old room, left much as it was in my schooldays, memories of the lessons, the good times, and the dear ones I had known there came back poignantly. On the familiar teacher's desk lay the guest book, before it the worn armchair. As I came to add my name to the list of visitors, Robert Louis Stevenson's lines, slightly rephrased, flowed from my pen:

> "Home is the hunter
> Home to her hill."

When, after much reminiscing, we paused outside by the rock beneath the maple, where we had picnicked so many happy times, I noticed a new groove and hollow in the whitened stone.

"Weather," our host explained.

And suddenly, a question of equal opportunities for all men, which we had been debating, resolved itself and came clear. The sun and rain fall upon rock and tree alike. The one accepts the gift and grows. The other, while seeming to reject, is cleansed and shaped thereby. Neither rock nor tree is sovereign.

"Did you notice our fossil?" the younger son, a college sophomore, inquired. "We found it on the stone pile out back."

To our interested questioning, he added, "It's a cephalopod four hundred million years old, a sedimentary rock from the Ordovician period." We had known it as just another piece of shale.

As we said goodbye, I looked thoughtfully at the present owners. Theirs are the faces of a man and woman and their sons and one son's wife who live secure in their love for one another, for the out-doors, for learning, and for all that is best as a way of life. I thought with happy satisfaction, "Our dear old Alma Mater instructs her brood of scholars still."

11

THE VILLAGE STORE

"Due Sam Leavitt for

	Hats and tea	$1.13
	6 Window Lights	.36
	2 Spelling Books	.25
	1/2 Pint Brandy	.38
	1Ball Candlewick	.10
	1 Pair Boots	4.00
	Dresses for Wife	2.00
Gave	2 Skeins Yarn	2.00
	Tub Butter, 25 lbs.	2.45
	1 Cord Wood	1.13
	4 Calf Skins	4.00"

So began Grandfather's store account in his Day Book for 1859. A busy place that store was, across from the old white church and next to the blacksmith shop, with the village pump and the watering trough between. A wooden building, twenty-two feet by thirty-five, with small-paned windows to the front only, it had been painted red on the outside.

One front corner had been partitioned off for a tiny milliner's shop, where the proprietor's wife made bonnets to order or to her own taste. Behind it was a small shoemaker's shop, conveniently looking out upon the town tannery.

An old store even in 1859, its dark, unplastered, rough-beamed interior held within its uncataloged cavern almost anything the townspeople ever asked for.

A Franklin stove dispensed heat and ashes in cold weather and soot tea in a summer shower. But its hearth was ever a comforting place to rest a pair of boots.

Barrels of vinegar, flour, molasses, kerosene, and salt pork, each identified by its own aroma, lined the rear wall where the fireplace had been boarded up. From the hooks above, an array of sheepskin moccasins, full-cloth overcoats, skeins of yarn, hanks of thread, bunches of herbs, and many another commodity were suspended at random.

At his high schoolmaster's desk, the proprietor entered his accounts in his own Day Book with a quill pen and the ink that he manufactured for himself and his patrons. If the latter preferred, he would sell them the ingredients and they might make their own by his "rule," which he generously shared. It read: "1 oz. nutgalls powdered; 1/2 oz. cloves; 1/2 oz. sulphate of iron; 1/2 oz. gum arabic; 8 ozs. water. Digest by frequent shaking till it has sufficient color. A good durable ink and will bear diluting."

Sam Leavitt extended credit generously to his farmer patrons, who could supply him with a considerable amount of his stock, but he was shrewd. He never accepted a tub of butter in trade until his capable thumb had gouged out a sample and his bulbous nose had sniffed along the rim. His Barlow knife also must deftly take a paring from each cask of cheese.

To one who slyly thought to exchange some green axe helves for a sheep there in 1863, the storekeeper was quoted as having shouted in righteous indignation, "Meaner than a dead dog rolled in tan-bark. Your credit ain't worth the powder to blow a mosquito over a tow string."

But when the small son of a widowed village dweller offered to sweep the floor, blackened with barrel drip and booted feet, in return for sheet wadding and thread for his mother's quilting, Sam Leavitt allowed the trade. And when he discovered the festered cracks in the small boy's bare feet, he even threw in a box of the Green Mountain Salve that he made as one of his staples in stock.

The directions for the Green Mountain Salve read: "1 lb. beeswax; 1 lb. soft butter; 1 1/2 lbs. soft turpentine; 12 ozs. balsam fir. Melt and strain. Use to heal fresh wounds, burns, scalds & all bad sores."

Another staple was his Magic Ointment made of 1 qt. alcohol; 4 ozs. gum camphor; 2 ozs. turpentine; 2 ozs. oil of organum; 1 oz. sweet oil. The "receipt" added: "For cuts or calks on horses or cattle in winter it has no equal but it must be applied often."

For more than sixty years, Sam Leavitt had been the town merchant, and it was said that he had been shrewd from the first day he opened his store. It was he who had first recognized the counterfeit silver coin that began to circulate in large amounts in Bennington County and over in York State's neighboring towns in the early 1800s. So clever a copy was it that the most wary had been deceived by it.

As soon as young Sam Leavitt had discovered the coin that did not ring true, he had pondered who had given it to him. Since most of his goods were paid for in trade, he soon suspected one Adonijah Crane, who lived with his two brothers and mother on a farm east of the village. Already the well-dressed young men had been considered suspicious characters, for they often loitered around the store and tannery instead of working their farm. Also, they had given money instead of scrap iron, wheat, or other produce, or such service as shearing a sheep to pay for their "boughten" goods.

Leavitt and two or three confidantes began keeping a strict watch over the Crane brothers and soon observed that these men took frequent walks into the woods near their farm.

Then, one evening when Leavitt had stayed late at his store, his friend David Sheldon had reported seeing a light up on the mountains near the Cranes. The adjacent area had previously been approached, and it had been noted that the mother often ran out with a pail, shouting, "Pig! Pig!" The listers had reported finding no pig, so suspicion had grown. This night, the village posse hastened toward the place where the light had been seen. Toward morning, after a diligent search, they came upon the men in an open cave at the base of Mount Antone. Beside them were their instruments and a pile of their spurious coin. By some strategy, the Cranes managed to flee, and no more of their counterfeit money went into circulation.

When the wind- and rain-battered building was swept clean of half of its shingled roof in an east gale in the late 1800s the stock was salvaged and a bigger store built hard by.

One of the greatest treats of my childhood was to go to that store.

Although Sam Leavitt had long before gone to balance his account in eternity, men waiting for the evening mail still warmed their boots upon a newer hearth, or chewed tobacco upon a longer settee out front, this time upon a veranda high enough for loading sack or barrel into a high-wheeled wagon.

Those philosophizing, guffawing men at times posed a problem for feminine patrons. More than one of the shyer younger generation preferred to drive around to the back when the male congregation was thickest. However, one aristocratic, middle-aged widow tartly remarked to the storekeeping postmistress, "*I'm* not afraid of those men, but when I come after the mail, I always put on an extra petticoat. They're not going to poke one another and grin because they can see between *my* legs."

A Vermont brand of Paul Bunyan tale also was often heard in that store in winter. I remember one of these that Bob and Joe and Sally and I heard there when we were youngsters. Two loggers, Payne and Barnes, were entertaining the assemblage with an account of their bringing two big loads down the mountainside. The climax was that Payne's logs had tipped over and pinned him beneath them on an icy road bank. Barnes had had neither time nor strength to lift the load, so he had resorted to another measure of rescue. Breaking a hole in the creek ice, he had stirred so mightily with his axe helve that his combined dexterity and cuss words had caused the water to boil. This he had scooped out in his cap, cussing the while to keep up the boiling, and poured it around Payne. Repeating the operation, he had caused the ice to melt sufficiently for the victim to extricate himself.

Drummers with their black bags of samples had taken the place of the peddlers with their waterproof packs, and now and then the horseless carriage drew up by the water-box, but inside the store the scene remained much as in Sam Leavitt's day.

A long counter ran the length of the store, from one big front window where a two-pound Great Divide potato or seven-foot dent cornstalks with their giant ears were sometimes displayed at harvest time.

The showcases, at right angles with the far end of the counter, were a museum of delight to us six- and eight-year olds. Plump, gay-colored gumdrops, choc'late creams, pep'mint or strawberry sticks, or, at Christmas time, wonderful chocolate boys and brightly striped ribbon candy, filled one case. Jewelry, ribbons, dolls, tiddledywinks, painted tin engines, and many other enchanting treasures beckoned us back and back again.

Miss Belle, the retired village schoolteacher, "kept the store" in my childhood. In her starched white shirtwaist and long black skirt, with a black bow and her pencil in her high grey pompadour, Miss Belle was a genial keeper of the store. Never too busy to listen to a customer's tale of joy or sorrow, she angled graciously and adeptly for all the latest news.

When the Dupliss boys from a neighboring lumber camp were involved in a nearly fatal fight over the queen of the ball at a Beartown shindig on the other side of the mountain, Miss Belle was among the first to hear of it the next morning. She had liked those three black-eyed, smooth-spoken young men and had tied a neat four-in-hand for one the evening before. She had even let them oil down their hair to patent-leather perfection; in front of her own little looking glass over her private wash dish behind the cellar door. Yes, and she had unsuspectingly sold them several big bottles of vanilla extract, just as they were leaving. She had supposed they were for the camp cook, but when the empty bottles were found over by the church sheds, the good fathers of this town, that "voted dry," knew otherwise. Miss Belle grieved that her sale of vanilla might have helped to send those "poor boys" to jail.

I can remember her once "covering up" for Sally and me, when I was a twelve-year-old. It was one Saturday afternoon in late May that we had been sent to do the week's trading. Across the back of the buggy was roped our crate of twelve dozen eggs, packed in oats, to be exchanged for sugar and matches and sundry other items.

About a half-mile from the village, we pulled over to the left of the recently "worked" road to pass Martha, a neighbor girl about my age, also going to the store, driving her old Fan. "Slow Poke," Sally taunted, but Martha and Fan had no mind to let either us or the challenge pass. Away we went, urging on our respective mares, which were sending up flying stones and clouds of dust and turning buggy tails into jack rabbits. In spite of our best efforts, Fan and Martha won, and we arrived at the store hilariously. But hilarity turned to distraught dismay for Sally and me when we saw the eggs, not a whole one in all that mass of shell and sticky oats.

"We'll empty the crate and wash it out over at the trough," said resourceful Miss Belle. "Then I'll give you some oats from that bag the mice gnawed. I'll put up the things your mother has on her list, and this summer you girls can pick me some blueberries to pay for them."

That we gladly did, but kindly Miss Belle sent Sally and me each a flowered china plate from the oatmeal premiums at Christmas time, that we might not feel she had been too severe in her accounting.

Long hours went into Miss Belle's day. The farmers began arriving in the village for factory or creamery delivery soon after six o'clock on a summer morning, or seven in the winter. By the time her first patrons began lifting the front door latch, Miss Belle had donned her ample gingham apron and swept out the center of the floor and the steps, using wet tea leaves or newspaper bits to lay the broom's dust.

So many children came in at recess and the noon hour from the village school that she always ate her lunch after one o'clock. Spreading her big white-linen napkin upon one end of the counter, she would set out her sandwiches and pie, brew her tea over her alcohol burner, and finish off with London Cream crackers from the barrel by the stove and cheese from the box on the counter.

Her sister, Miss Jennie, always brought her supper from their home up the street. Devotedly that older sister plodded through sleet, snow, or rain with her big willow basket on her arm.

The store closed as soon after nine in the evening as the seven o'clock mail could be given out and the most social customers would leave. Then Miss Belle and Miss Jennie, in cape, or fascinator and shawl, would turn homeward, contented at being in the center of the town's ever-revolving wheel.

Once, when Miss Belle was laid up with her one attack of the grippe, an experienced clerk, Mr. Don, took over the store. His chief assets were originality and high-pressure salesmanship.

Grown up by then, I had gone to investigate a newly stocked commodity, one spring rocker. After it had been separated from its associates of several cans of maple syrup, a demijohn of molasses, a fly trap, a keg of nails, and a hunk of salted salmon, we discussed the chair's good points. When I sat down to try the seat, my spine nearly went through the top of my head.

"I thought you called it a *spring* rocker!" I exclaimed. "This doesn't bounce at all."

"That's only your state of mind and a matter of relativity," Mr. Don pointed out suavely. "If you'd jest thought you were going to set down in a hard chair, when you set 'twould have seemed soft." The chair stayed on with the fly trap and the dried salmon.

Unnumbered tons of grain and salt have been among the staples dispensed from that store's great dark backroom. They were doubly valuable, for those sacks and bags have increased many a wardrobe and beautied many a home. We made place mats and doilies edged with crocheted lace from the oyster-white linen containers for Worcester salt in my childhood. Crib sheets, embroidered bedspread blocks, dish towels, and pillow slips for everyday use, as well as petticoats and bloomers, came from the cotton bags for Calf Feed. True, it required long boiling in a tub of suds, and an even-longer bleaching on the sunbathed meadow grass, to remove the big black or red letters from those pieces more than a yard square, but the results were rewarding. The burlap sacks from the cracked corn, we also discovered, made perfect foundations for hooking rugs as well as strips for rewebbing a worn chair seat.

In these latter years, the Homemakers' Units soon discovered the bonanza when a milling company began to sack its grain in beautifully printed cottons. These the women have reused for dresses, aprons, blouses, handbags, curtains, and numerous other projects.

"My wife wants me to get my feed this time in the blue morning-glory print," I heard one farmer comment, as he hoisted and sorted through the hundred-pound sacks to find ten to match.

"We sometimes take our washed sacks to Home Bureau meetings," one of my cousins explained, "and trade around to get enough of one kind, if we're short. That's the way I got enough to make that pink rosebud skirt for my dressing table."

There is one sometimes-requested commodity that the store does not stock. When "summer people" are in town, one or two of the patrolmen find sport in sending the growing boys in for a "left-handed monkey wrench." The present owner eased one such youngster's embarrassment by saying, "Tell Mr. A— that all we have today are ambidextrous ones." Never having heard of "ambidextrous," Mr. A— met with as much confusion as the youngster.

Among the many services the store renders the community is bride-groom and paternal "setting up the cigars." When a popular young lady of an outlying district was married recently, her city-bred husband had never heard of the custom, and the bride forgot to tell him. Home from their honeymoon, the bridegroom was surprised by a telephone call from the storekeeper saying, "When the boys found you hadn't set up the cigars, some of them began plans to horn you and Joan tonight. I knew her mother thinks considerable of her flower beds, so I set up a box of White Owls in your name. They're five dollars. I hope it's all right."

When the young husband learned what a "horning" would have entailed, he gladly paid for his reprieve of White Owls.

The present owner enjoys recalling an amusing episode with an aging bachelor of the town a few years ago. Cal, who was a gallant admirer of many a good cook and attractive housewife, came in one quiet morning and asked to see some "long-legged stockings."

"Are they for yourself?" inquired the proprietor.

"Yeah," Cal answered, and Mrs. S— hauled out box after box of the longest men's socks she could find.

"Ain't ye got no ladies' stockings?" the slightly irate customer finally demanded.

"Why, yes," Mrs. replied, "but I thought you said they're for yourself."

"So they be," Cal replied curtly, "but I dunno's it's anybody's damned business who's goin' to wear 'em."

"After that," said Mrs. S—, "I was careful not to ask *him* many questions."

Last summer I stopped to buy gas at the pump, which now stands where the watering trough once mirrored the sun. An amazing array was coming out of the store's front door. Buggy whips and nose feed bags; a rusty black bonnet and a faded brown derby; a linen duster as of 1910; a buffalo robe, moth-depleted along its edges; a faded paper bag exuding dusty tea; a flail and some posters of the Gold Dust Twins.

Inquiry revealed that the motley collection was destined for the Lord's Auction to be held that afternoon on the church lawn across the street. "They'll go like snow in the sun for souvenirs," the auctioneer said with a grin, as the stack grew. "Anything that don't sell, just put it with something else, and you'll be sure to get a bid."

As I watched the store door open and close and open again to patrons bearing market basket and mail, I thought of the long cavalcade of American living that had crossed its worn threshold.

Turning to the auctioneer, I said with a reminiscent smile, "I'll give a dollar thirteen for the hats and tea."

12

THE BLACKSMITH SHOP

"The Forge," the signboard states above the door of a friend's summer home in a town in southern Vermont. The transformation of a blacksmith shop to a private dwelling significantly marks our present changing era. Recollection of the building's former service provides its present owner with an interesting tale.

The summer of 1815 Preserved Wright opened the first real blacksmith shop in Rupert township. Noted in the early village history as "poor but honest, and held in high esteem," he was, by his craft, a leader in community enterprise.

By peculiar coincidence, his name was particularly suited to his calling, for a wright in olden days was defined as one who wrought. The term blacksmith had also early been applied to one who wrought with black iron, and charcoal smudge and soot.

Preserved had long been assisting his farmer neighbors with the shoeing of horse and ox. Finally, at the age of forty, he had laid aside the wherewith to build his own small shop beside the village pump. Constructed of hand-hewed timbers and plank from White Creek saw mill, it was fourteen feet long, ten wide, and ten high. There was no window, but it had a wide door at the front.

Chimney and forge were of field stone from a nearby mountain meadow, and his anvil was a broad flat rock set upon a two-foot hickory stump, within easy reach of the forge. The latter, a four-foot-square arch three feet high, faced the door.

The first faint light of dawn was tinging the treetops that July morning when Preserved came to kindle the fire in his forge. The night before he had filled its cavern well with the charcoal of his own burning, the only fuel then available that would sufficiently heat a blacksmith's irons.

Four days and nights he had spent charring the great mound of logs he had cut and rolled through the cold winter months, and piling great shovelfuls of dirt upon the smoldering logs to smother the flame for the charring. He had stored a year's supply of the precious charcoal there on the woodlot, to be carted as needed to his shop yard.

Before unbarring his newly hung door that summer dawn, he peered into the rotted stump that served as a rain barrel at the back of his shop, and found it half full of water. No need to draw any today from the well out front. He settled the heavy ladder that his son had just finished pegging against the side of his shop and placed a wooden bucket of water nearby. If sparks should fly too high from the forge and shower upon the shingles, he had the equipment ready to save his roof.

Pride shone in Preserved's sharp eyes and surged beneath his coarse brown jacket as he knelt upon the packed earth floor to ignite his charcoal. The night before he had placed a bunch of "swingling tow," the refuse of the stalk after the spinnable flax had been removed —dry, light, and highly inflammable—upon an iron hook over his forge. Now, bringing his "Long Tom," companion of hunting days, from its hook behind the door, he poured a little powder from his pocket horn into the flash pan, and holding it under the tow, snapped the old flintlock, setting powder and tow ablaze. That blaze applied to shaving and charcoal, his forge glowed with its life's beginning.

Before a horse or ox would be brought to his door before sun-up, there would still be time to iron a wheel. Preserved worked the great bellows, or "leather lungs," that pumped air into his forge, till the coals burned bright with their keen red heat. Onto the wide bed of glowing charcoal he laid a band of iron, and while it "het" he turned to the waiting wheel. A heavy wooden contrivance was that wheel. Its hub, spokes, and felloe or "felly," sometimes called the rim, all were shaped by hand from a stout ash tree. To iron it or fasten its tire of iron upon it, Preserved placed it upon his wheel holder.

This was a huge stump cask, hollowed from an oak tree, which he had hooped with iron and nearly filled with rocks to steady it. For further steadying, he had thrust a heavy timber diametrically through its base and spiked it to the corner beams. With wheel hub in the hollow and spokes supported by the top of the barrel, he could work upon his wheel.

Donning his worn leather apron over his homespun breeches, he lifted his white-hot iron from the forge with hand-made tongs. Upon his rock anvil, then, with ringing blows of his ten-pound sledge, he wrought the band of iron to the desired width and length. Into another stump barrel, half filled with water, he plunged the writhing band to cool it, and with nails he had pounded out at his winter fireside, applied it to the waiting felly.

He shod that day three oxen before his evening meal, as well as a horse that had pawed at the hitching-post outside, awaiting its turn, while its master chinned with the smith and ox-drivers within.

Preserved had installed special equipment for the shoeing of the "neat critters," who could not stand on three small feet while the fourth was shod, as the horse could on his larger hoofs. This ox-sling or strong scaffold stood just inside the open door, along the west wall. It was a massive wooden frame into which the ox was led and his head secured in a stanchion at the far end.

Broad straps or belly-bands, attached to a great strip of the stoutest cowhide from the village tannery, suspended by other straps from a lofty timber, were then buckled securely beneath the animal's body. Up the rough ladder beside the stanchion its owner climbed and cranked the wooden windlass, which turned an enormous wheel made of shaped planks, high above the ox's head. From this wheel a timber extended lengthwise above the ox, and to this timber the great strap was attached.

As the ponderous wooden wheel was revolved by the windlass, turning the huge timber, the stout cowhide straps tightened and raised the floundering ox a foot or so in the air. To prevent his hampering struggles during his shoeing, posts with leather thongs stood near each corner of the frame or stall, and to these the animal's legs were tied in an easy position, and his horns secured with other thongs to another part of the frame.

One after another, Preserved then beat and shaped two footpads for each cleft hoof out of the white-hot iron from his forge with heavy blows of his sledge upon the anvil. When each of those four hoofs was carefully fitted, with its iron shoes nailed on, Preserved holding the animal's hoof in the vise-like grip of his knees beneath his cloven apron as he worked, the ox was released from thong and sling.

But shoes for horse and ox, and tires for a multitude of wheels were only a part of all that was beaten out upon Preserved's rock anvil. Spikes and nails for building also came from his two-pound shaping-hammer. Ten pence a dozen, eight pence a dozen, or whatever the price might be, due to the cost of the iron that went to their making, gave rise to the terms for the sizes of nails today. In 1815, a dozen of those handmade nails, the size now called ten-penny, cost as much as twenty feet of two-foot cherry boards. A few years later, Preserved bartered thirty-five pounds of those sweat-wrought nails for a curly maple chest of drawers for his daughter's "setting-up." In today's exchange, that would equal about a dollar a nail.

Broadaxes for hewing timbers, bridge-irons, plowshares, cow-bells with chunk-iron clappers, HL or Holy Lord hinges, all came from the blacksmith's clanging anvil. So, too, did the spacious frying pans with handles a yard long, the long-handled forks, ladles, and skimmers for reaching into the cavernous black kettles also of his forging, and the broilers, spits, and sundry other cooking utensils of those early days. At the smithy, too, a lumbering covered wagon was equipped in 1849, when one of Preserved's neighbors set forth to take up a homestead in the West.

Custom prohibited a lady's entering the shop without masculine escort, nor was she warmly received even then. Seldom, therefore, did a petticoat brush its doorway. On rainy days, or when teamsters must wait for their horses' shoeing, the news of town, state, and nation were there conned well. There, too, the town officers often were really chosen long before the annual Town Meeting convened.

When Great-Grandfather proposed to ride to Connecticut the fall of the "frost-every-month-of-the-summer" in 1816 to obtain seed corn for the next spring's planting, it was Preserved who shod his bay Morgan, Prince, for the journey.

Although he encouraged gregarious gathering, nevertheless Work and Piety were the smith's watchwords. When Eben Harmon there loudly protested the fence viewers' decision upon his and his neighbor's wall, Preserved offered only a mild reprimand. But when Eben's continued abuse provoked a brawl where the smith was paring the hoof of a fidgety mare, Preserved seized a tub of black and sooty water and heaved its contents upon the thumping, cussing men: Snorting and dripping, they vanished through the doorway. With never a word, Preserved returned to his shoeing.

In 1853, the wright's aging muscles could no longer swing his sledge, so another smith came to the village. Hardly more than a boy, young Byron Scott had served as apprentice in a neighboring township. Youth demanded a bigger and better smithy, so the seldom-used Select School building, constructed of brick, across the street from the meeting-house, was converted into his shop. Brick, instead of fieldstone filled into a plank frame, formed the new forge, and slate from a nearby quarry protected his roof. Beside the door, the townsmen piled the worn horseshoes, ox shoes, and wagon tires accumulated through the years at Preserved's now-abandoned shop. Old iron must not be wasted, for it could be heated and wrought again into many a useful article.

An iron anvil was fastened with clutches and bolts upon its oak stump pedestal, set less than an arm's length from the forge. A great block of granite, with a hub-hole in its center, now replaced the cask of rocks for ironing a wheel. The ox-sling, however, was brought from Preserved's own shop and put in its place, with but few reinforcements or repairs. Two granite hitching posts were deeply set in the ground at the front, a gigantic horseshoe nailed upon the door, and with friction matches young Scott then lighted the charcoal in his forge.

A five-foot-long and three-foot-wide bellows of light wood and leather, brass nails and thongs, suspended from a heavy wooden rack, was connected at its pointed end with the lower part of the forge chimney, so air could be forced through its metal tube into a small opening in the bricks.

A six-foot wooden pole attached to the bellows provided the handle, over which the young smith hooked his elbow to pump the air into his forge. It was so placed that his hands might work at forge or anvil while his elbow worked his pump.

In the 1850s, more than one face, black as Scott's own smutted one, peered in at the smithy door. The fear in those faces there turned to gratitude as Byron Scott skillfully filed off broken shackle or iron collar, and hurried the refugee into a passing load of hay or corn. Many an escaping bondsman was thus helped along the Underground Railway, with its cave for a hideout at the foot of Mount Antone, by the mercy of the smith.

Through the years, the men congregating at the blacksmith shop drove away with many a truth of their own conning, as iron-shod as beast or wheel or sled or plow.

"There's more pleasure in sweating an hour than in yawning a century."

"I'd rather wear out than rust out," and "I ain't got time fer the lolling log, humped up like an old burnt boot."

"Time's the rider that breaks the youth."

In my girlhood, Amos Cruikshank there pumped the bellows and clanged the anvil. Though women and girls still waited at church or store instead of inside the blacksmith shop, Sally and I once peered from the depths of the buffalo robe, as we curled up on the cutter seat, while Father took Old Fan to be shod.

Through the wide-open door we gazed, fascinated, at the clouds of red-orange sparks flying from the forge, fed now and then by soft coal from a nearby bin, as the smith's crooked elbow pumped the bellows. From the long rows of shining shoes hung from the overhead rafters, we watched him select one of the biggest for Old Fan. Onto the forge it went to heat for its fitting. With long pliers he turned and returned it till the red-white iron was "het" to his liking. Swiftly, then, he laid it upon his anvil, and with ringing blows of his hammer sending more clouds of sparks flying upward, he pounded it to the pattern of Fan's wornout shoe. Into the tub of scummy black water beside him he dowsed it, and brackish steam rolled to the rafters.

As Amos picked up Old Fan's hind foot and pressed the hot iron against her hoof, we girls shuddered at the sight and sound of the burning hiss, although we knew her shoeing was not hurting Old Fan. Into the previously drilled holes of the shoes, sweat streaking his sooty face the while, Amos pounded the nails that sent their points through the outside of the mare's hoof. Twisting off the protruding ends, he gave them a final filing and set Old Fan's newly shod foot down on the hard earth floor.

As truck and tractor brought the farms mechanical power, as automobile displaced the horse and buggy upon street and road, the blacksmith practiced a dwindling trade. Burdock and thistle grew high among the rusty wheels and horseshoes piled beside his door. The ox-sling Amos gladly gave to the county museum, but he sighed as he sold the last iron from his cobwebbed rafters to a teamster who thenceforth would do his own shoeing.

When, in 1930 Amos disconnected his bellows and let the fire die in his forge, it was never again rekindled. The spiders spun their webs where men had spun their yarns, and desolation blackened the windows that had glowed from the reflection of live coals and shaping iron.

Preserved Wright's tongs and ox-shoes could be seen upon the walls within for some time after its closing. The ankle iron that Byron Scott long ago filed from a foot seeking freedom and the shoe that Amos Cruikshank once removed from Dan Patch's famous hoof were unwittingly lost, however, when debris was cleared from the corners.

The deserted shop was finally torn down, its bricks going to the building of the present summer home, but memories linger beneath the tall elm where the smithy stood.

13

THE OLD MILL AT HAGAR BROOK

Although Great-Uncle Zachariah had gone to his rest, and his mill to Mother Earth, long before my generation came into being, we grew up loving the legend and the gifts of the miller and his mill. Named for his Grandfather Harwood, who had helped open the first Vermont colony at Bennington in 1761, pride in that name and achievement was strong within him.

On May 5, 1832, his twenty-first birthday, young Zach had opened his mill. Twenty by thirty feet, with twenty-four-foot uprights, its hewed frame stood solidly there between the winding Valley Road and the churning white falls of Hagar Brook. For months he and his father and brothers had toiled at its building, and now the first rumble of his own machinery brought it alive. Joy surged through the young miller as he watched the rushing mountain water pour its power upon his wheel.

Ever since the October day in 1815 when as a four-year-old he had first gone to the mill with his father, he had hoped and planned to become a miller. How well he remembered that first real glimpse of the grinding of a grist. Fascinated, he had watched the sacks of corn that he had so tediously helped to shell emptied into the wooden, flared-top box called a hopper, with a hole the size of a rabbit's burrow where the grain had poured out down through the center of a great, round rotating stone.

His father had pointed out that this was an old mill, one where the great four-foot stones in the big oak barrel banded in iron had been set in '72, before the Revolution. Those granite Buhr stones, each eight inches thick, had been brought from France by Remember Baker. It had been Baker himself, also, who had tanned his best cowhide for the leather belt and pounded out the iron bolts that held it together. From the heaviest tin he could find, he, too, had soldered the fifty-five cups, bolted two feet apart, on that belt.

In silent wonder, the small boy had gazed, enchanted, at the wide belt with its cups (the size his grandfather used for ginger tea, that whirred busily, round and round, catching the golden meal that the upper stone's revolving shot off the outer edge of the stationary under stone, and conveying it down a wooden trough into the previously emptied sacks, to be taken home for the good brown bread and johnnycake.

Grist from that mill always measured true and never tasted of cob nor mould, young Zach remembered his father's often observing. The same should be said when he would some day have his mill.

In the little log schoolhouse at the foot of the hill, he had learned to figure the facts that a miller must know. Through long months, from dusk of dawn till dusk of evening, he had learned his trade, helping an uncle with his grinding and a neighbor with his saw.

He himself had chosen the stoutest hides at the tannery, to be cut into six-inch strips for these belts in his mill. On long winter evenings beside the kitchen hearth, he had "het" his iron and pounded out not only the precious bolts and screws, but a supply of nails as well.

While his two older brothers, Joseph and Franklin, and the two younger, Oliver and Seymour, had planned for the farms their father would give them when they would come of age, Zach had planned for his mill. His father was glad to have him a miller and would set him up, also, in a business of his own as soon as he reached his majority.

So it was that, the autumn of 1831, ground had been broken by Hagar's Falls for the raising of his mill. The gigantic water whed at its side would power not only quern and saw, but also his turning-lathe, for Great-Uncle Zach had decided to make furniture in his mill, when the season was slack for the sawing and grinding.

One carefully pegged half was tightly enclosed, except for doors and window, to house Buhr stones and hoppers, belts and chute, as well as a wooden windlass with great iron tongs. The last would be used to lift the upper stone when the grinding surfaces must be pecked with a special hammer and chisel every three or four months, to retain the several grooves in each of its sections that radiated from its center. He had set two pairs of Buhr stones: the great four-foot ones to be used for corn and oats, wheat, barley, and rye; the twenty-inch ones for the buckwheat that supplied the community's hot cakes for breakfast. Its kernels less resistant to the crushing of the stones, it required less surface over which to be milled. There was a crank for adjusting each top stone, and it seemed to be working well.

Each hopper, that he had planned and carefully constructed himself, was now supplied with a one-and-a-half-inch pipe to run the grain cleanly through the upper stone onto the lower for spreading it there for grinding. A screen, or bolter, made of a thin piece of wood closely perforated by the slimmest nail he could make, would now sift the grain as it was shot from the belt cups down the wooden chute into the waiting bag.

Sister Harriet had given him, for spares, a dozen of her towcloth grain bags, newly woven for the opening of his mill. One must be filled for her with the first grist of the new wheel's grinding. He would lower the upper stone well for that grinding, for Harriet liked her wheat meal fine. He must not set it too close, however, lest stone dust be ground from the sharp new grooves to spoil the meal and dull the grinding surface.

He'd have a cooking fire, too, over there near the brook, and hang a pot on a pole above it. There'd be lots of things a man could cook without much bother—cracked wheat right off the stone any day, coarsest grind and no bolter for that. Many times he'd cooked it already, putting five large spoons of wheat into a two-quart earthen jar with a tight-fitting cover. After adding a large spoon of dark maple sugar and a small teaspoon of salt, the jar would be filled with water. Into his iron kettle he then would put a handful of nails and set in the jar, with water halfway up the outside of it. Covering jar and kettle, he could leave it to cook for hours, when the wheat would be like a thick jelly, ready to eat with cream and sugar.

Yes, he was his own boss here, and here he would be measured by all that he did in this mill.

He crouched by his beautiful overshot wheel, to watch with pride its steady, perfect rhythm as the water pouring over the falls filled the evenly spaced buckets bolted upon its rim, causing it to turn and sing with the power of Green Peak's rock springs and melting snows.

"The strength of the hills is his also," he meditated half aloud, and added a thought of his own. "When earth gives such bounty to man, man must make wise use of its bounty."

A shout from the road told him that his brothers had come with his grain barrels. There were five of them, one for each kind of grain and each made by himself or a brother from the trunk of a big maple. It had been a job to make them, but they would last a lifetime. Each one four feet high and three to four feet in diameter, where the trunk had grown thickest, pretty fairly rounding for big ones, too, they would hold a goodly number of bushels. Later he would make more if he needed.

Twelve-year-old Oliver's barrel had turned out a mite the best, but he had had the hardest time getting the fire started to burn out the center before he began the adzing. Finally, the coals from the kitchen hearth had taken hold in a slow fire, though, and burned down a good two feet by the time it had eaten a hole that size in diameter. Oliver had a way with an adz, and he had done the smoothest job of all the boys, chipping out the rest of the wood till he had the required shell three quarters of an inch thick all around and at the bottom.

Zach ran his hand over the smoothly chipped interior free from hump or knot. The boys had done well, but it had been their father who had nailed on the strips of tin all around the bottom to prevent cracking and keep out the grain worms. No matter how well a miller swept up his floor each night, the grain pests always got up through the cracks. But they'd done their best, the barrels were tight, and tomorrow Zach would begin to grind. He closed the wide doors where for many years to come the grain would be brought in, pushed the bar across the latch so wind would not shake them open, and stood in the other half of his mill, where the east and west ends were left open.

Here his up-and-down saw with its shining four-foot blade had been newly set, with its deep pit beneath. He fingered with pride the clutch and hand irons, the handle and bar that would regulate his saw and the working of the log carriage upon its wooden track. He and his brothers had spiked those cog tracks down so every inch was true, and the seasoned timber that went to their building would never crack or warp.

As the tall, bronzed, blue-eyed young Zach shut off the power that drove the series of graduated wooden wheels with their connecting belts, he knew an almost-reverent gladness that now he owned his mill. The waning day was filled with the promise of good things yet to be.

Throughout the next several decades of his life, that promise was fulfilled. Three, and sometimes four, times a year, the grinding of the farmers' grain was interrupted by the necessary chipping of the Buhr. That had to be done by a man who made this his business, a skilled little hunchback who periodically made his rounds from mill to mill that he served. At such times, Great-Uncle Zach stood by, resharpening the chisels, as they all too quickly were dulled by the pecking of the hard Buhr stone. He prided himself upon his never-dull grooves, and this was his contribution. From up and down the valley, the loads of grain poured into his mill, because he kept his grinding best and his grain barrels sunned and clean.

He often had new ideas, also, for utilizing the product of his mill. From the patrons' sacks that were his fee, he one winter produced "Crust Coffee," which he sold for less than the store variety and wh;ch tasted just as good to his provident neighbors. He and his young wife, Sarah, worked out the formula, which she then followed in roasting the "coffee" in her kitchen. "Take 2 cups Graham meal, 3 of cornmeal, mix in 1 of maple sugar draining, burn carefully, like common coffee. Use about 1 teaspoonful to 1 pint of water." After the babies came, however, there was no more chance to "burn carefully" the meal, so Great-Uncle Zach gave the recipe to his patrons, who sometimes continued to make their own "Crust Coffee" for years to come. More than a century later, his brother Oliver's daughter served our family a most delicious brew made from that recipe.

He also contrived new mixtures of grist for his own and his neighbors' flocks and herds. If brown bread made from cornmeal, wheat, and rye was especially good for man, why not blended grain for beast and bird as well? So out of his sacks and barrels he concocted various feeds: more corn for fattening purposes, more wheat at breeding time, more oats when the shortening days increased the highland cold.

When, in the 1850s, a fellow Vermonter revealed to Great-Uncle Zach that flour could be produced much more rapidly and efficiently by a steam-propelled roller than by the water-wheel stone, Uncle Zach was skeptical of the proposed process. Furthermore, after carefully observing a demonstration of the new method, he was convinced of the value of his long-used way of grinding. As he pointed out to his inventor friend, the millstones run by water rotated more slowly and remained cold, thereby preserving the rich germ of the kernel. In the more rapid milling, the grain became so heated that the meal would soon become rancid and the germ would clog the grinding. The necessary discarding of the germ, before crushing the kernel in the new process, seemed wanton waste to one who thought to make wise use of earth's bounty to man. So it was that the overshot wheel in Hagar Brook hummed on till the end of Uncle Zach's life.

Although the children long remembered Great-Uncle Zach after his going, for the grain dust as well as the icicles in his beard, the half of his mill that contained his lathe, his plane, and his saw was his chief delight.

The first day after the opening of his mill that May 5, in 1832, the shining blade of his new pit saw cut planks for flooring a covered bridge in the neighboring township. One after another, great pine logs were rolled in the east end of the mill and onto the carriage for sawing. As Great-Uncle Zach set the irons and moved it into place by hand-control handle and bar, his whirling water wheel gave its power to carriage, belt, and saw. And as the shining blade sang along the forest monarch's length, smoothly slicing its first great plank, after the cutting of the outer slab as regulated by the carriage guide, the young sawyer knew the joy of might here supplementing might.

His older brother Frank was tail sawyer for that day. As he caught one after another of the 2-inch by 2-foot planks falling upon the platform on the other side of the saw from the carriage, his hard young muscles bulged with the burden of carrying it out, and when each log was finished, with the equal burden of piling all twelve planks upon the carriage for the trimming of the bark from their edges.

The trimming, however, did not finish the sawyer's responsibility with his lumber, for each piece must be thoroughly seasoned before it was ready for use. This could be accomplished in those days only by "racking" the planks or boards. To do this, one was laid upon another, separated by three or more cross strips of edging between, until the pile was as high as sawyer and tail sawyer could make it.

"Always rack 'em one board higher than is an easy reach," Uncle Zach told his many helpers through the ensuing years.

June, July, and August were the best months for the curing, left to the sun and the wind there at the end of the mill. Bridge plank and joist, flooring and two-by-four, beam and rafter, timber for every kind of building rumbled away in endless loads along the Valley Pike. It was timber that never warped or cracked when properly treated, through the long years to come.

Grist and lumber were not the only products which left that mill. Slabs and shavings he sold for fifty cents a load to widows who had no one to chop their wood, and many a family whose wage-earner had been injured or taken ill were given those makings of "the poor man's fire" that Great-Uncle Zach often left when he chanced to be passing such a home. Sawdust, too, as tawny as the backs of the Jerseys it would bed, was shoveled from the incessantly replenished pile at the end of the mill, to disappear into the thriftiest farmers' barns.

From the very first, however, Great-Uncle Zach found his greatest joy in his cabinet work. While sawing and grinding were slack that first summer, he turned gladly to some choice logs he had saved. Sawing these into boards three-fourths of an inch thick, he racked them up to season. His blue eyes shone with pride as he gazed upon the beautiful grain of the bird's-eye, buckhorn, violin, and curly maple; upon the satiny pine; and upon the red-brown sheen of the cherry. He would make desks for himself and his brothers, and bureaus for his mother and the girls. For his father, a medicine cupboard big enough to hold a year's supply of the herbs he loved to gather, and with a drawer for every herb after it had been dried and pulverized with the big iron mortar and pestle.

Happily, then, in spare moments, when his woods were cured to perfection, the young Zach turned to his plane and his lathe. The medicine cupboard he finished first from his best white pine. A curly maple bureau with Sandwich glass knobs he fashioned next for Great-Grandmother. Carefully turning the pillars and legs on his wheel-belted lathe, he felt again the miracle of the power of rushing water. Only a short time since, these parts must all have been turned by hand. Yes, knowledge of earth's resources was a wondrous gift to man. Four drawers, each nine inches deep, the young craftsman topped by one twice the depth to hold his mother's spare coverlid and the blankets and comforter for the coldest nights of winter. He added a small drawer at each end of the broad top also, for her caps and gold beads. Great-Grandmother prized that handsome bureau, not only for its daily convenience but even more for her son's fine workmanship that went to its making.

Harriet, Abigail, and Ruby, receiving theirs in turn, prized theirs as well: Harriet on her thirty-first birthday, Abigail and Ruby when, as brides, they went down the mountain to homes of their own.

By the end of his fifth year in the mill, Great-Uncle Zach was well established and ready to take his bride. From saw and lathe and plane then came the furnishings for their home at the edge of the meadow by the mill.

The piece over which he worked longest was the secretary where he would keep his accounts and the numerous other items that a man with a thriving mill was always needing to keep. He fashioned its frame from the darkest strips of the wild brown cherry, its ends from the heart of a great white pine. Panels for the bookcase doors and the dropleaf for writing he smoothed from the buckhorn maple, the narrow drawer beneath and the supporting columns from his choicest piece of bird's-eye. Violin maple went to the making of the two wide bottom drawers, and, for the whole, hours of loving labor on these woods that he had collected as a boy from his home hill. Brown cherry knobs turned on his lathe and strap hinges cut from a pulley belt remnant completed his secretary.

A schoolmaster desk for each of his brothers, blanket chests, taper-legged tables, and many another piece, fashioned with painstaking care from the choicest logs brought to his mill from the mountain's virgin forest, found their way into his family's homes throughout the next three decades. Each was a piece that has been cherished now for three and four generations.

One August day, as he racked his lumber "one board higher than was an easy reach," Great-Uncle Zach knew that this time was his last. His years in his mill were over, but they had been good years, and in it he had given his best. He shut off the hum of his machinery and paused again by his weathered water wheel.

A great peace filled his being as he gazed upon Green Peak. Yes, "The strength of the hills was his also," as he turned and smiled at his youngest brother, Seymour, who that day had come to help him close his mill.

Today I write at Great-Uncle Zach's secretary, and scores of his other grandnieces and nephews still treasure the pieces that came from his lathe and his saw. Today, too, thousands of tourists, as well as his descendants, journey to a remote country store where grain from the water-powered stone's cool grinding, that he so staunchly advocated, still gives its undiminished gift for man's sustenance.

14

THE DEPOT

Rupert Depot now sits like an old man at the edge of life, reflecting upon the past. Hatted with overhanging eaves that have protected many a patron from snow and rain, its small-paned windows peer out like glazed eyes from the turned-up collar of its weathered buff coat.

A puffing freight train twice a day and the American Express truck each noon are the only functional interruptions to its reveries these days. But the 107-year-old can recall eighty years or more of teeming activity across its wooden platform and along the shining rails at its western door.

Those were the days when the Delaware and Hudson Railroad maintained the only connecting artery between northwestern Vermont and its essential markets, Boston and New York. Known also as the Rennselaer and Saratoga from 1865 to 1871, it was originally the Rutland and Washington.

What excitement marked its opening in mid-April 1852! The depot had been completed only the day before by a "bee" of eager farmers—just in time for the coming of the long-anticipated steam cars! Every man and woman, boy and girl who could crowd into a surrey, buckboard, "democrat," lumber wagon, or ox-cart had flocked in from the countryside almost before daybreak.

Horses and oxen were securely tied in church sheds and to meadow fences some distance from the tracks, that the animals might not be terrified by the thundering approach of progress.

Townspeople arrived on foot soon after an early breakfast. Puffing, white-bearded Eli Holcomb trundled his ailing wife to the depot door in a red wheelbarrow, newly painted for the occasion.

At ten o'clock the train was due from the north. Would it really come? It was now two years and four months since the ground had been broken for beginning the 45-mile line which was to connect Rutland with the western boundary of Vermont where it joined New York State in Washington County.

Grandfather glanced at his big silver watch. Fifteen more minutes. His hand touched his wallet as he returned his timepiece to his inside coat pocket. In it were the precious shares of railroad stock, costing eighty hard-earned dollars each, which he had bought in January, 1851, when the first rails were actually laid. Now the track had been extended to Eagle Bridge, where it connected with others leading to the big cities.

"Do you cal'late Tom Canfield'll be aboard this first run today?" his brother Oliver boomed in his ear, as voices all around them swelled loud with suspense.

"He'd ought to. He's earned a free ride after all his trouble. Getting the money together. Fighting taxes. Bringing those hotheaded Irishmen over to do the digging. Keeping order in all our stock-holders' meetings, too. Tom's made a good president and superintendent of the road so far, he has. Hope nothing'll go crosswise today." "Who'd a thought 'twould take all this time when the Legislature passed on it? Five years ago come November since those papers were drawn up and passed on. When the telegraph line went through that Feb'rary, I supposed we'd be shipping our next year's wool by steam for sure." Brother Oliver stamped impatiently into the packed waiting room.

Grandfather smiled to himself as he recalled the day the telegraph line was finished. The second of February, 1848, it was. He and his bride, Mary Ann, had been visiting Uncle Phineas in Burlington that day when the first message came over it. He had set it down on paper and it was here in his wallet now. He knew it by heart.

"From the city of Troy to the city of Burlington—We do sincerely congratulate you as having become, at this early day, one of those favored communities, united by the life blood of speedy com-munication, and as sincerely congratulate ourselves on being able to salute, face to face, the Queen City of Lake Champlain."

Professor Morse had some head on his shoulders when he worked out that invention, code and all.

Tom Canfield and Professor Benedict, Ezry Cornell and Colonel John Peck worked pretty hard, too, to get up that line between Montreal and Troy, Grandfather reminisced. He had had his doubts when he bought a share of that stock, just to be accommodating and aid progress. He wondered how long it would be before Rupert would have a telegraph office, with those keys clicking news clear across the nation faster than you could think.

"It almost seems the whole county's turned out," Grandmother observed, drawing her best black cashmere shawl more closely against the chilly April breeze.

Through the depot and neighboring barn doors the anxious crowd milled across the wide green separating the tracks from the village street. Even the gnarled branches of the nearby tall old elm provided a lookout for a dozen popeyed boys.

"She's coming round the bend!" came a hoarse shout.

Down the shining rails roared the gigantic monster, flames and black clouds belching from its smokestack, cowcatcher aproning its front.

As the great thundering miracle of transportation shrieked and clanged to its cinder-shooting stop, cheers and yells of welcome broke from the assembled throats. The shouts of relief, hope, and delight echoed and re-echoed down the newly steel-opened valley way.

No longer must weary teamster on plodding horsedrawn-lumber wagon make the tedious weekly trip to haul potatoes and butter, maple sugar, cheese, and wool to Troy markets or to Whitehall station on the Barge Canal. No. The railroad would now open a local market where buyers would come to load the township's produce aboard the great boxcars. Here, also, the daily running powerful giant would bring all a body could ever want to buy, right at home.

The gleaming windows of the passenger coaches held promise, too. Relatives in far places could now be visited and come a-visiting. Fairs. Fashions. City sights. What dreams could now come true at last!

Tom Canfield appeared on the rear platform. He waved his hat, smiled broadly, and signaled to the conductor. The whistle blew, and cheers followed the thunder of a New Era along the gleaming rails.

An almost equally excited crowd milled around Rupert Depot one noon a month later. That May 15 was the day of the record-breaking run from New York City to Burlington. At six o'clock that morning, Tom Canfield, two or three newspaper reporters, and the superintendents of the various other sections of the line had boarded the train to make the speed-test run. They alone were all who would risk their necks on such a crazy experiment.

"She never stopped panting all the time she was taking on wood and water," the station agent commented with satisfaction. "And when she took off again, you should've heard her paw and snort. She fairly flew up Sheldon Hill."

The "noon flier" arrived in Rutland at 1:25, having made the 62-mile run from Eagle Bridge, including its stop at Rupert Depot, in eighty-five minutes. For the first time in history, man could ride at nearly fifty miles an hour. Such speed! Such progress! Nat Gooken, engineer, and Amos Story, conductor, were proud men that day. So was Tom Canfield, superintendent, president, and builder. And so, too, were T.S. Beebe and a dozen farmers in the town of Rupert. Theirs had been no small part in establishing the record.

Even before Rupert Depot was built, a huge water tank with a thousand-barrel capacity had been erected near the station site. The steam locomotive, when it came, would have an enormous thirst to be quenched. T. S. Beebe's never-failing rock-spring, high on the mountainside, therefore began sending its clean, bright water into that tank in early 1852. For nearly a century, through all the years that it was needed, it never failed.

Nearby also was the wood yard for supplying fuel for those early engines. Rupert farmers tiered it full of "body maple" (wood from the trunks of large maple trees), and it was the wood from their pasture slopes that fed the "flier's" locomotive for a section of its speeding run.

The railroad company later gave prize money to the engineer who made his run on the least fuel, so each inspected the wood all along his line and chose the station for taking it on by the quality of its product. "Maple body" at Rupert yard was found to give the best mileage, and until coal displaced it in 1888 the Rupert woodlots supplied "body maple."

One supplier of body maple at Rupert station, however, soon had a complaint. The railroad bisected his pasture. On cool nights that next early fall his sleek Jerseys found the ties, which had retained the sun's heat, a more comfortable bed than the chillier grassland. The rushing locomotive's cowcatcher picked up one after another of said farmer's herd. In vain did the owner and his friends congregate at the depot and petition for fencing the line.

"No fence, no wood," was the final edict of those dour-faced owners of the woodlots. When the tiers of "maple body" showed signs of dwindling, the fence posts began to appear.

So great were the demands of the woodyard that by 1870 the influx of teamsters and choppers supplying the need had increased Rupert's population by eighty-five residents. Their shanties sprang up like mushrooms along the track near the depot.

There, in one woodchopper's shanty, a future engineer of the road, John Hinds, was born. There in the woodyard, as a boy, he ran errands for his heroes, the engineers. There he heard the thrilling tales of Thomas Hawley Canfield's successes. His early days as operator of a boat line on Lake Champlain. His record run on the rails right past these shanty doors. His leasing this railroad and operating it on his own, the first line ever to be leased by a private individual. And of his later exploits in promoting the Northern Pacific in the Great West.

There, too, he learned of the colorful career of Jay Gould, who had also been in control of this line, not long after Tom Canfield. And as the trainmen said, he had here "cut his eyeteeth." All the available news of Gould was relayed in detail by the engineers, who manned the engines named for him and for the other superintendents and directors of the road.

Throughout his boyhood, as the "Horace Clark," the "Timothy Strong," the "Jay Gould," and other engines made their daily stops at the depot, young John dreamed of the day when he, too, would ride the cab and rule the engine. And his dream came true. He served his apprenticeship and got his locomotive. During the early 1900s he was considered one of the best engineers on the line. He and the thirty or more other engineers who made those daily runs during the eight decades encountered many a challenge. Now and then a horse or cow which had broken through the fence would be picked up on the cowcatcher. Frequently some engine detail would require attention while the train was moving, so the engineer would climb out his cab window to check on it. Switching operations were also often hazardous in those early days of few safety devices and controls. Records show that, consequently, one conductor, two purchasing agents, and seven engineers lost their lives on those forty-five miles of curving tracks between 1853 and 1927.

One of these was Sumner Hitchcock, whose name is still remembered for his courage and daring. As he swung around the bend not far from Rupert station one day, he saw a little child sitting in the center of the track only a few rods ahead. The whistle screamed. Brakes ground. But the tiny figure sat motionless. Hitchcock knew his speeding train could never stop in time. What to do? With a mighty leap, he bounded through the cab window and onto the cow-catcher. At one swoop he snatched the blue-coated little boy to safety. The two-year-old proved to be Jimmie Layden, son of another railroad man, who was later killed near the same point.

Young Jimmie, however, lived to a ripe old age as a merchant in the neighboring town of Salem. He often spoke admiringly of the brave man who saved his life. In recently recalling the story, his daughter said her father always concluded the account with, "It's a good thing I've always been the lean kind. If I'd been a plump baby, Hitchcock never could have jerked me out from between the wheels that day."

Not long after his rescuing young Jimmie in 1884, Sumner Hitchcock himself met death not far from the same curve. He had crawled out through his cab window to check a connection, lost his balance, and was thrown beneath the moving wheels.

The Rupert stationmaster, William Austin, frantically summoned his son, a doctor, from across the village street. Emergency relief was all that could be given the poor fellow, as his mangled body was taken from beneath the engine.

"Take me home," he begged, quivering with pain. "And hurry if you can."

Knowing that his time was short, the rest of the train crew took over. Down the flashing rails sped the "Jay Gould," setting a new record for the road. And Engineer Hitchcock's last wish was grati-fied. He saw his wife and children before he died within the hour.

Hazardous though railroading was in those earlier days, the system brought prosperity and expansion to a growing America. Six passenger, two milk and express, and four freight trains daily made their run from Rutland to Eagle Bridge until the mid-1920s. Theatre specials and excursion trains frequently provided additional accommodations as well, in the late 1890s and early 1900s.

Each September, for many years, too, cattle, colts, pigs, and sheep for exhibition at the state fair were driven up the stockyard chute near the water tank into the allotted cars. And driven down again a few days later, many proudly wearing the winners' blue or red ribbons.

Previous to the coming of the railroad, huge blocks of marble from West Rutland quarries were dragged overland by oxen for loading on canal barges at Whitehall. But with the arrival of the Rutland and Washington Iron Horse, fed and watered at Rupert Depot, speed and volume developed in the marble industry. A thousand carloads of the great white blocks for the construction of the Supreme Court Building alone in the national capital sped along the echoing route. So, too, did countless thousands of tons of the beautiful white stone for Capitol extensions and other famous Washington buildings. And so, too, did the marble for the Crocker First National Bank of San Francisco, for mantels in fashionable Baltimore mansions, for the Porter Mausoleum in New York City, and for millions of monuments, tombstones, tabletops, and architectural needs throughout the growing nation.

When Union Station in Washington, D.C., was erected in 1905-1907 white granite for its exterior had been borne from Bethel quarries northwest of Rutland along the Delaware and Hudson by way of Rupert Depot.

In 1869 the Rising & Nelson Slate Company near West Pawlet began to operate. From then on, great loads of slate for roofing this nation's and Canada's buildings flew along this route. Mainly they came from this and other quarries in the neighboring towns of Granville, West Pawlet, and Wells.

The National Express Company established an office in the depot about as soon as it was completed, so buyers from Troy, Albany, New York, and Boston almost immediately made their appearance.

For many decades, glad-faced farmers with their horse- or ox-drawn loads of potatoes, wool, maple sugar, cheese, apples, and other commodities crowded into the convenient near-home market-line. The hawk-eyed buyers there flocked around the loads, vying with one another for best price and best produce. Smelling and tasting the cheese and butter, feeling the rolled-up fleeces for foreign matter that might increase their weight, pouring potatoes across a great wooden grader, and constant superintending of operations all marked shrewd dealing at the depot yard.

Among the first consignments shipped were 600 pounds of potatoes at 33¢ per cwt. for a Boston market. In the spring of 1918 Father there sold a 50-bushel lot @ $3 per bushel.

One who there shipped his product without inspection, however, was Norman Jenks from over the hill. Each November, for many years, he brought his boxes of spruce gum, for Boston and New York dispensing, and ginseng for the China trade. The dealers paid him twenty cents a pound for those amber lumps of hardened pitch he pried from the bark of the evergreens in his own and his neighbors' woodlots. And five dollars a pound for his "ginshang" spelled wealth from his digging in many a mile of mountain pasture.

Back to the hill and valley farms and to the village homes, the teams conveyed as much as they brought. The cars on the siding unloaded treasure unobtainable from peddler's pack or local store. "Fluid burners" or oil lamps, kitchen range and parlor stove, iron and coal for the blacksmith shop, horse-rake and mowing-machine, Gold Drop, a $1000 ram from Spain to sire the Merino flocks of the township, flowered wallpaper and ingrain carpet, the latest fashions from the National Cloak and Suit Company.

As late as the 1930s farm produce borne in motor trucks was being packed into the cars at the siding: dainty boxes of maple-butter-nut fudge; crates of eggs, brown for Boston and white for New York; and ferns for the city florists by then supplemented the earlier produce.

The diesel-hauled freight cars, loaded with lime and grain for the farmers or with road-building supplies for the town have most recently there tendered their service.

From the treasure-freighted boxcars of my girlhood came the Montgomery Ward and Sears Roebuck ruffled curtains, mattresses with a real bounce, peek-a-boo embroidered blouses, and many another dream-fulfilling commodity. Bags of clover seed and bundles of young apple trees, stacks of books for the district schools, as well as numerous other aids to prosperity and knowledge were stored in the baggage room to await the owners' call.

From the first, those boxes and bags invited mouse and rat to gnaw and nibble, so the station agent always kept a cat. The first to install his stray feline as watchman found that his pet needed outdoor exercise as well as a place to hunt for a living. Business at desk, telegraph key, and ticket or baggage window left him no time to wait upon a cat. So before starting his day's work at six o'clock one morning, Mr. Austin diligently whittled a cat hole out of one bottom corner of the freight-room door. There it still is, providing a handy exit and entry for every feline protector of railroad storage.

Uncle Washington Kinne was buyer and weighmaster at the depot for many years. Living just across the street from railway and storehouse, as did the stationmaster, the two men were credited with saving the lives of several teamsters and travelers who were marooned at the depot in the famous Blizzard of March 11-13 in 1888.

For two days the trains could not get through the six- and eight-foot drifts and the more than three-foot-on-the-level dense white deposit. It was the first time in thirty years that the trains had not run!

Maple trees had just been tapped, and two enterprising buyers from New York rode the last train in to Rupert station. With a dozen or so other stranded ones, they crowded around the big wood stove and took turns feeding it chunks from the provident pile at one end of baggage room and platform, for those forty-eight hours of whistling wind and entombing snow.

Uncle Washington opened his stores of potatoes, butter, and cheese, and Mr. Austin shared the tea he kept in his office for emergencies, brewed with water from T.S. Beebe's unfailing mountain spring. Never had potatoes tasted better than those baked on the top of the depot stove. Never had bed provided greater security than did the waiting-room benches with potato-sack covers, those three wind-and-snow-racked nights. And never had the New Yorkers wiped such perspiring brows as when they, too, manfully plied the shovels to dig out when the storm had at last abated.

From the first, the depot was alive with people, some arriving, some departing, and others just "to see the cars come in."

The first to set forth to New York on the steam cars were young Sam and Lucindy Parker for their honeymoon in June, 1852. In spite of their gay smiles, Sam's hands were seen to tremble as he clutched his valise, and Cindy Ann's bonnet plumes went all askew as she clung to Sam when they climbed aboard. But when they returned the next week, they gave a glowing report of "seeing the sights," including the clipper, *Flying Cloud*, back from its record run of 89 days from Sandy Hook around Cape Horn to San Francisco. Old and young alike were fired with an increased desire to visit far places.

Widow Hale's five sons were among those who heard and who set forth as soon as each turned eighteen. Ed and Lorenzo were the first to go in 1861. With the Vermont enlistees' badge of sprigs of evergreen in their caps, they there set forth on the Railroad Company's free fare for soldiers, to join the Boys in Blue. The Town Band assembled at the depot to celebrate their departure, as it did for every other soldier boy's, when townsmen turned out full force to bid them "Godspeed." From the station steps, bugle and drum sent inspiring echoes down the ringing tracks: "No Surrender," "We Stand Here United," "Hail to Liberty," and "Battle Hymn of the Republic." The cows in the pasture facing the depot came to the fence, lifting soft eyes and inquiring noses to join in salute and farewell.

When Grandfather, as Town Representative, set forth for the State Legislature one bright morning that following October, some of the town mothers also tearfully gathered there to see him off. Could he, on his way, visit the camp ground at Burlington, where their sons awaited departure for battlefields to the South? Supplies of clothing, food, and arms were reported pitifully meager. Many of the boys were sleeping on the cold ground without even a blanket. Would Grandfather personally deliver their numerous parcels of socks and mufflers to their sons? And would he "get after" the Legis-lature to end such uncalled-for misery right away?

As the "Tom Canfield" shrieked for its puffing start north, Grandfather assured them that he would.

Proof that someone had interceded was evident in the ensuing months, as friends returning from army visits and eagerly awaited letters brought somewhat more comforting reports to the depot, from Fort Dummer, "Camp near Fairfax," and other army posts.

Tears streamed down the leathery cheeks of even the laconic town constable when happy-go-lucky Lije Dean's father in a halting voice there read aloud from his son's letter.

"At last the Quartermaster has received most all of our equipment & they are good aside from the guns. They are rifle muskets not worth much. (Some that were captured on a vessel coming from Europe to the Confederacy.) Our company is said to be the best drilled in the Regiment & that our officers are the best. Now about our fare—it is bread, beef, potatoes & beans, tea & coffee, salt & vinegar, mostly beef & bread. We are faring better now than at first. Merritt and some of the other nine months' boys died for lack of vittles before they got here. I would like to see you very much."

At the station, too, the Boys in Blue who returned from Gettysburg, from Richmond, and from Libby's Prison were welcomed home with warm handshake, eager greeting, and anxious question.

How often the scene was repeated in 1898 and again in World War I.

Shortly after Lorenzo Hale's return in 1865, he set forth again, this time for Wisconsin, where he established a vast dairy farm.

His younger brothers, Clark, Lee, and Sam, in turn boarded the cars at Rupert station for the Great West. Clark ultimately established a hotel in Pasadena; Lee helped to build the first transcontinental telegraph line; and Sam labored in the opening of the Oregon timberlands.

Besides being a vital link in the nation's growth, Rupert station was a local center of social and civic activity, as well as mercantile. There, on step and platform, in waiting-room and on the green be-neath the elm, men gathered for train arrivals, often assembling early and lingering late. With them, by Civil War time, mingled suave, smooth-shaven drummers or "knights of the grip," complete with top hat, plaid vest, flashy tiepin, fragrant cigar, cordial handshake, and endless flow of tall tales. Although by the early 1900s many such travelers had turned to Ford and Overland, they still frequently stopped at the railroad station. There they added welcome variety to the assemblage awaiting the mail and conning the day's news, business deals, and political issues.

Greatly impressed by the Western Union Telegraph Line, which had been operating efficiently for many years, about twenty families in the village decided in 1879 to set up a network of their own for local communication. Known as the Rupert Telegraph Company, their lines to private homes connected with Western Union at the depot. Although the private company disbanded with the coming of the telephone, from 1879 to 1895 those busy little instruments clicked out many a message of birth, death, marriage, burning barn, quilting-bee, church social, and shrewd Yankee trade.

Even though the depot is only a story and a half in height, a club room was finished off above waiting room, baggage room, and office in 1869. Here the Odd Fellows met each Monday in 1880. Here, too, the Independent Order of Good Templars convened from 1870 to 1872. And here, "on the first Thursday evening on or before full moon in each month," the Masons of Morning Flower Lodge held their meetings for an interval of transfer between other regular quarters.

In my girlhood, the town's teen-age boys were now and then nabbed "red-handed" there in the midst of a game of "penny ante."

Those were the years when a dozen or so boys and girls boarded the 10:15 train at Rupert each schoolday morning for the half-hour run to Granville High School, returning at 4:30 in the afternoon. If one chanced to be late or had to run back for a forgotten book or lunchbox, Conductor John Wilson and Old Peter, the brakeman, would hold the train or even stop, back up, and take on the puffing, panting, belated one. Those two dear old gentlemen, in dark blue uniforms with gleaming brass buttons and shiny-visored caps, were our pals and confidantes. They knew our report card marks before our parents did. They smiled but refused to co-operate in our forging an excuse for a stolen holiday. They shared our bags of fudge, popcorn, and peanuts; indulged us in our cheers and singing, but frowned us into order whenever we became too boisterous. Everyone loved and admired Conductor Wilson and Brakeman Peter.

The depot doors and walls in those days were well-punctured by the tack-holes of three generations of townsmen's notices. Warning for Town Meeting; auction bills; bounty notices for bear, panther, and bobcat; Fish and Game Laws; and even our own geometry assignments and Caesar translations were posted there. All were there read and verbosely considered in detail by the heterogeneous group who daily congregated around the potbellied wood-and-coal stove or outside the small-paned windows that were washed twice a year.

A crowd of the younger villagers and country folk congregated there to meet the seven o'clock train one February evening in 1932. Judy, the prettiest and most popular girl of her day, had married Bart Cane, the wealthiest young man in town, at a quiet home wedding the week before. The newlyweds had left for their honeymoon without "setting up cigars" in the village store. Tonight they were returning home, and they must pay the penalty for not "standing treat."

At one end of the station, the groom's father in fur-collared coat and fur cap huddled among his buffalo robes in his top cutter behind his restive bay, King, awaited their coming.

The seven o'clock clanged to a stop. The mail sack thudded onto the station agent's truck. The passengers descended the steps. Last of all came Bart and Judy, unsuspecting, toward the crowd.

With a deafening roar and bang, the "shivaree" let go. Amidst hoarse shouts, resounding tin pans, horns, cowbells, and every other noisemaker imaginable, Judy was lifted on two pairs of stalwart shoulders and romped around the depot. Bart was rushed to his father's sleigh, from which King and his driver were unceremoniously separated, and the bridegroom was hitched between the shafts. Judy was deposited among the robes and, escorted by more than one rejected suitor, transported to her father-in-law's home by manpower, chiefly her husband's. In vain did Bart protest that cigars would be set up this very night. In vain did vivacious Judy freeze to stony silence. Kitchen band, whooping boys, and laughing girls brought a half-contrite, half-indignant young couple to their door. There the rancor ended, however, for Bart's mother, having "gotten wind" of the horning, invited the score or more noisy rebels in for hastily assembled cookies and coffee.

A kiss for the bride, a handshake for the groom, and well-wishing all around finally ended the "shivaree" in an aura of good will.

The following June, the last passenger train made its final run. It could not compete with the family car. Gradually, express, freight, and telegraph services likewise declined following World War II.

A young lady who grew up in Rupert has been the station mistress for the past twelve years. She recently said, "I have 'cinders in my blood' and I count the former years, when I had dealings with train crews, the happiest of my life.

'The milk train and 'The Slate Picker' (express trains) have been abolished. A year ago the Railway Express Agency instituted a truck route from Saratoga Springs to Fairhaven, Vermont, and back.

"There is one freight train a day north and back. I can't help thinking it will be a tragedy when no more trains run on the Rutland and Washington Branch of the Delaware and Hudson, and the grass grows on the right-of-way. But that's the way the signs point."

Rupert Depot now sits like an old man reflecting on the past. Its glazed eyes are now dulled from disuse, and its overcoat is patched and faded. But the remote little figure will stand forever among the cornerstones of our America.

15

THE CHEESE FACTORY

Dawn was just greyly breaking over the hills to the east of Rupert the first morning in April, 1870, when a strange clatter broke the customary morning quiet of the village. The slow clop-clop of hoofs, the rattle of a jolting lumber wagon, and the rhythmic clink-clank of tin cans announced the arrival of the first load of milk at the new cheese factory, which was opening that day. Hope sang in the driver's heart, jubilant as the waking chorus of the song-sparrows and the chickadees in the spring-sweet mountain air. I was reminded of Grandfather's account of that opening day at Rupert Cheese Factory when I recently visited the one next to the Calvin Coolidge Home at Plymouth, Vermont. That building has just been restored by the former President's son John, who now operates it as a private business. In various other sections of our dairy states, this old-time method of cheese making is also still in operation and its product still in great demand. Some of Grandfather's papers tell a typical story of the establishment of such factories. In late June, 1869, the Rupert Dairy Association, which was made up of about thirty farmers, had met at the depot and voted to build a factory at the east end of the village. Already more than eleven hundred such Yankee cheese factories had sprung up in the country since the first one had been built at Rome in the neighboring state of New York in 1851.

Although that was the first one to be called a cheese factory, the first real community making of a cheese had occurred at Cheshire,

Massachusetts, fifty years earlier. In the early summer of 1801 on an appointed day, the women of that locality had sent their curds to the cider mill, where they were packed into the great press. The sides reinforced with stout hoops, it had taken a month to form the cheese, which was as big as a huge bass drum and weighed about 1,450 pounds when finished.

After several months of ripening, well wrapped in its white calico bandage and well rubbed with whey butter, it was taken to President Thomas Jefferson at the White House. A four-ox team hitched to a pung carried it in early December to Hudson, New York. From there it was transported by sailboat to New York City, where it was met by a heavy wagon drawn by six horses with beribboned bridles. Traveling days and resting nights, the teamsters brought their precious freight into Washington, D.C., on December 29.

On New Year's Day, 1802, President Jefferson, wielding the biggest knife to be found, cut the enormous cheese, saying, "I will cause this auspicious event to be placed on the records of our nation and it will ever shine amid its glorious archives." He then gave Elder Leland, who had presented the cheese, a large piece to take back to the people of Cheshire as a proof of its excellence and token of his appreciation. Likewise, he sent a generous sample to each state governor.

Grandfather and many another cheese maker had read an account of that famous experiment in an 1835 issue of *The American Magazine*. In spite of the satisfying results of that community cider mill pressing, however, cheese making had remained a farm home industry for the next half-century and more.

In the cheese room of our old saltbox home, a flat-topped, wood-burning stove, the Olive Branch, supplied the heat for the big pan wherein milk was daily transformed into curds. These, in turn, were broken and drained in a cheese basket, and then pressed and shaped in a cheese press containing a hoop, its pressure tightened by a rope.

This cake of cheese was placed on a wooden ladder to cure, being turned and rubbed with whey butter each day. The hoops and ladders were whittled by the boys of the family in spare moments. The press, however, was not so easily obtained, as it was more complicated to make.

Thousands of pounds of cheese were boxed or casked in that farm cheese room between March and December each year. Both farmers and their womenfolk participated in the drudgery. Besides making, curing, boxing, and delivering the commodity to customers or to the depot for shipping, at seven to ten cents a pound, the cheese-room must be kept clean of contamination, especially in hot weather. It had been backbreaking work, indeed, to start the cheese making at five o'clock each morning, carry it through to the pressing, and flush the whey out by pump log to the pig sty, after skimming off its thin skin of cream for butter. Then the vat and tubs and all the utensils must be scrubbed and the floor mopped, after the stove was cleaned of its ashes and soot and the wood laid for another early morning fire.

So, when in June, 1869, the Rupert Dairy Association met and voted to build a factory, both men and women felt a great sense of relief in their progress. Gladly Grandfather noted in his diary for the 17th of that month: "Took $100 in a cheese factory association."

On August twenty-first of that year the work was begun. That bright afternoon the men of the township met at a bee for digging the ditch for laying pipe from the spring across the nearby creek to the building site. Of first importance was the assurance of an adequate supply of water for vat steam pipes as well as for cleansing factory and equipment.

The water assured, the building progressed rapidly under the hands of those thirty farmers. Logs from the upland pastures, sawed in the Hollow Mill, provided the well-cured lumber.

By November, the great new factory, forty by eighty feet and three stories high, with a square cupola for ventilation rising from the center of its roof, stood majestically there between creek and high-way. On November 11, 12 and 13, Grandfather joyfully wrote in his diary, "Worked at grading around the cheese factory with my team."

A coat of red paint covered the exterior "before snow fly," and during the winter days the men completed and plastered the interior.

Because the cheese maker must live near his work, it was decided to finish off the east half of the first floor for his living room, bedroom, and pantry, with two more bedrooms on the second floor directly over these. The making-room would serve as the kitchen. A small porch was added to shelter the living-room entrance.

In my childhood, the biggest, most beautiful morning glories in town twined their luxuriant green tendrils over that latticed veranda. We believed that they were well-fed with whey. A barn and meadow for the cheese maker's horse and a generous space for a garden were also included in the three-acre plot for the building.

A pleasant home it was for a family, so the Rupert Dairy Association was never "put to it" to find a skilled cheese maker.

Eugene Bizallion was the first to kindle the fire and set the steam hissing through the walls of the vats. Trained at home in his boyhood, and later by one Jesse Williams at Rome, New York, he was a master at his craft.

On the first Monday of April, 1870, the factory was opened for business. It was an eventful day, indeed, in that mountain township, when the teams drew the buckboards loaded with tall tin cans up to the receiving door.

Grandfather had a slow old team, Vic and Peter, so two of his neighbors had engaged him to carry their milk that summer for thirty dollars. In those days of rough, steep roads, only slow horses could be used to draw the cans to the factory, for a fast-stepping team would have churned the rich Jersey and Ayrshire milk into butter long before it could have reached the receiving door.

When the teams headed for the factory that memorable April morning, all the scholars in the little red schoolhouse, where Mother and Aunt Ida went, flocked to the windows to watch the great event.

At the factory, Grandfather as treasurer of the R.D.A. helped with the recording of each farmer's weight of milk in the big ledger that first morning, for Eugene Bizallion had his hands full with checking spout and vat for their initial operation.

As the head team drove up to the receiving door in the middle of the north wall of the second floor, the talons of the great hand-worked windlass at the left gripped a twenty-, thirty-, or forty-gallon can and lowered it to the spout between two windows just below. Through this galvanized spout, the milk poured into the weigh can, and after each man's name in the book, Grandfather recorded the amount of milk brought to the factory on that date. Each day thereafter the cheese maker would make a similar entry.

From the weigh can, a turn of the faucet sent the milk down the spout into one of the two vats, each set with one end beneath a front window for the cheese maker's convenience. Each of those vats was four feet wide, twelve feet long, and two and a half feet deep, and held about five thousand pounds of milk. Wood outside and tin within, steam pipes passed between the two layers for heating the milk. When one vat was filled, the milk poured through the spout into the other by a simple manipulation.

Before each farmer's can was turned to pour into the spout, its contents must be smelled or tasted. It was too cool for souring milk to appear that first day, and it was not yet time for leeks or other tainting forage, so no man went away, downcast or indignant, to carry home his unacceptable product, as he sometimes did in years to come.

All that morning, Bizallion tended his wood fire and watched the thermometer that he used to test the temperature of the milk. How well he remembered that, as a boy at home, he had had to test the heat by his hand. He was glad not to have to risk the milk from thirty dairies by that test.

After an hour or so, when the milk registered eighty-five degrees, he added annotta, a coloring prepared with lye from the flesh of a tropical plant, and the rennet, a third of an ounce to every hundred pounds of milk.

"Considerable rennet," he contemplated, "more than a half pound in one day." He would have to watch the supply, for it came from the patrons.

Each had brought in a piece prepared from the inner surface of the stomach of a young calf. The outer skin and fat had been carefully scraped off, while fresh, and the remainder kept in salt for several hours, after which it had been dried and brought to the factory. Previously, the cheese maker had cut off a piece of this membrane and soaked it in brine. This juice, poured into the milk, contained much pepsin, which caused the casein of the milk to coagulate. As soon as it was firm, in an hour or so, Bizallion cut the great mass with a "gang knife" into half-inch cubes. With a wooden rake, he agitated these thickening curds while his well-tended boiler fire brought it to a ninety-eight to a hundred-degree temperature. It took nearly three hours for that process, while the eager-faced farmers intermittently peered in to see how well the curd was working.

It was long after noon before he could roll his ten- by three-and-a-half by two-foot drainer, set on casters, around to the vat to dip out huge handfuls of the curds. Kneading the mass thoroughly to accelerate its draining, he sprinkled it well with salt, three pounds to a hundredweight of the curd.

Into the waiting hoops, each of heavy galvanized steel sixteen inches in diameter and fourteen high, lined with a twenty-inch strip of cheesecloth, he then packed the slightly warm curds, set the wooden press or follower upon them, and adjusted the two-inch iron screw to press out the remaining whey.

He filled eight of his twenty hoops that day, calculating that each cheese, when finished, would weigh about forty pounds. Four hundred pounds of milk to a cheese was what the men had estimated in buying the hoops, and their estimate had been about right.

After an hour or so, he turned each hoop of cheese and again put it to the press, to remain till the second day. When he would again remove them from the press, he would trim the cheeses, grease them with whey butter, and pleat down the bandage on both the top and bottom sides. These he would then place on the cheese-box covers and carry them upstairs to the curing rooms. One occupied the west half of the second floor, the other all of the third, where the cupola ventilator greatly aided the process.

Turning now to the make room, he skimmed the cream from the cooled whey and set it aside to be churned that evening into whey butter. It was so like other butter that he and his family usually used it on their table. Releasing the plug in the bottom of the vat, he let the whey run out through a wooden trough to a wooden tank out back. There, in the morning, the farmers would dip the whey into their emptied milk cans with a pail, and cart the still-nourishing fluid home to their fattening pigs. The men would settle their shares among themselves, portioning it according to the amount of milk brought and to their current need.

By May 1, a matter of three and a half weeks, more than three tons of cheese had been cured or was still curing there on the factory's open shelves. Three to four weeks were required for sufficient ripening, and already several lumber-wagon loads of the boxes had been shipped from the depot to New York and Boston.

On May 22, Grandfather "added up the weights of milk for the first month preparatory for a dividend to be made next week." The figures were posted on the factory door, where all might audit them. Proceeds and expenses likewise were posted, and each member of the R.D.A. knew every month all the facts of cost and income when he received his share of the dividend.

For many years, those dividends were so great a part of the family income that hope surged high with the beginning of the season. "Went down street, took our milk—got fooled & brought it back. Got pretty well chilled," was Grandfather's entry in his diary for April 2, 1872. So glad had he been at the sudden news from a neighbor boy of the factory's opening the day before that he had forgotten it was April Fool's Day, practical joker though he knew the boy to be, and had not investigated further.

Although he "felt shiftless" from his cold for several days, he was on hand with his cans when the factory did open the following week. In fact, before going home that day he drove into the village and had "Vic and Peter shod all around," "got 200 lbs. meal for the old horses," and "Engaged Dr. Guild to send for a melodeon—$85."

In May of 1874, the price of cheese had jumped from ten to sixteen cents a pound for the factory product sent to White and Douglas in New York. By now, the members of the Dairy Association had voted to sell all their cheese to the city market and to buy what they needed for personal consumption from a family who still worked up theirs in their home, the price being three and a half cents less per pound.

Sage cheese was also a popular commodity from that factory. Each August, one vat of warm curd was liberally sprinkled with chopped sage from Grandmother's herb bed. Worked in along with the salt, this lent a delicious flavor to the ripening cheese.

One of Grandfather's nephews, Burr Harwood, who was himself an expert cheese maker, still likes to recall that more than one first premium for cheese at the county fairs was won by the product he made in Rupert Factory.

His record achievement there came one June day in the 1890s when nearly six tons of milk poured from the farmers' cans into the yawning vats. Burr pressed, banded, and shelved twenty-two forty-pound cheeses with no assistance that day.

Burr also recalls with relish some amusing incidents of patron irregularities. "One day," he once reminisced, "a man brought his milk, and I dumped it as usual. Suddenly I noticed something flip into the weigh-can. I let it into the strainer and caught it in a pail. It was a fish! A good-sized bullhead! I went out to the whey tub where the patrons were collecting their whey, called to one side the man who brought it, and showed him the fish.

"'Where'd you get that?' he demanded.

"'Out of your can of milk!'

"'Gol!' he explained glibly, 'There was some fishermen down by last night and they probly put that in my can for a joke!' How he laughed, but he kept watching me out of the corner of his eye.

"A while later that farmer's hired man told me that the old fellow had had that fish in the watering-trough where he cooled his milk. He used to rinse his pails there and put the rinsings into the cans. For once the old codger dipped too deep."

Burr's eyes held a faraway look. Then he chuckled as he continued.

"Another time two ten-year-old boys brought in their father's can of milk. It was a hot morning after a warm night.

"'Your milk is very nearly sour,' I pointed out to them by way of warning.

"'I told Tom we'd ought to put some sugar or sody in it when I smelled it this morning!' Willie exclaimed, 'but Ma was all out. Don't make us take it home, Burr. If you do, we won't have nothin' to eat but bannocks and pot cheese till it's all et up. And it does make Pa awful ugly to have to eat just pot cheese and bannocks.'

"I was going to keep the milk anyway," Burr concluded, smiling a little at his reminiscences.

Recently, as I watched a cheese maker in another Vermont town working at his vats of curd, I thought how little the method had changed from that of our old factory. True, rennet and coloring are now shipped from laboratories, instead of being supplied by the farmers, but wooden rake and trough and tub are still in use among the few Yankee cheese factories that dot our American landscape.

Though home drudgery was lightened by the community enterprise, it still was a task to market the milk. The man who drew it two or three miles to the factory with his slow horse team lost most of the forenoon from barn and field. Through two-foot snow, axle-deep mud, rain, wind, and hail, as well as scorching heat, the daily trip must be made. True, the sundry errands at store, post office, and depot could be attended to on the same trip, and visits with neighbors could be enjoyed along the way, but it remained a toilsome job. The months-long waits for dividends were likewise most dissatisfying.

When, therefore, the motor truck provided easier transportation of milk to the depot for shipment to Boston, with monthly checks coming in on time, in the early 1900s the Rupert Dairy Association voted to disband and patronize the newer market.

The factory became a tenant house and later a barn. In its time it had housed a lucrative though laborious craft, and had given to millions its nourishing Cheddar of pleasing taste and texture.

Now it is good, indeed, to see the old art being more and more frequently revived and flourishing throughout our northern countryside.

16

R.F.D. "MAGICIAN"

"There's a big box on a post right outside the gate!" Bob excitedly pointed out one August morning in 1904 as we ran out into our dooryard to look for ripe apples under the Red Astrachan tree. "It wasn't there last night."

Cautiously, we went nearer. It had a big, black 49 on it, and our father's name. "Maybe," we agreed, "some magician left it." Rushing back to the kitchen, we breathlessly made the announcement.

There, however, we learned that this was a mailbox into which a carrier would put our letters, papers, and magazines thereafter, instead of Father's or the neighbors' going to the village post office for them.

"Uncle Sam's your magician," the hired man observed with a grin. For a long time, we thought "Uncle Sam" was the mail carrier only. Even after we learned otherwise, the thought persisted. Many a time through the years, as the dauntless carriers rendered service far beyond what was required of them, we were reminded of our hired man's words: "Uncle Sam's your magician."

How we watched that first day and many a succeeding day for the event of the mail carrier's coming. What fun it was, when our mother was sending letters or cards, to stand on tiptoe and thrust them into the roomy interior, slam the door shut, and insert in a small hole for that purpose a heavy wire holding a strip of red calico, as a signal for the carrier to stop. How anxiously, too, we would run out later to see if the flag were still out, indicating that there was mail for us. If not, we must get the bit of red bandanna out of the box. Whether there was mail or not, the flag must be brought in and tucked away in the desk for the next time it would be used.

It was an unwritten law on our route that when a money order or stamps were wanted in cold weather, some member of the family must watch for the carrier and go out with the money to get what was needed. On warm days the request and payment might be left in a tin cup, with a handle, in the box. But never on a freezing one. Too many times we heard of other route carriers' having to remove gloves from already chilled hands to struggle, fingers half numbed, with loose change. Worse yet, on a windy day stamps might fly out of the box before the door could be closed. Then the exasperated carrier must extricate himself from the mail bag on the seat beside him, sundry boxes and packages on the carriage or cutter floor at his feet, his lap robe, and his leather reins tied around the dashboard, while he retrieved the refractory paper.

Mr. Porter brought our mail the first eight years, making his daily round, except Sunday, behind his faithful horse Bill three days a week and his black mare Molly, with the white strip down her face, on alternate days. We at midpoint of the route expected his arrival regularly between three and half past, for the stage from the railroad station at Granville reached Pawlet a little before noon. Having packed wagon or sleigh, eaten his dinner, and hitched up his horse, Mr. Porter would be ready to start his two-mountain climb and descent by half past twelve.

A wise and kindly man he was. When I was a four-year-old he settled a tantrum of mine. The evening before, Bob's red globe bank, Joe's and my black iron dog and cat, and baby Sally's little red and green tin house all had been carefully opened by my father and the contents emptied on the kitchen table in separate little piles of patiently hoarded pennies, nickels, and dimes.

"They're to be put into a bigger bank," Mother had explained, as she counted each pile and recorded the amount on a sheet of paper after each of our names. Satisfied, we had gone to bed.

But doubt and misery developed that afternoon, when I saw my mother heading toward the mailbox with a small grey cotton sack of jingling coin. Tagging along behind her, and half hiding beneath her checked gingham apron, I heard her instructing Mr. Porter to carry away our precious hoards to some unknown place called Rutland. Outraged, I clung to the sack, refusing to let it go, while I frantically protested that it was Bob's and Joe's and Sally's and mine, and we weren't going to let any old Rutland have it. Astounded at her child's distrust and wrath, and disturbed by such an unexpected outburst, Mother was momentarily at a loss to clarify the situation.

"Well," said Mr. Porter, with a twinkle in his grey eyes, "it seems your little girl wants to go along with her money. Shall I put her into my mail bag and take her to the Rutland Bank today? Or do you think we'd better wait till she gets her bankbook and has her face washed, before we let her see where her pennies have been put for safekeeping?"

"Bankbook," "face washed," and "safekeeping" must have made an impression. Or perhaps it was a greater fear of being carted off in the dark mail bag. Anyway I let go of the controversial sack and retired behind the lilac hedge, awaiting further education.

A neighbor boy owed his life to Mr. Porter. Unbeknown to his parents, three-year-old Eddie had gone fishing at the edge of the deep pool beside the bridge at the foot of our mountain. As the carrier neared this spot, where he usually watered his horse, he saw Eddie's red straw hat bob forward and heard a splash. Jumping from his carriage, lame though he was, he ran down the bank, grabbed the small boy, and rolled him over a barrel that lay near, until the water was forced from his lungs. Then, although responsibility for the government mail forbade any "riders," the rather shaken carrier delivered peaked Eddie straight into the midst of his mother's cookie baking.

Returning to his horse, which was enjoying the grass at the dooryard's edge, Mr. Porter resumed his reins and drove, whistling, on his way.

For a couple of weeks before Christmas each year, it would be nearly dark before the mail carrier's sleigh bells could be heard. We depended upon those silver-toned bells to let us know when we should dart out for stamps or to mail the holiday packages.

Although there were close to thirty stops along his route before he came to ours, it was not always business that delayed our carrier. The telephone had not yet reached some of those rural homes, so news items of local or wider interest must often be relayed, a friendly chat indulged in at a lonely door, or an opinion given on some important matter.

One young mother once ran out to get Mr. Porter's advice on the proper treatment for her baby's colic; Bob called him into the barn to ask what ailed his calf; and Joe often took him around to see a litter of pigs or the chicken coop he was building.

The day before Christmas, too, Joe would represent the family in presenting our token of appreciation to our carrier. Donning his Santa Claus mask, he would run down the path to the gate with a sack of the choicest of the Northern Spies, their red cheeks polished till they shone; a birch-bark box of butternut maple candy; a jar of spicy mincemeat or a dozen jars of the finest herbs. They were homely offerings, but given with genuine feeling and so received.

In the summer of 1912, Mr. Porter silently retired. We grieved to have him go, but the new carrier impressed us greatly. He drove a Steamer, the first one we had ever seen or heard. A full hour earlier each day he arrived at the top of our hill, making a stop at our watering trough as well as at Box 49. He told us he was only trying out the route, for he was debating whether to take it over permanently or to buy more land and give his full time to farming.

Unexpected trials beset his carrying of the mail, so he finally chose the land. His first discouragement was having to have his Steamer hauled up the steepest grade repeatedly by our neighbor's team or ours. When he subsequently started out one afternoon with his father's horse and buggy that had long been standing in their wagon shed, more trouble developed. The wheel spokes rattled so loosely that he dared not go on until he had driven his gig into the deepest part of Hagar Brook, beside the bridge, to soak wheel spokes and felly until they were tightened.

Although he whiled away the time by reading the postcards and the patent medicine ads in his mail bag, it was a tedious wait, and it was long past dusk when he completed his round.

Worst of all, however, was one day of heavy snow a few weeks later. The farmers had not had time to break out one quarter-mile stretch on the side road where he had to deliver a box marked "Perishable." His sleigh could never get through. Blanketing his horse, he tied it to a tree and stepped out with his load into a drift. In he slumped, hip deep.

"Not snow nor rain nor gloom of night stays these couriers from the swift completion of their appointed rounds," flashed through his mind.

Though he vowed that he would hand in his resignation that very night, he would not have it said that he had failed to perform his duty. What should he do? Kneeling in the white depth, he discovered that he could work himself along on his knees, dragging his feet, without sinking in. Thus he made his way to his destination, delivered his burden, and at long last crept back to his sleigh. Small wonder that he chose the land.

Two or three other temporary carriers brought the mail in other interludes. One, who was in his late middle years, confided to us one day, when he was making out a money order, that he had hoped he might meet some eligible and "willing" lady on his route. He concluded, however,

"There are as good fish in the sea as have ever been caught." Though he remained "in the sea," he never missed even one daily round of his three months on Route 2.

It was in 1916 that young Chriss Monroe took over this branch of Uncle Sam's R.F.D. And romance did develop for him. A pretty, vivacious, black-eyed girl, famous for her cherry pies, lived up one lane along his route. The neighbors soon noted that it took an "unconscionably long time" for the handsome new carrier to make his trip up that lane. Besides, Marie's family had never before had mail EVERY day. They guessed that something besides the mail was being delivered up there. Their conjecture was confirmed when Chriss joined the armed forces the next year and left his favorite horse with Marie.

When he returned to his route at the end of the war, he was also returning from his honeymoon. That first week his bride had to wait supper for her husband every evening. The men, women, and children along the remote hill route must welcome their carrier back and hear as much about Overseas and the War as the young veteran felt able to tell. He, in turn, must catch up on their special events of the long months he had been away.

Although duty demanded only that mail be delivered at the box, Chriss more than fulfilled his duty. His buggy, and later his sedan, often wheeled into a dooryard or drive to deliver a package too large for the mailbox, if the ground were wet or the signs pointed to a storm. As his patrons on Windy Summit grew older, he often drove to the door to take care of their business, that they might be sheltered from gale or cold.

Registered letters he seldom left with another member of the family but delivered them himself to the person addressed. In cornfield, hayfield, sheep barn he would find them. He had such knowl-edge of his patrons and their activities that he could locate them by brief search.

Although latterly Chriss could make his rounds in his sedan the entire year, until the late 1930s this was not possible. Even after his high-wheeled Model-T could chug through early winter slush and spring mud, there would be two or three months out of the twelve when he must depend upon his horse.

In the time of heaviest snows, when no amount of shoveling and breaking could keep the mountain road passable, he still would manage to cover at least half his route each day. Driving his bay Morgan, Howard, as far as he could up the east side one day, he would leave his horse in a patron's barn, shoulder his mail bag, and snowshoe to the top of Windy Summit and to side-road homes where he had mail to deliver. The next day he would cover his route from the west end in similar fashion. Often it would be many hours after dark before he reached his home in Pawlet.

On one such occasion, he had been delayed an extra hour and a half by delivering a picture postcard to a little lame girl from her uncle in Canada.

"It was worth all the extra effort to see her so happy at getting her only mail this winter," Chriss told Marie later. No doubt he felt the same after wading to an aged couple's hillside cottage to deliver their *Sears Roebuck Catalog* another challenging night.

But Chriss performed many another service besides carrying the mail. Whenever he saw sheep tearing barley sheaves at harvest time, cattle trampling the young corn in a spring field, a stray animal at the roadside, or anything else amiss in pasture, meadow or barnyard, he would quickly identify the offenders and notify their owners. Thousands of dollars' worth of damage to property he thus prevented, and an incalculable amount of damage to human relations. To Chriss, however, it was just a part of his daily rounds.

One of the most widely publicized of his good deeds was his retrieving a pig in the grass. As he was driving along North Rupert Flats one summer afternoon, his sharp eyes spied a queer movement at the edge of the road. Climbing out of his car, he stealthily approached it. A small black pig with a white face and pink nose was crouching back into the clover.

"Pig, pig," Chriss murmured soothingly, stretching a lean brown hand toward it.

"Oink! Oink!" responded the eight-week-old fugitive, burrowing deeper into its green refuge. Then, with a startled jump that tripped its pursuer, sending him headlong against a pole, away it bounded toward the stone wall. Chriss grabbed his cap, ignoring the lump swelling up over one eye, and took after it. Barred from all but racing along the fence, the pig was finally captured, squealing, by one hind leg, and stowed away in the rear of the carrier's sedan.

At the next farmhouse, Chriss inquired but no one knew a thing about any such stray. Telephone calls up and down the valley produced no information, so Chriss left his captive freight in the farmer's pen and drove on.

News of the pig was noised about, and after some days the mystery was solved. The "Rawleigh Man," who periodically peddled spices, extracts, and various other household necessities in that vicinity, had taken the shoat from a farmer farther north in exchange for liniments and tea. That night, many miles to the south, he had discovered that his four-footed currency had rooted its way out of the bran sack in his truck and was nowhere to be found. Appreciatively, he paid the impounder for keeping his pig and rewarded Captor Chriss with his biggest and best bottle of Pain Killer.

Sally still recalls the time Chriss taught her a lesson in humaneness by interceding in behalf of a spotted adder. She and her twelve-year-old classmate were preparing cudgels to belay the interloper when they were going home from district school one afternoon.

When Chriss met them, he turned his horse aside, that hoof and wheel might avoid the reptile sunning itself in the middle of the road.

"Don't kill it," he urged. "It's a harmless snake and couldn't possibly hurt you. Besides," he added, smiling at the perspiring, agitated little girl faces, "it helps your fathers' crops."

The girls laid down their cudgels, and their fear of an adder disappeared behind the carrier's black buggy top.

Once when I was at home from college for the holidays I had an assignment to write for sociology. The topic was "Adoption," and I was frantic the last Saturday morning of vacation. The return trip would occupy all of the next day, and the paper was due Monday morning. A lengthy search through all available books, magazines, and papers had been barren of information.

"Why don't you ask Chriss?" Mother finally suggested. "He and Marie have just adopted a baby."

More eagerly than ever I watched for our mail carrier's coming that day and hustled out with a long list of "leading questions." But I didn't use those questions—I was too busy writing what the new father had to say, as he glibly gave me a detailed account of adoption procedure. He even explained why all those steps were necessary and valuable.

After that fifteen-minute interview, the paper practically wrote itself. I used my mentor's own closing words for its conclusion: "A child has to have kindness and good care all the time, if he's going to grow up right."

Incidentally, his two adopted children have "grown up right," and the son is following in his father's footsteps in a neighboring town's post office. Chriss and his present wife, who came into the home after Marie's death, when the children were still small, are now enjoying four grandchildren, whom they are also helping to "grow up right."

When I read the numerous appreciative comments of Chriss' service upon his recent retirement after forty years of fulfilling far more than his duty, I recalled our mother's tales of how the mail first came over the mountain a century and a half ago.

In 1803 a biweekly stage was lumbering over this road from Manchester to Salem, connecting with others to Boston and Troy. Somewhat later, and until 1853 when the railroad took over, the stage arrived every second day, leaving mail at the taverns at the foot of each side of our mountain. Relays of four-horse teams brought the precious load of papers and letters, sometimes as many as eight or ten of the latter at one time for Rupert folks, all the way from Boston through Bellows Falls.

I recalled a margin note printed on Grandfather's receipt for *The State Banner* in January of 1848. "Terms: By Carrier $2 (half yearly in advance). Sent by stage and left in the immediate vicinity of the subscriber $2. By mail at our office, or to those residing at a distance from the place at which the paper is left, $1.50." Grandfather got his by stage.

"Those heavy, cumbersome Concord Wagons didn't much resemble the smoothly purring sedans of Chriss and his successor," I meditated. "But they, too, brought the world to the remotest countryman's door. And who knows? Perhaps in another hundred and fifty years, mail delivery on Rupert Mountain may be by helicopter."

Whatever the conveyance, of one thing we may be sure. Dwellers on this country road, as well as many another in America, will never lack the daily communication service of Uncle Sam, "R.F.D.— Magician."

17

THE TOGGLERY

Only a gnarled Red Astrachan apple tree now marks the place where Grandfather's shop once stood. Yet vivid in my childhood memories are the weathered silver grey clapboards of that 24-foot square hub-of-activity that stood at the edge of our hilltop orchard and that was sometimes called the Togglery.

Vivid, too, is the memory of the rosy glow of the "six-over-six" wrinkled glass window panes as they reflected the light of the morning and of the evening sun. And of the blue puffs of smoke that curled upward from the fieldstone chimney on many a frosty day.

"Your grandfather built the shop in 1846," Mother used to tell us. "That was the fall before he brought your grandmother here to live right after they were married in March."

Thereafter, the shop served for nearly ninety years as a place of masculine refuge and creative effort.

Grandfather Seymour's first achievement in his shop was a yoke for his oxen, Duke and Major. In late August of 1846, he selected two straight limbs about three inches in diameter from a green hickory in his woodlot. These he peeled and cut to the right length to loop around a nearby tree which was similar in circumference to the necks of his oxen. He firmly bound the protruding ends of each of these U-formations with spruce rootlets. There he left the cuts to shape and season in the wind, the dew, and the sunshine.

At the end of a week, Grandfather untied his hickory loops and took them to his shop. At his recently completed workbench, he adzed and whittled with axe and jack-knife on a piece of hickory, about six inches thick, a foot wide, and five feet long, that had seasoned for a year in his woodshed. This he shaped into a cross-piece to fit over the shoulders of Duke and Major while holding them a foot or so apart. In this shoulder piece, he bored holes with a hand augur at the proper places to insert the loops, ends up. In the loopends he also bored holes for inserting pegs to lie parallel with the yoke top.

Pegs for securing these loops he whittled from a piece of maple saved for the purpose. His father had taught him that hickory was light and tough enough for the yoke, but maple was best for pegs, as it was harder and would not split even under the finest whittling. These six-inch-long pegs would need to be durable, for they would be pushed in and out of the holes every time the oxen were yoked or unyoked.

In the center of the under side of the crosspiece, he drove in a stout iron pin attached to a heavy iron ring, both of which he had forged by the fieldstone fireplace. To this ring would be fastened the tongue of his ox-cart or the heavy hauling-chain for drawing logs or stumps or rocks. What scores of houses and barns that ox-bow helped to build in the ensuing years! And what thousands of tons of food for man and animal it helped to produce and harvest!

Young Seymour's main project in his shop that winter was his ox-cart. No longer would he need to borrow one from his neighbor, Amos Clark. A pair of wheels, five feet in diameter and with an axle fitted into their hubs, had been given to him by his brother Zach, in exchange for the second ox-yoke that Seymour made. Grandfather whittled two maple linchpins, or rods to insert through the ends of the axle where they protruded beyond the hubs. Setting these in place, he then whittled another to fasten the cart-body to the tongue or drawing-pole, attached beneath the center front.

This cart-body was an eight-by-five-foot ash box, nearly two feet deep. Forging a heavy U-bolt and ring or "eye" from old iron, by his fireplace, he inserted the U through the ring. The former he drove into the center bottom of the box and the latter into the center top of the axle. When the cart was thus joined and "center balanced," the tongue was pegged on. Seymour then spiked a heavy iron chain along the drawing-pole for additional security when the oxen would be hauling an extraordinary load.

To unload wood, hay, pumpkins, apples, and turnips, as well as count-less other kinds of cargo, the driver would pull out the pin that fastened the cart to the pole, thus permitting the box to tip back and the load to slide out at the rear.

To facilitate the dumping operation, Grandfather contrived a removable tailboard that slid up and down in the grooved ends of the sideboards. He likewise set in some pegs to hold stakes along the sides of the box to permit piling on higher loads when such need arose.

This ox-cart was an indispensable vehicle for nearly a half century! Its two high wheels easily straddled the stumps and rocks that at first studded the meadows. They rolled well, too, in deep mud, over rough roads, and across pasture hummocks. Always the axle and hubs were kept well "greased" with a mixture of pine pitch and tallow. For many years, the cart carried grist and apples to mill; brought home the meal and cider; drew potatoes, grain, hay, and other produce from the fields; and hauled wood from the woodlot.

The farm implement that Seymour prized perhaps the most among those that he contrived in his shop that winter of 1846-47 was his grain cradle. It was so called because its "fingers" or "arms" caught and held, or "cradled," the grain upright, while its three-foot blade mowed the stalks.

This long blade-and-handle could sweep across a field in less than a quarter of the time required by any earlier "sith" (scythe). How many long hours Seymour had spent previously in cutting grain with a sickle held in his right hand, while he caught and drew the stalks within reach by means of a "mathook" held in his left.

Having studied the year before the first cradle that he had ever seen, owned by a cousin in Connecticut, he had collected his materials the preceding summer. Digging around the ash stumps at the edge of the meadow, he obtained sturdy roots for the three "fingers," all of which must curve parallel with the iron blade. For the handle, he chose a hickory sapling. Roots and sapling were left to cure for many weeks beside the shop. Ash and hickory he had learned would give the essential strength coupled with minimum weight (though we children found this ponderous cradle too much to lift) for cutting and laying the heavy grain in swaths so it could be bound.

With utmost care, Seymour pounded his iron, heated on the shop hearth, into the desired blade. He then assembled blade, "fingers," and the essential slim wooden braces. To these, he "ironed on" (fastened with iron bands) the four-foot snath or handle, with its pegged-on hand grip or hand hold. The "hang" or balance of his new implement pleased him.

Five acres of wheat fell before Grandfather's cradle in one day during that summer of 1847. Soon afterward, he swept across four acres of rye between sunrise and sunset. "Without the help of any rum or cider, either," he used to observe to his hired men, with the hint of a grin behind his beard. Amos Clark who bound the grain into sheaves with strands of grass as Seymour mowed, vowed to have a cradle of his own before the next reaping season. So did several other neighbors who watched its miraculous performance.

Consequently, that November the shop was a center of community activity as Seymour instructed the others in shaping and assembling the parts. As the five men planned and wrought together, they little dreamed that within a quarter century they would consider their cradles cumbersome and slow because a horsedrawn reaper would by then be revolutionizing the harvesting of grain even more than the cradle had revolutionized the reaping in the early 1800s.

Certainly Grandfather would have been pleased could he have known that his grandsons and nephews would still be using his cradle to "pick out" the edges of their hillside fields more than a half century later. And certainly he would have been highly amused could he have known that it would be honored as a museum curio by the time it reached its century-mark.

A chest for Mary Ann was Seymour's next production in his shop. From pine planks three quarters of an inch thick, he fashioned her "keepsake box," eighteen inches wide and deep, and twenty-eight inches long, bordering the lid and bottom with carefully applied strips of "half round" molding. The finish was a dark-on-light red spatter stain made from boiled spruce roots and bark;. Below the big iron-inlaid key-hole, he set his wife's initials, "M A H," in large, close-together dots of the darker tone.

At the top of one end of the interior, he inserted a lidded compartment, eight inches wide and deep. Therein Grandmother Mary Ann kept some of her smallest treasures. How we children used to love to have her show us those: the wee brown linen shoes that her first baby wore; the white matron's cap that she donned on her wedding day; the shell-handled silver spoon on which all of her six children cut their teeth; a flying eagle silver penny; a half dozen letters from her brother who never returned from the Battle of the Potomac; a china-headed doll with blonde hair and rosy cheeks that was given to her youngest daughter, Vetty, when she was two; and the little soft grey shoulder shawl that her mother had worn in her last illness. Wool for it had grown on the back of Mary Ann's pet ewe in her father's flock when she was a girl. Together, she and her mother had cleaned and carded and spun the wool into yarn. Together, they had knit the shawl which had comforted many an ill member of the family before it was worn too thin for further service during Great Grandmother's last illness in the 1890s.

The bed of the chest held other treasures of Mary Ann's. Beside the shuttle that Seymour had made for her loom lay her best indigo and ivory coverlid, woven in the Double Chariot Wheel pattern, and her best linen tablecloth, done in a creamy M-and-O design and bordered with wide fringe. These were brought into use only for such important guests as The Minister, The Teacher, and Aunt Vesta.

In our childhood, Aunt Vesta was a favorite visitor. She always asked to be shown "what's going on in the shop now," soon after her arrival on her annual "family round."

Seeing the handwoven tablecloth and coverlid brought out in her honor, she invariably recalled countless tales of "the earlier days." How our spines would tingle when she told of the bobcat that came to the shop door when Grandfather was working on Grandmother's chest one winter evening.

"Your grandpa just grabbed a fiery brand off the hearth and yelled like Satan as he made for the door. You should have seen that bobcat scud, and he never did come back," she would conclude. She always declared that "the shop doings" primed her memory.

The shop work of which Grandfather was most proud, perhaps, was the ballot boxes for Rupert Election in 1860. (Although this occurred in the church, the boxes were later used for many years in the Town Hall.)

A Vermont State law, enacted the preceding year, stated: "Every organized town in this state shall provide one box to receive votes for a representative to represent such town in the general assembly of this state....; one box to receive votes for governor (and other state officers) . . .; one box to receive votes for justices of the peace; one box to receive votes for representatives to Congress; and one box to receive votes for electors of president and vice president of the United States, and in the lid . . . of each box there shall be a small aperture, sufficiently large to receive such votes, which said boxes shall be properly designated and kept by the town clerk in each town, for the purpose aforesaid."

In compliance with the law, Seymour sawed the parts for each of the five boxes from a pine board slightly less than an inch thick and about ten inches wide. These he pegged together into receptacles fourteen inches high at the front and twelve at the back. To facilitate the ballots' falling, he sloped the top behind the flat front section containing the aperture. At the rear of each box, he hinged a door and secured it with a wooden button for use in the removal of ballots for counting.

At the front of each, he painstakingly carved its designation:

"T. R." (for Town Representative); "S.O." (State Officers) and so on to "Electors."

That first November, much to the maker's exultation, the Electors' box was packed with ballots for the electors of Abraham Lincoln for President.

For many succeeding years, those ballot boxes fulfilled their function at the September and November "Freemen's Meetings."

One of the pieces that Grandfather most enjoyed making was the feather bed patter. Every bride in the community for several years received one of these as a wedding gift from him and Grandmother. The last one that he ever made in his shop was for his son Frank's wife. That was the fall of 1869.

Grandfather and Grandmother were setting stakes around the Red Astrachan sapling at the corner of the shop, to protect it during the winter, when their son brought home his bride Adell from Western New York State. They had first become acquainted the preceding summer when the vivacious eighteen-year-old had been visiting relatives in the neighborhood.

As bride and groom helped with the staking, they smiled when Grandfather observed that perhaps their children would be among the first to eat the fruit from this little tree.

That evening, Grandfather whistled happily as he shaped a patter for smoothing out the humps in Adell's feather bed before she would be spreading it with her blankets and quilts. On this flat beech paddle, six inches square, with a yard-long handle, he tenderly carved the initials of his son and wife, and beneath these, the date of their wedding.

When the marriage ended in divorce a few months later, Grandfather found the patter on his workbench one evening. On it lay a note: "If Frank and I had been like his parents, we, too, might have made a good home. Adell."

Grandfather shaved the initials and date from the patter and re-inscribed it when his son remarried a year later. "This is a warning," he told Frank and his second wife, who had been a close friend of Adell's, as he and Grandmother again presented the feather bed patter.

Sunshine, candlelight, and lantern glow illuminated many an ingenious hour in Grandfather's shop throughout a half century of his life and also several years of Father's.

The piping of the peepers, song of birds and hum of bees, the croon of the crickets and the whine of the snow-wind all marked the passing of the seasons outside its door.

Crops sprouted and grew lush in the meadow. Fruit trees bloomed and bore in the orchard. The jingle of cowbells, bleat of lambs, and whinny of horse and colt in the pasture all carried the music of farm wellbeing through the open windows of the shop.

The hill men whistled tunes of contentment as they bent above the work-bench inside. There they labored to produce the facilities for seedtime and harvest, for the welfare of their animals, for progress in their township, and for health and comfort in their home.

Bands of ash were whittled, steamed, and shaped into snow-shoes for "scholars" to make their way to school in winter. Hinged rods for flailing the grain from its straw; cheese baskets, ladders, and casks for the dairy; snaths for scythes, helves for axes, and handles for rakes, hoes, and potato hooks, all were made and mended in the shop. Splinters of swamp oak were once split out for an obese daughter's corset stays. Candle box and sugar bucket, sap spiles and rattle-boxes, shoe last and baseball bat came also from the shop as need arose. So, too, did elder bobbin, poplar shuttle, and cherry reel to equip the spinning-wheels and loom.

Through the years, a motley collection piled up in the shop: cutter shafts and whiffletrees, to be mended, chairs for seats to be renewed, a scarecrow to be re-outfitted, and a kite to be re-strung were among the sundries. In one corner, a worn potato sack provided a drying-mat for some prized pumpkin, squash, and cucumber seeds. Nearby stood a leaky wooden sapbucket filled with grass seed. Directly above, hung ears of golden dent corn traced up by their husk. All evidenced more promise than fulfillment.

So, too, did a huge umbrella frame that appeared on the wall in the early 1900s. A once-inflated pig bladder was tied to the tip of each rib. As these hardened and cracked, they bore witness to a young boy's blasted hopes for aeronautical prowess.

In my childhood, a row of tallow candle stubs in drip-caked iron holders stood on the window sill above the wide-planked workbench that extended the length of the east wall. Awl and chisel, gimlet, whetstone, hammer, pincers, hinges, and much unsorted hardware lay ready to the owner's use, in a clutter of convenience. A square tin lantern with glass panels in its four sides was suspended from the ceiling at each end of the bench. The candle in each was reduced to a meager lump of tallow and blackened wick, but both had served well so were retained in their place below the rafters. Their functioning had been replaced in the early 1900s by that of a pair of kerosene lanterns, hung from wall hooks, with a tin reflector behind each.

When the globes became opaque from smoke and dust, a masculine hand would "rim" them out and polish them off with a wad of newspaper or a torn shirt tail kept on hand for the purpose.

This shop provided a center of relaxation as well as of work for the men and boys of Windy Summit. Here, beneath the smoke-browned beams, they oiled their boots and cleaned their guns, curried their dogs and strewed their harness mending, filed their saws and shaved their axe helves, secure from the antagonizing invasion of the mop or broom that reigned in the farmhouse.

Here many a small boy whittled and tested his willow whistles, pored over his disassembled watch parts, and spread bleached bones from the back pasture for juvenile research.

Even a small girl, if she were uninitiated into the holy rites of good housekeeping, might romp in the shop with the boys and their ever present dog, cat, pet squirrel, or tame crow in joyous abandon of scream and yelp and tumble. Here, too, we often investigated the mysteries of the fat grey spiders that spun their silken snares across the windows or among the rafters.

In a screen-topped sap tub near the east window, one summer Uncle Oliver penned the pink-eyed white woodchuck that he had captured in his garden. The shop door creaked on its hinges many a day and evening that July and August to accommodate community curiosity.

Shortly after Whitey had gone to his winter retreat under the meadow wall, a motherless little raccoon was nested in the tub and leashed to the workbench. Its tiny black hands often clutched the handle of vise or hammer as Father mended harness or "hung" an axe. The velvety pointed nose and beady, ringed eyes were glued to Uncle Oliver's elbow as he and Cousin John shucked the burrs off the hazelnuts that they had dried on the broad doorstone. The sharp wild teeth finally gnawed an opening into a wide white world one March night. The shop seemed empty after Ring was gone.

When Bob and Joe and Sally and I were children, a rectangular box stove stood in front of the old fireplace. How we loved to watch the flames leap when the front door was opened and a dry chunk of birch was thrust into the crimson pile of embers. And how we loved to hear the winter wind whistle down the chimney or wheeze in the stovepipe.

One day when no fire burned in the stove, we heard a strange noise in the pipe. Emboldened by curiosity, Joe jerked the stove door open. Out of the ashy cavern flopped a pair of panic-eyed, soot-covered squirrels. With a desperate leap through the partly open door, they disappeared among the Red Astrachan branches.

"Santa Claus sent' em," three-year-old Sally shouted gleefully.

On the broad hearth of that same stove, numerous boys roasted chestnuts or marshmallows or baked juicy, red-cheeked pippins, while they discussed topics or told tales that they never would in the presence of their elders.

"Are babies brought in the doctor's black bag, or do they really come the same way calves and kittens do?"

"My mother says eating too much pork pie will give me a big stomach. Your brother's wife Annie don't eat pork pie and her stomach's getting bigger every day. When I told Ma so, she said 'Sh-h-h!' So mebby Ma's wrong, and it don't hurt to eat pork pie after all. Whadda you think, Bill?"

"I brought in some corn silk to make cigarettes. Didja bring the paper to roll 'em? Pa sez if I'm going to smoke to do it right in front of everybody. I tried to, but the tobacco made me squirm so I don't want folks to see me. We've gotta practise if we're goin' to be any good at it."

An ancient cuspidor, blotched with telltale brown stains, and a heel of Town Talk tobacco on the shelf above, had companioned numerous boot-drying, story-telling sessions among the men. So had the musty cider keg, with its worn and pungent spigot, above which dangled a tin dipper.

Nearby, a sag-bottomed Lincoln rocker and a cobbler's bench piled with dusty Montgomery Ward Catalogs, *Poor Richard Almanacs*, Burpee's Seed Catalogs, *American Cultivators*, *Town Reports*, and *Police Gazettes* bore witness to several decades of masculine education and diversion.

Along the wall facing the stove, a broad-seated, feather-cushioned lounge, fashioned from a discarded four-poster bed and covered with faded brown denim, was reminiscent of hunters' naps in full dress; of haymakers' "forty winks" at noonday; and of small boys' escapes with, and internal atonement for, filched mince pie, watermelon, or green apples.

Flanking the window above the lounge hung two 18-by-24-inch pictures in walnut frames. One showed Grandfather's famous flock of Merino sheep. It had been banished from the saltbox parlor wall when Merino value tragically vanished back in the 1800s. The other was a hand-tinted photograph of Father's prized Duroc-Jersey pigs, named for nine gods and goddesses, busy at lunch with their auburn-bristled mother, Juno. Denied a place in Mother's parlor, Juno and her piglets brought color to the rough walls of the Togglery.

A smoke-brown cupboard with a heavy brass latch stood between the two west windows, filling the wall from floor to ceiling. Undefiled by feminine scrubbing or arranging, it provided a complete pharmacopoeia for the hill farmers' needs. Bunches of dried herbs were stacked in the top compartment: thoroughwort for cows at calving time, wormwood for a foundered horse, lobelia for the men's bee stings, and peppermint for overnourished boys, along with many others.

A mummified black can, relegated to the most obscure recess, bore witness to Grandfather's experiment in the medical science of the mid-1800s. Afflicted with a persistent racking cough, he had resorted to inhaling fumes of hot tar and nearly strangled himself to death. Thereafter, Grandfather majored in herbs.

On the lower shelves were a half century accumulation of patent medicine bottles. By the early 1900s most of these were empty or nearly so, the contents having already fulfilled numerous needs. Dr. Daniel's Spavin Cure, Merchant's Gargling Oil for Horses, Tattersall's Heave Powders, Sloan's Liniment, and Turpentine Ointment for lambs with ticks were among the motley collection. Tall black bottles, squat blue bottles in shades of cobalt and aquamarine, amber and amethyst glass containers for various elixirs, were all mingled higgledy piggledy, and all were sealed in a long acquired coat of oil and grime.

On the unpainted back of the cupboard door was penciled a nostalgic breeding record: "Wild Air's first calf due in mid-March, 1872"; "Duchess to foal about May l0th, 1884"; "The Shropshire Ewe Peggy to lamb in early April, 1890-twins again, probably"; "Holstein Daisy - March 25th, 1901"; "Jersey Queen - April l2th, 1902, gave 36 quarts a day besides her calf, part of 1900." Each lamb and calf and colt and pig in stable or pen was a pet, and we loved to read the records inscribed on the mellow pine planking of the cupboard door in Grandfather's and in Father's writing.

Along the dusty sleepers, scores of paint pails were efficiently filed by their identifying drip: Venetian red for the barn doors and the cutter thills; sky blue for the old well sweep; apple green for wagon boxes and motor truck cabs; and russet for the fringe-topped surrey were among the hoarded pails.

Those containers once yielded an amazing nest of Easter eggs to eight-year-old Bob's assiduous exploring. His shirt and overalls, his hair and ears, his boots and nose all aided him in his artistic efforts with the shop paint brush. Boy and eggs vied for first place in applied art that April day, and the entire family were thoroughly impressed, Mother most of all.

After a destructive gale in the 1930s it was decided to raze rather than to repair the badly damaged Togglery. The last day before the demolition I spent in the familiar old room.

Early in the morning, I set to work cleaning and burnishing the handmade five-gallon brass kettle that had been in family service since the 1770s. According to legend, Great Great Grandfather Zachariah had taken it from his home in the Bennington Grants to the battlefield a few miles from there, to boil potatoes for the Green Mountain Boys in mid-August of 1777.

In the early 1800s, it had been brought to Windy Summit and used during the next three quarters of a century in the saltbox house for the production of tallow, soft soap, maple syrup, and apple butter. Relegated to the shop when it was superseded by more modern equipment in the house, it first replaced a leaky rain barrel at the corner near the door. Latterly, it had been used to cache euchre cards, pulley ropes, and dog collars. At the bottom was a sheepskin folio which I resolved to explore as soon as the kettle was done. As I scoured away its crust of grime and smoke, I marveled at the soundness of the metal and at the golden glow of its patina. How I looked forward to using it to hold the logs beside the hearth of my new home.

When the burnishing was finished, I pulled the Lincoln rocker out under the apple tree and untied the sheepskin thongs that bound the folio. Almost reverently, I gazed upon a half dozen of Grandfather's diaries.

As I turned the crumbling, yellowed pages, and read the faded script of two of the last ones that he ever wrote, I felt the innermost being of the writer intimately revealed:

"If pure necessity had not drove me to it I should have suspended my personal labors today, for I was more fit to be on the bed than behind the plow, notwithstanding my illness did a pretty good days work. My flax is in the blow. Spring wheat is heading out."

"I cut about 2 1/2 acres grass by scythe today."

"Got in about 6 Tons hay in P.M.—clover. There's some swaths look like a poor old Horse's ribs. I have salted a 19-load stack."

"Alas, the deep bereavement meted out to us, we are now bending under. Our little girl is dead - died at 11:30 A.M. Our Father - Thy will be done."

"Our Frank and Adell are too thick to be decent for any but lovers, and even them."

"Frank is off again today with his precious company. God only knows the end —."

"Frank wants my consent for him to marry this winter coming. He is too young at 19—yet my opposition might do him more harm than good. I will trust to God and let him go."

"Got in our turnips & carrots. 53 years old today— time passes along moving me on to Eternity."

Tangy red apples have plopped into the August grass, bringing happy gathering to numerous young ones, for many seasons since the shop went down. Among the children's chief delights are tales of the weathered building that stood for so many years beneath the Red Astrachan tree. We who knew it can still feel the presence of those who wrought in that old Togglery.

18

THE TOWN HALL

On March 5, 1872, Rupert voters assembled for the first time at their Town Hall. Red cutters, grey bobsleds and sleighs, piled deep with straw and buffalo robes, crowded the church sheds and the new Village School House yard. Horses snorted, jingled their bells, and subsided into their blankets.

Two hundred or so ruddy-faced and mustached or bearded men, between the ages of twenty-one and ninety-six, stomped the snow from boot and moccasin, turned up the earlappers on their heavy caps, and poured in through the schoolhouse door. Though it was only a little after nine, some of the earliest arrivals, plodding across the street from store and blacksmith shop, had been there arguing the items in *The Town Report* for more than an hour. Others, who had brought their womenfolk to the church basement to prepare the noonday meal for the voters, now came breaking their way across the intervening yards.

Stacking overcoats and an occasional big black shawl worn by an oldster, on schoolroom benches and desks, the throng trooped up the stairs. Guffaws and garrulous voices mingled with the clatter of feet on their way to their new voting quarters.

For more than a hundred years, the town's voters had been assembling in Moore's or Jenks' Tavern, the church, store, or some spacious farmhouse. Now at long last they had a suitable and permanent place in which to carry on the town's business.

And well had they earned it. In a series of bees between planting-time and harvest the summer before, the men had framed and sided, roofed, clapboarded, and ceiled the forty- by thirty-foot building. Men and women together had painted it, white on the outside, grey within, and had polished its many-paned windows. Scholars from the village district had begun using their classroom on the first floor the preceding October. Today, however, the voters had taken over both it and their second-floor hall.

"Frank voting his first time this year, Seymour?" a cracked voice queried in Grandfather's ear. "Look'sif he's going to take Freeman's Oath."

"Shouldn't wonder if he is, 'Riel." Justifiable pride gleamed in Grandfather's eyes as he glanced toward the corner of the hall, where his son and a half dozen other twenty-one-year-olds had gathered around the Town Clerk, Ab Hopkins. Grandfather himself, when Selectman, had administered the Oath to so many new voters that he knew it by heart. He followed the words to himself, as the Clerk spoke them to Frank, whose right hand was raised to "swear."

"You solemnly swear (or affirm) that whenever you give your vote or suffrage, touching any matter that concerns the State of Vermont, you will do it so as in your conscience you shall judge will most conduce to the best good of the same, as established by the Constitution without fear or favor of any person."

This Hall made a good place to take the Oath, Grandfather thought to himself. He and other selectmen, justices of the peace, and town clerks had administered it in numerous other "public places" —the store, depot, church basement, and once even at the blacksmith shop. That was in 1848, when Sam Noble barely got his name on the check list the required four days before National Election so he could vote for his former commander in the Mexican War, Zachary Taylor, for president.

He was glad a man could vote at Town Meeting the same day he was sworn. Studying *The Town Report* that came in the mail in early February every year was what fired some of the fellows to want to vote.

Grandfather pulled his own worn copy out of his pocket. He knew almost by heart the items listed in "The Warning" (or notice of the meeting) published therein. So probably did most of these other men.

He looked at his watch. Ten o'clock. Time to begin. He pulled out the chair behind the Moderator's desk and brought the gavel down hard.

"The meeting will come to order."

Bill Freeman closed the front draft of the big chunk stove at the rear of the room, turned the damper in the pipe, and pushed a spittoon into the center aisle between the numerous rows of chairs. Feet shuffled across the sawdust-covered floor as the men took their seats, and the din quieted down.

One by one, town officers were nominated and voted upon, the first by the men's lining up along the wall assigned to respective candidates. Sam Bardwell glared at his hired hand who joined the ranks along the opposite wall when the lister-for-three-years was being elected. But said hired man showed no sign of cringing. He was casting his vote "without fear or favor of any person." Sam might prefer the other candidate for listing his stock lower, but the hired man knew that his candidate would "most conduce to the best good" of the tax list. And his candidate won.

The ballot slips arrived just then, so the rest of the voting was done by dropping the written ballots into the slotted big, square, dark wooden box on a table at the front of the room. As the men filed past it, Grandfather remembered the times when voters had used beans to indicate their choice for one candidate and kernels of corn for his opponent. "No more ballot-box succotash," Judge Burton had observed when paper ballots came into use.

By eleven o'clock, selectmen, overseer of the poor, school director, lister, auditor, next year's moderator, town clerk and treasurer, road commissioner, constable, tree warden, fence viewers, pound keeper, hog howard, and the rest of the town officers had been elected. No longer were the four tythingmen, eleven surveyors of highways, and two leather sealers of earlier days required for the town's functioning.

Just as Grandfather opened his mouth to read the question of license for selling liquor in Rupert, 'Bijah Dean arose and called out, "Mr. Moderator." Being recognized, he proposed with some emphasis, "We need some cuspidors."

Dan Meehan's brother-in-law, voting for the first time since immigrating from Europe, had been much impressed by "First Selectman," "First Constable," and the rest of the official titles. He now arose, and with warm fraternal feeling announced, "Mr. Moderator, I nominate Dan Meehan for First Cuspidor."

When the uproar died down and the cuspidors had been provided for, without the personal assistance of Dan Meehan, the license question was read and warmly debated. As the argument grew heated, beetlebrowed and ruddy-faced Elon Clark stood up. He and his seven sons owned an equal number of farms in the township, and they usually stood together on their vote.

"I like a drink now and then myself," he boomed. "But I don't want it sold right here under my nose nor my hired men's noses, so we can't get our work done." That brought a final vote of "Nay," and the "Nays" have had it ever since.

A watch case snapped here and there. Noon and time for dinner. Over to the church parlors the men flocked. Each deposited his ten cents in the sugar bowl on a stand near the door and eagerly approached a loaded table. The church women's "Food Committee" hovered near and helped pass the pans and platters of home-donated baked beans, brown bread, scalloped potatoes, cold ham and corned beef, pot cheese, baked apples, pickles, conserves, chopped cabbage, corn pudding, and huge slabs of pie, all accompanied by steaming cups of coffee. Over well-stacked plates, seconds and thirds being taken for granted, taxes were the main subject.

Back in Town Hall promptly at one o'clock, that major issue was announced for discussion. More than once Grandfather had to rap his gavel for order, but every man had his say. From the first Town Meeting in Rupert in 1769 every man had had the right to be heard. Once he had stood and been recognized, no one could challenge such right until he had finished what he had to say. Such freedom of speech here spelled the first phase of democracy.

By sundown, also choretime, the town issues had all been thrashed out, many opinions changed by convincing argument, and business completed. Satisfied or resigned, depending on how the vote related to personal point of view, the men trooped down the stairs just as dusk was thickening. Horses pawed, runners squeaked, and sleigh bells jingled. The Yards would not be so crowded again, nor Town Hall so odorous with tobacco, wet moccasins, and other fumes of democracy until next March Meeting Day.

The 1872 use of Town Hall has been similarly followed ever since, with Primary and Caucus likewise occurring there. Though the Rupert citizens differ widely in many of their views, they have been able to resolve most of their differences amicably by "getting the rile out of their systems" on the Town Hall floor.

The approximately 70-page *Town Report*, annually issued in early February, has aided the cause considerably. Those well-thumbed and thoroughly digested reports, stowed in handbag, in coat or overalls pocket, often accompany the voters to the Hall. It contains "The Warning" (copies of which are likewise posted in three public places, usually the store, post office, and depot) or notice of the time, place, and items of business to be considered at the Meeting.

Each issue also carries a detailed account by each current officer of the exact sums in dollars and cents paid out, to whom, and for what. Thus no padding of expense accounts or partiality in distributing town jobs can possibly occur. Birth, marriage, and death statistics are included. So, too, are the names of delinquent taxpayers with statement of amounts unpaid, as well as the names of those receiving public support and classification of such expenses.

Besides these basic facts, special data is presented at intervals, so that all may be well informed regarding their town. One such early report included a map of the township and its 44.86 miles of "Traveled Highways excluding pent roads and trails." Each type of road, as well as every bridge, was indicated by name or symbol.

During each war, *The Report* has also published the Honor Roll of boys in service or honorably discharged to help on home farms.

In 1936, when Vermont "left the Union" by its adherence to Republicanism when the Nation experienced a landslide for the Democrats, the ballot roll was proudly summarized on those pages: "Number of Republicans—284; Democrats—39; Communists—2; Total— 325. (No Communists have registered for many years now.)

"The Agricultural Census," featured the following year, showed: "Number of Hens over 3 Months—4054; Number of Steers and Bulls —64; Calves Under 1 Year—349; Heifers 1-2 Years—346; Cows— 1731; Trees Tapped—15,800; Acres of Maple Orchard Tapped—345; Acres of Maple Orchard Untapped—15,100; Gallons of Syrup— 7,819."

Some sugar bush owners squirmed under that subtle rebuke considering that their taxes were in arrears.

Another year's notation, however, registered complete approval:

"A vote of thanks was given to the efficient town officers who have so conducted the affairs of the town as to clear Rupert of all indebtedness."

The Treasurer's Report that year carried no recommendation for the raising of funds for "Interest at—% to—for Town Indebtedness," as it so often has.

Those same *Town Reports* frequently have provided the voters with verbal ammunition as well as facts. In the 1890s, certain controversial issues listed were once postponed until the dissenters who lived several miles over the mountain had to leave for evening chores. Those independent farmers made provision for late chores thereafter and stayed until adjournment. The kerosene lamps in tin sconces more than once lighted a wrangle over taxes. However, funds for road building and maintenance, bridges, schools, fire protection, support of the town's unfortunate, officers' salaries ranging from $20 to $600 a year, and town indebtedness always have been raised.

The three Selectmen, five Justices of the Peace, and the Town Treasurer, who constitute the Board of Civil Authority, often have hastily swallowed a box lunch there in Town Hall and met during the mid-day adjournment of the March Meeting to hear personal protests regarding taxes. More than one white-haired citizen has there been advised that his poll tax (a personal assessment on each voter under seventy years of age, ranging from $1 to $10 through the years, depending on the current budget) would be cancelled if he could prove that he had had his seventieth birthday before August first of the preceding year. Many another plea has been denied.

To reduce the list of taxpayers in arrears, however, it was once voted to give delinquents the first chance "to work out their taxes on the road." The provision proved highly satisfactory all around.

On one occasion, Tom White, who enjoyed the reputation of always "making ends meet," arose and challenged the Road Commissioner's Report. In scrutinizing the figures, he had discovered a discrepancy of $2 favoring the Commissioner. That officer promptly rechecked his account, admitted his error, and made a refund.

"Take care of the pence, and the pounds will take care of themselves," a prosperous, bright-eyed matron in the back row was heard to murmur as the matter was concluded.

The Overseer of the Poor's report that tramps and other transients were being lodged overnight at $1 each with a widower, Stillman Smith, who lived alone, provoked brief discussion. The use of barns and haystacks by such travelers, as had been the custom formerly, was pronounced a violation of the town's dignity, safety, and humanity, so the additional expenditure was cheerfully admitted to the budget.

So, too, was continued support of an aging town pauper, although much dissatisfaction was expressed at the additional burden imposed by his having brought into his mountain cabin, without town approval, a wife he had won through a "Lonely Hearts" correspondence, from the state of Montana.

When the First Selectman proposed spending $6,000 for Snow Removal Equipment, those astute voters took precautionary measures. A representative from each of the three sections of the township was elected to serve as a Committee to assist in selecting the machinery and to supervise its use, "its services to be fairly apportioned among all rural roads as well as village streets."

A motion for transportation of scholars from district schools to a centralized one met with long and stormy debate before its attainment in the mid-1930s.

"Just a lot of froth we'd get instead of good milk," our father argued. 'They'll learn their ABC's and multiplication tables a damn sight better nearer home. The more young ones you pack together, the more deviltry they'll hatch up."

"In another twenty or thirty years, it will be the fashion to have our district schools back again. Then look at all we'll have to raise for repairs on buildings that'll be gone to rack and ruin," spoke up another strong opponent to the centralized movement.

Only men had been fully qualified voters at Rupert Town Hall until 1920, although women with children were permitted to vote on school matters, if their husbands had fulfilled the requirements. After the passage of the Nineteenth Amendment to the National Constitution, women likewise might qualify for full suffrage. The requirements included citizenship in the state for a year and in the town three months, attainment of "one's majority" (age 21), and having taken the Freeman's Oath.

The Oath may be administered by any member of the Board of Civil Authority in any public place. There are no fixed days for such registration, except that it must be before ten o'clock on Town Meeting Day and at least four days before Election. No man need leave potato field or threshing, no woman her preserving kettle, to insure their suffrage right and privilege. Having made the state's required affirmation, one's name is permanently on the check list if his taxes are paid. But each voter is wise to inquire at the Town Clerk's office in advance of Election Day to make sure that his name has not been inadvertently omitted when the year's Check List is copied from the preceding one.

Although most Rupert women had staunchly maintained that "woman's place is in the home," seventy-one of them had taken the Freeman's Oath by October 28. Mother, Aunt Cornelia, Aunt Delia, Aunt Martha, and twenty others were among the first to do so. Enthusiasm was running high because Cal Coolidge, originally from nearby Plymouth, was a candidate for national vice president that year and would be needing votes on November 2. Aristocratic, 82-year-old Thankful Flower declined the new privilege, but she gladly gave her shy little Negro helper, Molly Jackson, "time off" both to "swear" and to vote.

Four years later, when her fellow statesman was up for election again as president, even Mrs. Flower put aside her reluctance to be "less feminine," subscribed to the Oath, and cast her ballot. That year the Australian Ballot system was introduced. Bob and Joe and I were among those voting for the first time in a national election, along with another score or so from our mountain district. As we lingered in the yard afterward, our one Democrat neighbor drawled, "Gol, it gives you a queer feeling to do yourself up in a curtain and know you're all alone with your conscience, especially when a fellow from your own state is up for president." As we discovered later, 80-year-old Norman's "conscience" had caused him to desert his party that day, the only time in his life.

Cal's winning somewhat mollified Tom Kellogg, who had been dead-set against women's "putting on the pants." The day the first contingent took the Freeman's Oath, he had glowered darkly from the blacksmith shop at the approach of "petticoat government" over at Town Hall. "You'll find out," he grumbled to any who would listen, "that no man can call his soul his own from now on, and them women won't even know what they're voting for, neither."

Regardless of Tom's prediction, Vermont remained as much of a Republican stronghold after Woman's Suffrage as before. However, Rupert Town Hall was the nucleus of an overwhelming upset for the party on November 2, 1958. Bill Meyer of West Rupert was elected the State's one Congressional Representative. The first Democrat to win the honor and office in well over a hundred years!

As a matter of fact, Bill had pressed his candidacy as a "liberal Northern Democrat" on his own independent beliefs—that the ideals established today determine the realities of tomorrow—rather more than on a party platform. A goodly number of staunch Republicans who could not deny the soundness of that line of thought deserted their ranks to vote for Bill.

When Bob, who had worked daily with Bill for six consecutive years at the Forest and Farmland Foundation, was asked if he had voted for him, his reply was a concession. "Hell, yes, the only Democrat I ever did vote for!" A thirty-five-year record broken by "so as in your conscience you shall judge will most conduce to the best good of the same!"

Although Town Meetings, Primaries, and Elections have often shown some effects of "log rolling" at blacksmith shop, depot, store, and post office, the voting has been kept orderly, and disappointed candidates have for the most part been good losers. One voter, who placed his bet on such a loser some years ago, had to pay the same by trundling his 240-pound candidate in a wheelbarrow from the Town Hall door to the depot at the lower end of the village amid the hoots and guffaws of his opponents. Two years later, however, the scales of fortune were balanced in his favor. He himself won the election to the State Legislature.

Cuspidor, chunk stove, and kerosene lamp all have gone the way of the ballot box at School House Hall. Old-time buckboards and sleighs with blanketed horses have yielded their place to today's motley throng of motor vehicles. But Yankee equality and forthright speech mingle in the valley air with chug of truck and purr of sedan as freely as they once did with clomp of hoof and creak of sled and axle.

Likewise, this township's voters still read *The Town Report* and troop to March Meeting and to fall Election with true, well-informed civic interest. Their belief in their responsibility as American citizens is as firm as was that of their forebears, who wrote in The Vermont Constitution: "That frequent recurrence to fundamental principles and a firm adherence to justice, moderation, temperance, industry, and frugality are absolutely necessary to preserve the blessings of liberty and keep government free."

Consistent adherence to that belief has long maintained Rupert Town Hall as a symbol of uninhibited and simple but fundamental democracy.

19

THE OLD WHITE MEETINGHOUSE

"I will lift up mine eyes unto the hills whence cometh my help. My help cometh from the Lord which made heaven and earth."

Those words from the One Hundred and Twenty-first Psalm came poignantly to my realization one glorious summer day when, as children, Bob and Joe and Sally and I came out from Sunday School in the old Congregational church at Rupert. All at once I was aware of what the wide front doorway framed—Mount Antone and the somewhat lesser neighboring hills of the Taconic Range, green and gold with light and shadow, serene, steadfast, enduring against the sky's deep blue.

From early childhood we had known the sense of peace, security, and fortifying strength to be found in our village church among the hills. Years later I came to realize that this old meetinghouse has from its 18th-century beginning filled a significant role in our American culture and growth. Although it is a comparatively remote and simple edifice, its ministers and its people have made a vital contribution to the development of human democracy and spiritual integration.

In its 175 years, innumerable gales have roared down the mountains and hurled their fury against the four solid walls. Shattering bolts from crashing thunder and forked lightning have barely missed the steadfast steeple. Frost has heaved the nearby road and freshet flooded near. But the skilled work-knotted hands of the pioneers built for their God and built to endure.

How many times during the centuries have red man, black man, or white man felt the comforting presence of those mountains and their Maker, from the very spot where we children stood that revealing summer's day?

Certainly that same Psalm must have rung in the hearts of the seven early settlers who, on June 6, 1786, met at the home of one of their number and organized this church. Why else had they chosen this site for their building?

Like all first settlers in Vermont, they were a religious people. They had recently sought the hills for physical security for themselves and their families; the God of the hills would give them spiritual security as well.

With this in mind, one of the bereaved young pioneers the year before had laid his girl-wife Abigail to rest beneath a great pine here in the valley facing these hills.

The practice of uniting church and graveyard was universally prevalent in those days, and so one of the leading landholders of the town was persuaded to deed the whole plot of ground for "God's acre," the church and horse sheds to the "West Society," as this section of the township had been designated for convenience of worship, at a proprietors' meeting about 1768.

Not far away on Indian River stood some Algonquin wigwams and huts, frequently visited by Samson Occom, the Indian preacher and educator who in the 1780s had a parish near Albany, New York. The seven founders of Rupert Congregational Church had often worshiped with their Red Brothers and had found the Reverend Mr. Occom an inspiration, indeed. As well they might. Occom, born in 1723 the son of a Mohegan hunter in New London, Connecticut, had spent four years as the first Indian pupil in Moor's Indian Charity School established by Dr. Eleazer Wheelock in 1754 in his home at Lebanon, Connecticut.

First as a licensed Congregational minister and later as an ordained Presbyterian preacher, Samson Occom had been the first Indian of that profession to visit England. During 1766-1768 as he traveled in Great Britain, he helped to raise 11,000 pounds for Dr. Wheelock's School. This school, transferred in 1769 to Hanover, New Hampshire, where it would be nearer the Indian tribes, became Dartmouth College.

Records state that the Reverend Samson Occom watched with keen interest as his White Brothers toiled to erect this 48- by 30-foot boxlike wooden edifice for their place of worship. They felled giant pines and oaks which were hauled by straining oxen from the forested hillsides. Thoroughly seasoned by wind and sun on the West Society "Flats" or valley meadows, the great trunks were then laboriously sawed and hewed by the townsmen into strong timbers for the building. When mortise and tenon, rafter and beam were at last truly and stoutly fitted and pegged into place, the huge framework "raised" by bulging muscle and earnest prayer, was ready to begin its community stewardship.

When the last hand-rived shingle was laid in place, this was the finest roof for an altar that had ever been dreamed of here among the few log huts, wigwams, and increasingly numerous plank houses.

Although there is no record of the earliest services held in this first meetinghouse of the township, some old papers show that the Reverend Increase Graves "remained with his flock" until 1793.

All of the people being of one faith, church and town government in those days were closely united. From the tax of "one penny on a pound to be paid in wheat at 4 per bushel, rye 3-6, and corn 3-, to be paid in the fall next coming to defray the town charges," voted at the 1789 March Meeting, one year's expenses of the church had been met.

From 1793 to 1798, the little mountain parish had to depend upon visiting ministers to bring them The Word. Among these was one Lemuel Haynes, the illegitimate son of a full-blooded Negro slave and a white hired maid of West Hartford, Connecticut. Born in 1753, the boy had lived with a pious farmer of Granville, Massachusetts, in whose home he had acquired a rudimentary education. At the age of twenty-one, he joined the Minute Men and as a Continental soldier had accompanied the Massachusetts troops under Benedict Arnold against Fort Ticonderoga.

Returning home, he studied for the ministry, was examined, and was admitted to preach in the Congregational church in 1780. Three years later, at the age of thirty, he married a white girl whom he had converted. After his full ordination in 1785 he took his first parish at Torrington, Connecticut. There, however, some of his parishioners objected to this colored minister with his pronounced African features.

Remembering that the State of Vermont had always espoused the Negro, the Reverend Mr. Haynes moved on to a Congregational church in Bennington County in that state. During his residence there, he occasionally preached also at Rupert. His witty though sometimes sarcastic touch in his delivery was well received, and his powerful sermons showed intellectual insight and conviction. A magnetic revivalist, he doubled and tripled the congregations of the churches he served especially at Manchester, and West Rutland, Vermont, as well as his later one at South Granville, New York. Having earned the degree of Master of Arts from Middlebury College in 1805, he became an intimate friend of many faculty members there, of the Governor of Vermont, and of Chief Justice Royall Tyler, who was also a writer.

One of the greatest honors accorded Mr. Haynes was his appointment in 1814 as delegate of the General Convocation of Ministers in Vermont to the General Association of Connecticut. That august body, greatly impressed by this Negro scholar who possessed no sense of inferiority in his profession nor in his social relations, invited him to preach. His sermon was well received, and warm tributes were paid it by Dr. Timothy Dwight and Professor Silliman of Yale and by President Humphrey of Amherst College.

In his periodic appearances in Rupert pulpit from 1794 to 1833, the Reverend Lemuel Haynes greatly broadened the viewpoint and deepened the faith of its parishioners.

There being no hall for public gathering except at a large dwelling used as an inn, this church was often used in those days for town business as well as for a place of worship. It was a meetinghouse in every sense of the word, a place for man's meeting with man as well as for man's meeting with God.

According to *The Town Record, First Book*, Rupert's inhabitants met at the "meetinghouse in the West Society" on September 28, 1795, to "see if the town will appoint members to sit in county Convention for the purpose of deliberating on the impending Treaty," that being the Jay Treaty with Great Britain.

At that church meeting a motion "to read the Treaty at large" "passed in the negative." It was voted instead to read the Treaty section by section, which was so done. Those astute pioneers preferred to be well-informed before taking action.

The following March 8 the "votable inhabitants" met again "at the meetinghouse on the west side of the mountain" at nine o'clock in the morning to choose town officers and "transact any other business proper for said day."

After electing a moderator, clerk, and forty-five other officers, including five selectmen, a treasurer, two constables, five listers, two collectors, two leather sealers, two grand jurors, two pound-keepers, four tythingmen, four hog howards, four fence viewers, eleven surveyors of highways, and one sealer of weights and measures, the "meeting adjourned for half an hour, then to convene at Ashur Huggins' store" a mile or so away.

Had rivalry for office elicited language unsuitable for a meetinghouse, or had cuspidors been limited?

Whatever the reason, the votable inhabitants did not hold a town meeting within the church again for more than sixty years and then not in the sanctuary.

Perhaps the new minister, who in 1798 came from New Jersey and was said to be a Princeton graduate, did not approve. For fifteen thriving years the Reverend John Preston served his parish. He conducted three services a Sabbath for his congregation that filled the four long rows of box pews before him. So ably did he deliver his message that there were few snorers or prankish small boys to be chastised by the crooked, five-foot staffs, one often tipped with a rabbit's foot, as the tythingmen circulated up and down the aisles.

Many, however, were the words of approval to be heard between morning and afternoon sessions from those who had driven the long miles to service from Windy Summit, from Oak Hill, and from Buck Hollow, and who ate their basket lunches in the churchyard. Or who strolled among the gravestones deciphering such epitaphs as appeared on one Sarah's marble marker:

> "Mourn not ye who stand around,
> Bid not time less swiftly roll;
> She a better world has found,
> Death is the birthday of the soul."

Though Parson Preston's chief concern was with the immortality of the soul, he believed that the Lord's house should be properly ordered. The sexton therefore was admonished to sweep the floor thoroughly more than the usual four times a year and to brush the cobwebs off the windows' small glass panes, in addition to his other duties, at five pence a week.

Those other duties included keeping the key, bossing all grave-digging, blowing the wooden pitchpipe and naming the psalms to be sung by the congregation, turning the hourglass on the pulpit, and handing notices up to the minister, as they came in, by inserting the paper in the end of a cleft stick and holding it up to the pulpit.

When a hand carved communion table was brought into use about 1810, one of the deacons persuaded his bride to weave a linen cloth for it. That creamy two-yard square of flawlessly woven M-and-O pattern, now in its hundred and fifty-first year, is still used at special communion service in this same church.

Though church funds were adequate, funds for the poor in those early times were not. And the meetinghouse one April afternoon in 1802 was the scene of what would seem in these days a strange proceeding for Christian brethren. One John Bunt and family were there being sold at auction.

The town meeting record twelve days before had noted: "4thly Voted that John Bunt his wife & three youngest children be sold at public vendue

& that the person who bids them off shall be intitled to all the services which they can reasonably perform & the use of whatever property yet remains in their possession & shall support them in sickness & health & shall have their apparel & property in as good repair when returned as it is when they are taken by the said bidder, the term to extend one year from the time at which they are taken. And it is to be understood that if the said wife of him the said John behave disorderly the said purchaser shall return the said woman and her said youngest child to the overseers of the poor at any time."

It was further stated that even in those days of extensive use of "spirituous liquors," the poor masters should prevent the Bunt family "from having any drinking with any person whatsoever."

At the same town meeting the very landholder who had deeded the church ground had been appointed "vendue master," and the "said vendue after proceeding a while" that day, had been "adjourned to the fifth of April next at three on the clock in the afternoon then to be opened at the meetinghouse in said Rupert."

Did John Bunt, his wife and three children lift up their eyes "unto the hills" that April day? There is no record of that, but it is recorded that seven years later there were surveyed to John Bunt eight acres of land adjoining "at a Beach saplin" his oldest, married son's 75 acre farm at the base of the hills that face the church. And the Surveyors' Committee was headed by the man who had served as "said John's vendue master."

Perhaps Parson Preston had preached to good effect from "Wine is a mocker," "Suffer the little children," "Honor thy father and thy mother," and "Thou shalt love thy neighbor."

Recently another auction was held on the meetinghouse lawn. As I watched the present pastor wield the auctioneer's hammer, and as I heard the townspeople hilariously bid off the "white elephants" to swell the home missions fund, I could but compare this sale with that "public vendue" nearly a century and three quarters ago.

In the years between, many a doctor, nurse, clergyman, lawyer, teacher, farmer, and other good citizen has been spiritually nurtured in this church that faces the hills. And the people of its and the neighboring parishes have learned to dwell together peaceably.

Perhaps much credit for this is due to the "assistant labourers" of the church. For many decades, in the early 1800s, numerous complaints were brought before the Congregational Society or Board of Administration, as was provided thereby, for settling such disputes. Those complaints covered a wide variety of sins: profanity, intemperance, fornication, adultery, and many another.

One such complaint, dated March 26, 1816, read: "To the Church of Christ in this place, Reverend and Beloved Brethren, I have for some time been burdened with our brother Truman Smith and that in two respects, In sin of Intemperance in the use of ardent spirits and in second, for Giving an Incorrect statement with regard to a horse he was about to sell, all which is contrary to our holy Religion that we have professed. I now tell it to the church. Nahum Gurley."

The complaint was received and a committee appointed to "labour with Brother Truman Smith in behalf of the church."

Another such "labour," begun by one of the brethren on March 14, 1814, had resulted in an Ecclesiastical Council composed of twelve ministers from neighboring parishes and headed by the Reverend Lemuel Haynes, convening at the Rupert church on August 31 of that year. Quotations from the published proceedings still filed at the Congregational Library in Boston tell of that famous Case of Discipline.

"The Church of Rupert having pursued a painful course of discipline, are induced to publish their proceedings for the purpose of giving general information respecting the principle on which they have acted....

"The difficulty under which they have long laboured was occasioned by a criminal intercourse between two persons of respectable parents, belonging to this place.....One of them was a member of this church. He was about twenty-three years old; and his unhappy associate about sixteen. He had reportedly visited her with a view, as was thought, to form a connexion for life. He had several interviews with her after the birth of their illegitimate child; but at length he forsook her under pretext of being destitute of any affectionate attachment to her.

"The following expresses the views of the Church and Council: Exodus XXII,16: 'And if a man entice a maid, that is not betrothed, and lie with her, he shall surely endow her to be his wife.'

"What if the seducer does not love the person he seduced? What if a man does not love his wife? Must he abandon her? Certainly not. God commands all, who sustain this relation, to love their wives. Hence, conjugal love is voluntary.....If the seducer had already married the disconsolate female whom he has covered with shame and confusion, he would be bound by divine command to love her.

"What if he has seduced two women? He is in a melancholy dilemma. But if his intimacy with the second is more generally known, or if he has done her the most injury, he ought to marry her rather than the first.

"It is deeply lamented that there is occasion to discuss this indelicate subject in any Christian church. But it is fervently hoped that the deplorable occurrence . . . will be so over-ruled as to subserve the cause of virtue; that it will serve to render all our churches more vigilant . . . lest there be any Fornicator or Profane Person, as Esau Who for One Morsel of Meat Sold His Birthright."

The outcome of that session with John T—,the seducer, is told in the Letter of Admonition to the Offender, which followed it.

"Dear Brother,

"We are under the painful necessity of addressing you once more in the language of admonition. Be assured that we are influenced to this by a regard for your best interest and a sense of duty for the great Head of the Church.

"When you first expressed a desire to join with us, in the work of the Lord, we cordially received you.... We heard with delight your serious exhortations and addresses to your young companions, and indulged the hope that you would contend earnestly for the faith, and be an ornament to this church, after most of us were numbered with the dead. But alas! how soon . . . our minds were filled with distressing grief, by that unhappy occurrence which, through your neglect, is already too well known.

"The succeeding death of our beloved pastor (the Reverend John Preston had died February 21, 1813) and some encouragement we had that you would make such amends as God requires, induced us to defer the discipline of this church. But as your subsequent conduct gave us reason to fear that you were disposed to put it out of your power to do it, we considered ourselves to be bound to proceed without delay.

"Accordingly one of the brethren, on March 14th, 1814, presented a written complaint against you.....Having ascertained that you acknowledged the facts stated in the complaint, the church unanimously voted that in order to give Christian satisfaction, you must not only make public confession of the crime, as you appeared ready to do, but discover a willingness to marry your criminal associate. At your request the meeting was adjourned for farther consideration.

"March 23. The church met according to adjournment. They entered into friendly discussion with you on the disagreeable subject, and sought without effect, to persuade you to do that which reason, humanity, and the word of God required.

"Being still desirous to afford you every reasonable indulgence, we consented July 13th, to refer your case to a mutual council, composed of such neighboring ministers and delegates as were considered unbiased and disinterested.

"Aug. 31. The council met, and after hearing your defence, and that of the church, and taking into view all the circumstances..... Voted unanimously That the congregational church in Rupert decided correctly in requiring their brother to marry the woman he had seduced. But, as you have continued incorrigible, the church deem it expedient to send you their last admonition.

"We must believe that the excuses and objections, which exist in your mind, arise from a selfish, unhumbled heart; and that sincere repentance would render a compliance with our request agreeable to you.

"Your crime is of such nature as tends to subvert all government, and ruin the human race. At the time when you committed it, you professed to be a disciple of Jesus Christ, and well knew that the commission of it would rank you with that description of persons who, inspiration declares, shall not enter the kingdom of Heaven. We consider your criminality greatly increased, in that you do not design to confine your intercourse and affection to the one you seduced, but are willing, since you have ruined her, to rove in pursuit of another, whom the church are in special obligation to watch over and defend.

"Now while you have a space for repentance, and opportunity of retrieving your character, and satisfying the church, we entreat you, by a regard for your reputation and that of your friends', by motives of benevolence for her whom you have seduced, and for the infant child you have been instrumental of bringing into existence; by the solemn profession you have made, and the interest of religion in this place; by the authority of God's word; and all the solemnities of eternity to repent of your past wickedness, publicly confess your sins, and in a penitent, affectionate manner solicit this injured disconsolate woman to unite with you in the sacred bonds of marriage, and then act the part of a faithful husband to her, and a kind parent to your child.

"Joseph Leavitt, Moderator
"Rupert, December 12, 1814"

Brother John T—having continued in his refusal to meet the demands of his church, he was publicly excommunicated on January 8th, 1815.

However, the other, "whom the church" were "in special obligation to watch over and defend," came in for her share of punishment also, once she had become his wife.

On April 10, 1816, Prudence C. T—was publicly threatened with excommunication "for marrying and cohabiting with a man that was under an indispensable duty, by the laws of God and by the votes of this church being approved by an Ecclesiastical Council to marry a girl with whom he had committed fornication."

When, on the following October 31, Prudence stood in the "broad aisle" of the church, confessed, and begged not to be excluded, the Reverend Lemuel Haynes, former Negro pastor of the church, to whom the case was referred, counseled the officials to accept her confession and retain her in good standing. That advice was followed, and her children were brought up in the church.

Whether due to churchly labours or to the efforts of town officials, or to both, the "lawsuit a week" of 1819 has dwindled, until in late years there is seldom one.

Conflicting ideas regarding forms of worship, however, left their mark upon this church in the early 1800s. In 1803, a Baptist church was established two miles to the westward near White Creek Meadows, and there was considerable dissension pertaining to ritual among the remaining parishioners as well. Nevertheless, in 1826 a minister from the nearby town of Hebron began a successful pastorate of twenty years.

Not long after his arrival the first Sunday School was organized. And the following year the humble little wooden edifice was extensively repaired and improved.

Throughout the 1790s and early 1800s, the meetinghouse door had served as the town's newspaper or bulletin board, as well as for the entrance to divine service. Upon its wide, hand-hewed planks had been posted not only announcements regarding church worship and business but also notices of land sales and stray animals, "warnings" for town meetings, and many another item of public interest. When the ponderous weathered grey portal, with its great home-forged iron latch and hinges, was replaced by a similarly fashioned one in 1830, the first was so thickly studded with nails and nail holes that it was deemed fit only to burn in the deacons' fireplaces.

The box pews also were relegated to the woodpile. No longer would each parish family huddle around a foot stove with its basin of coals from the home hearth, while the swinging door of the pew shut out the worst of the winter cold creeping along the meetinghouse floor. Nor would the hinged seats crash into place at the parson's "Amen" to the standing congregation. New-styled benches, each deeded to a family head, and a fashionable Franklin stove were the new order for Sabbath comfort.

A gallery and a front porch with a flight of steps and a carriage block were also added, as a convenience in getting into and out of the high-wheeled vehicles.

Most magnificent addition of all in that year of 1831 was the stately square steeple with its melodious deep-toned bell, which for more than a century and a quarter now has rung for the mountain hamlet the message of worship, of Christmas joy, of the changing year, and of more than one war's end. Well into the twentieth century, too, it tolled for the death of the townsmen, the heavy slow reverberations scoring the age of the deceased. The mountain-sheltered valley echoed longest in its history when 102-year-old Uncle Timothy Clark went to his last rest in 1840.

In spite of the parishioners' love for their pastor, membership was decreasing in his congregation during the 1820s and '30s. A general exodus westward claimed many from the town, but the pastor's scholarly influence also sent twenty-five or thirty of the young men away to Middlebury, Yale, and other colleges and universities.

One of those young men had been selected by the American Board of Foreign Missions to go as one of the first missionaries to India. On a memorable evening in 1833, while at home on a visit, he spoke in the little white church. Inspired by his vivid description of the need among their Asiatic brethren, the congregation became enthusiastic workers in filling missionary boxes and barrels with hand-knit mittens, outgrown baby clothes, crocheted rugs, and many another homemade offering to be sent into the field.

The minister from 1847 to 1855 served also as the town's superintendent of schools. For the first time, the teachers of all the nine districts' one-room schools had to be examined and certified by him each year that they taught. Many, indeed, were the certificates showing that those enterprising young men and maidens had been found "qualified to instruct in Orthography, Reading, Writing, Geography, Arithmetic & English Grammar; & satisfactory evidence being given" that each "sustains a good moral character," they were "hereby licensed."

Being a man of great energy and activity, both mental and manual, he often composed his sermons while pitching hay, filing saws, or swinging a scythe. But while those sermons were dynamic, they very often were not comforting. Like many another preacher of his day, his main theme dealt with Hell Fire and Souls' Damnation.

The first time Grandfather and Grandmother took their two small sons, aged four and five, to church in 1853, Grandfather reported in his diary, "—they behaved like little men. Of course, heard the Doctrine of Eternal Misery preached, right or wrong I cannot believe it. Lord forgive me if I am wrong." And he did not take his "little men" to meeting again for many weeks, preferring to read to them at home from the Gospels of St. Luke and St. Mark and from the "Sermon on the Mount."

On the infrequent occasions when Grandfather himself attended, his diary was eloquent with such comment as: "Went to hear the Rev.— preach today which was a mixed up mess with lots about Hell and the moral stupor of New England. What an old koot!"

"Went to meeting. A.M. heard a long roundabout discourse to prove that man does not get all his deserved punishment in this life. P.M. Chopped straw would be a fair illustration in my opinion."

That was a period of twenty or more years when many of the congregation were deeply disturbed by the doctrine of Eternal Misery and so turned away from regular attendance at Sabbath service.

As late as 1874, Grandfather's entry of March 2 read: "Worked for H.O.M. on his arch. Staid there in the eve on acct. of C.M. he is down & very bad—a state of despondency in regard to his future welfare—one of the fruits of a belief in eternal Hell—I pity him sincerely."

However the parish may have felt toward the preachers' sermons, they staunchly supported their church. On October 13, 1859, the Congregational Meeting House Dedication was a town event. The interior had been completely changed and redecorated, the old pews being replaced by more modern ones. A basement had been constructed beneath the sanctuary, and that basement, as the town's public hall during the next several years, became the center of far-reaching activity.

A series of lectures on "Phrenology," "Amativeness," and "The Generative System" held there soon after its opening ushered in a wholly new trend of thinking. Many were the townspeople of all ages who flocked to the church to have their heads examined by the phrenologist, and the other lectures were equally well attended by the grownups. So, too, were the numerous lawsuits, examinations of teachers, shows, and exhibitions that were held there in the ensuing years.

The fall of 1861, fifty-five pupils from Rupert and three of its neighboring towns assembled there two evenings a week at a "select school." And so popular did this project prove that it was repeated the fall of 1863 with forty registered under the instruction of Professor Wiseman.

Town meetings of various kinds frequently occupied this hall throughout its first ten years. There on November 6, 1860, at the regular Freeman's Meeting, one hundred-forty men cast their ballots for Abraham Lincoln. There, too, a few days earlier, a grandson of one of the founders of the church had taken the Freeman's Oath that he also might join in the balloting.

And there, on April 17, 1861, in that "terrible time when quite the whole South are in rebellion," a crowd assembled for the Raising of a National Flag. A foot of snow lay over valley and hill that April day, but a deeper chill shrouded loyal hearts as the Stars and Stripes lifted and billowed toward heaven amidst the fervent "Thy will be done" and "Deliver us from evil."

The next four years saw frequent war meetings held in the basement, sometimes two and three a week, when new recruits were needed to fill the ranks.

At one of the first of such meetings, a resolution was drawn up to be published in *The Manchester Journal* and *The Bennington Banner*, the newspapers locally subscribed to. It ran: "Resolved that the man who flees his state or country, or who shall refuse to contribute according to his means, or who by magnifying his bodily defects and infirmities, or who for any other trivial cause seeks to escape from his responsibilities to the government in this, its hour of peril, should be looked upon with distrust and is undeserving the respect of his fellowmen."

At the repeated calls of Governor and President for nine months' men and three years' men, those "patriotic and loyal" citizens met and called for volunteers. To encourage the young men to enlist, a bounty of $100 was voted for each of the first nine needed, and a committee of five circulated the subscription list throughout the township. A week later, $1,166.70 had been raised. So had the men.

Volunteers were scarcer in 1862, and on August 9 of that year the resolutions drawn up in the church basement read: "Whereas the President of the United States has called for 300,000 additional troops to be raised by draft from the several loyal States,

"And whereas we the people of the town of Rupert feel anxious to avoid the necessity of a draft upon our citizens:

"Therefore resolved that we take veritable measures to encourage the enlistment of volunteers to fill up the quota." The veritable measures consisted of appointing a committee of one from each school district to canvass the same for raising bounty money and volunteers. With few exceptions, the full quota of seventy-five men called during those four trying years was met by such canvasses. But those canvasses represented long, tedious, and often discouraging days, as more and more men were needed.

At some of the basement meetings, larger bounties were voted, and at one, the individual farmers reached into their well-worn pockets and drew out $10, $5, $2, and even $1 bills to encourage men to sign up. The doctors offered their free services to families of married men who would go forth to the battlefield, and all shared the burden of the war tax. By September of 1864, this amounted to 220 per cent on the Grand List, "any surplus to be invested in government bonds." By that time, it had become necessary to draft two or three men, but each draftee was given his choice "to go, furnish a substitute, or pay $300."

The young men to fill the ranks were disappearing from the farms all too fast, so the citizens finally passed another resolution: "Resolved that in the event the town of Rupert be requested to furnish nine additional men to fill up any quota which may be assigned to the town by draft or otherwise, the Selectmen be requested to notify the Adjutant General of this State in a respectful manner that the town of Rupert is unwilling to do more than its equal proportion according to its population, in raising troops in this present war."

One of the earlier volunteers had died of typhoid fever in the Hospital of the Army of the Potomac soon after his enlistment, and his body had been returned to his home for burial. Because of a heavy snowstorm, the girl whom he had expected to marry had arrived too late for the funeral, since she lived in a distant part of the state. As First Selectman, Grandfather had had a large share of the responsibility for making up the military roll, and the day after the young man's funeral, his diary showed an additional responsibility. "Went to the Street burying ground with G. Derby this A.M. to permit the disinterment of M. F. Kinne that his betrothed might look at him—she seemed very much affected."

But the evening of August 6, 1863, was a brighter occasion at the church. The National Thanksgiving service there celebrated not only the winning of the Battle of Gettysburg a month earlier, but also the Welcome Home of Rupert's Nine Months' Boys. Though the boys were pale and haggard, joy poured through every note of "Mine eyes have seen the glory" from the congregation that packed the church and overflowed down its front steps and onto the carriage block.

There, too, patriots assembled to celebrate the Emancipation Proclamation and finally the ending of the war. And there the saddened townfolk came to express their sorrow at the passing of the Great Emancipator.

Recollection of those stories of the Civil War years came to us as youngsters in 1917 and as adults in the 1940s when we saw the soldier boys make their last communion before going overseas to the battle-front. And also, in World War I, as we said a tearful farewell to our pastor, who was leaving for service with the Y.M.C.A. in France.

Later, however, we knew the joy of sharing in the glad all-day festivities on the church lawn when the marble monument was placed there to honor the World War servicemen of the town.

The pastor whom we welcomed back from the Marne has always preached the doctrine of a loving Father rather than of Eternal Punishment. That new trend of thought was ushered in in 1874, when Dr. Lambert came for a nine-year stay which brought new life to the church, though struggle marked his coming.

His predecessor, whose best achievement had been sponsoring an annual Christmas tree from 1869 on and participating in singing school, debates, and lyceums in the church basement, had to be persuaded to move to another charge because of lack of funds for another year. And by a donation party to bring his salary up to date. Then came the problem of finding the tremendously high salary of $1,200 a year for the new minister, who had won the congregation when, as a visiting pastor, he had preached "There is a hope in Christ." After an arduous canvass and recanvass of every member and possible member of the church, and after much debate by the Congregational Society, as the administrative body was called until 1910, the required stipend was guaranteed.

On May 7, seven of that Society set out with horse-drawn lumber wagons and hayracks to move the new minister in from twenty-odd miles away. Rain-drenched, they put up at the Hartford parsonage, and in the next day's clearing weather they loaded the goods and started for Rupert. A few miles on their way, one driver's "wagon ex broke, which caused a serious delay in our train," to quote Grandfather. "We could not get kept overnight at that place but did find the most hospitable entertainment at West Pawlet, 'without money and without price.' Would gladly have paid them but they refused. May God bless them and theirs."

In spite of rain and axle-deep mud, the next night the seven drivers "landed the goods mostly safe and sound at the parsonage and ourselves at home."

The following day Dr. Lambert's sermon from Matthew 10:29 and 31 was delivered to a full house, as were most of his subsequent sermons, which continued to present God as a loving Father.

Yes, the new minister was doing well as he began nine of the finest years for the little white church.

England, Scotland, and Wales supplied the parish with its next several pastors. They were men who brought greater international understanding and who carried on the spirit of good fellowship that had been so well begun, in spite of a second period of conflicting ideas for forms of worship.

Those conflicting ideas led to the founding in 1883 of the Methodist Episcopal church a few rods up the street. This has proved itself truly a sister church through the years. The hurt at the time of its establishment was greatly eased by the "wise counsel, careful ministry, and labor of love" of the Congregational pastor, the Reverend J. Loring Pratt.

It was his successor, the Reverend Bernard Copping, who in 1886 delivered the centennial sermon. After briefly tracing the history of the old white meetinghouse, he spoke inspiringly from the text, "Other men labored, and ye are entered into their labors." In closing, he reminded his congregation that their beloved church had justified all the personal sacrifices for its sake by its "divine working for human redemption."

A Sunday School library, opened about this time, began drawing increasing numbers of boys and girls, who found that its *Mrs. Wiggs of the Cabbage Patch, Hoosier Schoolboy,* and dozens of other fascinating tales could bring color to isolated farm weekdays.

The Woman's Christian Temperance Union and Loyal Temperance Legion were developing activities that were meeting there in convention and otherwise, as also were the Missionary Society, Dorcas Club, Mite Society, and various study groups.

Community suppers there each winter were also adding not only to the much-needed parish income but to the social life of the township as well. One of these, a conundrum supper in the 1890s, was of special interest. Cards sent to every family stated: "You are cordially invited to attend The Mystery Supper, Congregational Church Parlors Thursday, February seventh, seven-thirty to ten-thirty.

.... MENU ....

Three Fourths of the Globe, 1c.	Relics of Greece, 2c.
What Some Folks Don't Know, 3c.	
Women of Grit, 2c.	No Grounds for Complaint, 3c.
Dead Beats, 1c.	
Jersey Extract, 1c.	Boston's Overthrow, 3c
Fruit of the Vine, 1c.	
Bean Cake, 2c.	Seed Cake, 2c.
Chip of the Old Block, 1c.	
Home of the Multitude, 2c.	Chopped Creature, 3c.
Nature's Head Dressed, 2c.	Amaized Loaf, 2c.
Fruit Encrusted, 3c	

If this puzzle you should solve
Silent you will please to be
That on each person may devolve
The working of this mystery.

....

Note.—Please check off your order on this card, write your name at the top and bring it with you to the supper."

The highly amused arrivals at the church parlor on that February seventh found that the supper dishes consisted of:

Coreless Baked Apple	Sliced Cold Baked Ham

Baked Beans

White Bread and Butter Sandwiches	Fresh Graham Bread
	(from locally ground flour) Buttered

Hard-Boiled Eggs

Milk	Tea (With sugar and lemon or cream)

Grape Juice (Home-bottled)

Chocolate Cake	Coconut Cake

Slice of Aged Cheese

Fruit Cake	Mince Tart
Pumkin Pie	Indian Pudding
	(Made of maize or corn meal)

Apple Pie

In 1910, the present pastor, the Reverend J. Duke King, came with his young wife to begin more than a half century of ministry in the old "West Society." Fruitful years they have been, years of interpreting the Creator in relation to human need that extends beyond the immediate parish, which he has served with diligence and vision.

In my childhood memories, the village church stands out as a center of entertainment, as well as of spiritual instruction and enjoyable discussions with our well-loved Sunday School teachers. In the winter, there were the home talent shows followed by abundant suppers in the church parlor of the basement. In March came the Maple Sugar Sociable, when long tables were surrounded by young and old, briskly stirring great saucers full of creamy soft sugar or dripping the hot sweet amber liquid over hard-packed snow in soup plates to make wax. What a lull there was in the clatter of voices as the heaped-up pans of plump brown fried cakes and the plates of sour cucumber pickles went round and round, and tongues yielded to the delight of warm sugar and wax from the season's "first run."

On Monday evenings throughout the summer, ice-cream socials provided the only place in town where that delicacy could then be bought. The cone-shaped dipper would scoop a half-pint of banana, vanilla, chocolate, or strawberry frozen custard from a hand-turned freezer and pile it on each plate beside a huge wedge of homemade devil's food or butternut cake, and all for fifteen cents. Childhood bliss went with those sociables and with the-eat-as-much-as-a-body-can-eat chicken pie suppers that the Dorcas Society still serves at its annual fair.

The yearly picnic was also an event, even the rainy-day ones in the church parlor, instead of on the lawn or in a nearby meadow, as was the custom when the day was pleasant. The ten-gallon can of lemonade with its block of ice and floating slices of lemon tempted us to "dip" all through an afternoon of "Drop the Handkerchief," "Stagecoach," or a hotly contested game of baseball.

Charlie Pat, the town's crippled pauper, who lived by himself in a tiny cottage at the edge of the village, enjoyed those picnics, too. I still remember being sent by my mother, who was chairman of the food committee, with two huge, heaped-up plates of baked beans, deviled eggs, potato salad, cold ham, raised biscuit, pickles, cake, cheese, and watermelon, for the welcome but whiskery old man to eat by himself on the bench by the door. I still remember, too, his tap-tapping along the hall with his cane, to return those same emptied plates with a dignified, "Thanks for the bite."

Christmas Eve still brings young and old from even the most remote farm homes to the church tree and children's program. A gift and candy for every child in the parish supply an abundant harvest for the two tall evergreens, that there symbolize each holiday season the spirit of the Nativity. Never does one forget a Christmas Eve in the little white meetinghouse.

Children's Sunday is likewise a memorable occasion, when child voices ring from the church dais banked with flowers and ferns from pasture and meadow. But, Oh! the horror in our childhood when someone would forget his part. Then, indeed, not only the delinquent one but his parents and teacher as well would lift imploring "eyes unto the hills" outside the open windows.

I remember yet how proud we used to be on Children's Day to drop our pennies into the collection baskets, wreathed with daisies and buttercups, as the twin sons of one of the deacons would pass them while the chorus sang,

"We bring from the fields God's gifts manifold,
So give to the Lord your silver and gold."

And how glad we felt in knowing that those carefully hoarded pennies would bring happiness to some less-fortunate child somewhere away in the world.

In 1936, the "Church in the West Society" celebrated its 150th anniversary. By that time several of the horse sheds had been enclosed and ceiled as recreation rooms for the pastor's teen-age club, the Green Mountain Boys. Four-H Clubs and the Women's Home Bureau were now among the activity groups enjoying the remodeled kitchen and newly decorated parlor in the church basement.

Hydrangeas at the base of the triple flight of steps at the front and a lawn border of blue spruce had brought additional beauty to the grounds, as had tall trees and a white fence to the adjoining cemetery.

Most changed of all in that century and a half perhaps was the interior of the sanctuary, with its pearl-grey walls and its wine-colored carpet, pew cushions, and curtain back of the pulpit. Memorial gifts of stained-glass windows, a marble baptismal font, urns for the altar, a pipe organ, and other modern appointments had made this a house of worship far beyond any possible concept of Samson Occom and those seven early settlers who had laid its foundation.

On that golden June Sabbath that marked the 150th anniversary celebration, men and women from Alabama, California, France, and other far places returned to pay tribute to their childhood church. As their voices blended in "Faith of Our Fathers, Living Still," the hills returned the message.

And then the Head of the Congregational Church in Vermont stirringly brought the challenge, "If that which ye have heard from the beginning shall remain in you, ye also shall continue in the Son and in the Father."

In the hush that followed the sermon, a sense of rededication flowed through the hearts of those assembled there. And lingered.

Another anniversary service recently filled to overflowing the pews of the old white meetinghouse. Blue sky, blue hills, and bright fall sunshine blessed the crisp September morning, as Protestant, Catholic, Jew, and so-called unbeliever filed through the old church door.

"The Lord is in His holy temple; let all the earth keep silence before Him," came with a slight tremor of emotion from the pulpit. The pastor, bearing well his harvest of years, then told of his "Half Century as a

Country Parson." His reminiscence of his experiences in serving humanity, regardless of color or caste or creed, confirmed the sense of brotherhood among all men in those who had assembled with no barriers of faith, to join their good friend in celebrating the fiftieth anniversary of his ordination into the Christian ministry.

Afterwards, eighty or more of those who at some time had addressed him as "Father," "Rabbi," "Reverend," or "Brother," surprised the Parson with a Family Dinner in the church dining room. How the walls reverberated with anecdote of present and past as the steaming tureens of good country cooking went round and round.

Those same walls have reverberated for a hundred and seventy-five years now with the anecdote of a growing democracy. And with more: with the sacred ritual and music of baptism and marriage; with "Thy Kingdom Come," "In My Father's House Are Many Mansions," and with "The Lord Lift Up the Light of His Countenance Upon You and Give You—Peace."

But still they stand, firmly, solidly facing the mountains, sending up their square, staunch steeple toward heaven, symbolic of the Finger of God.

Although I now worship far from that little white meetinghouse, memory still brings me my childhood pastor's benediction mingled with the benediction of the hills.

TOPIC INDEX

Apple Paring 22

Ballot Boxes 180-1
Birds 42
Blizzard 154
Buhr Stones 140-1, 142

Candles 18,45
Charcoal 86, 134
Cheese-Making 29, 161-2, 163-4
Christmas 32, 37, 119-20
Civil War 29, 155-6, 209-10
Clearing Land 64
Concord Saltbox 16, 18
Cradle (Grain) 178-9

Deed 63
Diary Entries 28-31, 51-2, 53, 54, 55-6,
    70-1, 89-92, 93, 109, 186-7, 207,
    208

Evolution 82

Family Gatherings 27-8, 32-3, 46-7, 52
Flax 69
Freeman's Oath 189

Harvest 51, 59-60, 66-7
Harwoods 17, 18, 21, 25
Haynes, Rev. Lemuel 199-200, 203
Herbs 44-5
Hobo 109-10
Hops 66-7
Husking-bee 52-3

King, Rev. J. Duke 213, 215-16

Land Clearing 63-4
Lessons, School 33, 115-16, 120-1,
    123-4
Lillie, John 58
Lincoln, Robert Todd 111

Linen 18, 26
Listers 29-30, 108-9
Lyceum 121-2

Occom, Rev. Samson 198
Orchard 46, 67
Ox Cart 177-8
Ox Yoke 176-7

Paint Pails 185
Parlor 24, 26, 34
Patter, Feather Bed 181
Paupers' Auction 201-2
Pound 49-50
Pump Logs 73-4

Quilting 24, 80

Railway 151-4
Recipes 143
Remedies 19-21, 36, 43, 60, 68-70,
    77-9, 85, 126
Revolution 102-3, 186
Road Maintenance 105-6, 172
Rug Making 80

Saltbox House 15, 24-5, 26-7
Scarecrow 65-6
Seeding 66
Sheep 54-6, 74, 111, 184
Shoeing Horse and Ox 134-8
"Shivaree" 158
Soap Making 87
Sugar Making 94-6, 99-100

Threshing 59-60
Tree Planting 119

Wedding 23, 30, 31
Well 40-1
Whittling 22